W9-ACD-727

Cartographies of Desire

Cartographies of Desire

Captivity, Race, and Sex in
the Shaping of an American Nation

Rebecca Blevins Faery

University of Oklahoma Press : Norman

Also by Rebecca Blevins Faery

(ed., with Carl Klaus and Chris Anderson) *In Depth: Essayists for Our Time*
    (San Diego, Calif., 1990, 1993)

Library of Congress Cataloging-in-Publication Data

Faery, Rebecca Blevins.
    Cartographies of desire: captivity, race, and sex in the shaping
of an American nation / Rebecca Blevins Faery.
        p.   cm.
    Revision of thesis (doctoral)—University of Iowa.
    Includes bibliographical references (p.   ) and index.
    1. American literature—History and criticism.   2. Indians in
literature.   3. Rowlandson, Mary White, ca. 1635–ca. 1678—In
literature.   4. National characteristics, American, in literature.
5. Pocahontas, d. 1617—In literature.   6. Indian captives—
Historiography.   7. Indian women in literature.   8. White women in
literature.   9. Desire in literature.   10. Race in literature.
11. Sex in literature.   I. Title.
PS173.I6F34   1999
810.9'35297—dc21   98-54760
                                                                                                    CIP

ISBN 0-8061-3149-7 (cloth)
ISBN 0-8061-3150-0 (paper)

Text Design by Gail Carter

Contents

Figures

Acknowledgments

The research and writing necessary to complete a book often feels like a lonely enterprise, but it is one rarely completed without the support of many other people. Certainly that has been the case for me, and I want here to acknowledge a significant few of many sources of support and encouragement during the years of study and writing this project required.

To Mary Lou Emery and Ed Folsom of the University of Iowa, who directed the doctoral thesis that was this book's beginnings, my thanks for your encouragment, patience, and sustained support. My thanks also to my editor, Kim Wiar of the University of Oklahoma Press, who encouraged me with interest in the work early on and waited patiently while I completed it. I am indebted to the Center for Advanced Studies at the University of Iowa, where I worked happily and productively for a semester; to the Jamestowne Society of Virginia, for a generous grant-in-aid for research and travel; and to Mount Holyoke College, for a semester's sabbatical leave and a travel grant that allowed me to begin my research in London. Thanks to the many friends, especially Stephen Wootton and Richard Dillard, who brought useful films and texts to my attention and helped make them available to me.

My thanks to all my family and friends for their forbearance and for forgiving me for the many times when the necessity of work caused me to neglect the ordinary obligations of affection and friendship. Special gratitude and love to my husband Bill Nowysz, who made sure I always had a room of my own to work in. And last but not least, love and thanks to my children, Annemarie and Rick, who never lost faith in me or confidence in my ability to finish this project and who were my steady inspiration, because the future is theirs. This book is for them.

Cartographies of Desire

Extracts

I want to draw a map, so to speak, of a critical geography and use that map to open as much space for discovery, intellectual adventure, and close exploration as did the original charting of the New World—without the mandate for conquest.

—TONI MORRISON, *Playing in the Dark*

Ancient maps of the world—when the world was flat—inform us, concerning that void where America was waiting to be discovered, HERE BE DRAGONS. Dragons may not have been here then, but they are certainly here now, breathing fire, belching smoke . . . .

—JAMES BALDWIN, "Here Be Dragons"

Like the colonized country itself, the women [of both the colonizing and colonized cultures] become representative objects of desire, and their conditions are to some extent parallel.

—ABENA P. A. BUSIA, "Silencing Sycorax:
On African Colonial Discourse
and the Unvoiced Female"

Race and sex have always been overlapping discourses in the United States.

—BELL HOOKS, "Reflections on Race and Sex"

I promised to show you a map you say but this is a mural
then yes let it be   these are small distinctions
where do we see it from is the question
—ADRIENNE RICH, *An Atlas of the Difficult World*

Introduction

Here is a story, no doubt a familiar one: Growing up in the postwar South of the 1940s and '50s, I spent many sweaty summer afternoons playing cowboys and Indians. It was a routine social game, requiring a sizable group of playmates, and everyone's enthusiasm for the game was something that could always be counted on. I was a tomboy, everyone in my family told me so, and in those games I was always a cow*boy*, never a "cowgirl," one of those foolish hybrid creatures who, in the Saturday Western movie serials (to which I was devoted), were always too clean and weepy and afraid, who never had any power or any fun. Every Christmas of my childhood I begged and prayed for a real cowboy hat and boots, six-shooters in a hip holster, and real leather chaps. Year after year, I did get a toy hat and six-shooters in a holster that buckled around my hips—the pistols shot rolls of red paper caps whose acrid burning smell is still vivid in my memory—but I never got the boots or leather chaps.

Occasionally, absent a group large enough to make the cowboys-and-Indians game fun, I played with just my best friend and favorite playmate, Robert Lewis Treadway, who lived two doors up the street and was a few years older. Being a boy and being older combined to give him a certain amount of privilege, so he almost always got to say what we would play and who would be what. Often, armed with his real bow and metal-tipped arrows, he would be a lone Indian who stalked me through the large open field above his house, overgrown and dotted with ancient, twisted apple trees, or through the thick woods that crossed the ravine behind our houses and separated them from a horse pasture beyond. He was quiet and quick, and I never knew exactly where he was; he seemed to be everywhere at once, lurking and invisible, just like the Indians in the Western movies I loved. When Robert Lewis was the stalking Indian, I was the hapless white girl, his intended prey. Usually I was armed with his BB gun to defend my imaginary frontier home. It was never very clear why he stalked me or what would happen if he captured me—he never did, maybe because neither of us could figure out what would happen then—but the imagined danger, however vague, was thrilling.

I also spent many hours alone, and then my imagination had free rein. I read voraciously, and once, a children's magazine to which I had received a gift subscription carried a long story about Frances Slocum, a little white girl who had been captured long ago by Indians on what was then the frontier—the Wyoming Valley of Pennsylvania—and who grew up with them, married one, raised Indian children, and finally refused to be reunited with her white family, preferring instead her life among her adopted people. She was given an Indian name, We-let-a-wash, so was no longer "Frances Slocum," but someone altogether different. The story was filled with an irresistible romantic sense of adventure and mystery, but I remember feeling that there was also something in it that hinted of tragedy. How could a "white" girl become a "red" woman, "lost," as the story's title said, to her "real" family? And why would she want to?

The squat cardboard boxes that held my favorite breakfast cereal, large pillows of shredded wheat, were for a time during my childhood a treasure trove of "Indian lore." Cardboard rectangles divided the layers of shredded-wheat biscuits, and on each rectangle was printed some feature of traditional Indian life. An attentive reader—certainly what I was, as I crumbled my shredded wheat into a bowl of milk and crunched and read avidly—could learn to distinguish the tracks of deer, raccoons, wolves, and bears; could learn what it meant to wear a feather in the headband this way or that way; could find out what the Indians ate in summer and in winter; could see what the inside of a tipi looked like; could learn a few words of some Indian language, complete with phonetic spellings. (I wonder now if the language was identified. I can remember thinking, "This is how Indians say 'tree'"; I can't, however, remember a single one of the words I learned so diligently.) I saved the cardboard rectangles meticulously. I read that an Indian could walk through a forest wearing soft deerskin moccasins and make not a single sound from a snapped twig or a crushed leaf; I wrapped my bare feet in pieces of torn cloth from my mother's rag bag, gathered them around my ankles with old shoestrings, and stealthily crept through the woods behind the house, tensing every muscle and moving with painful deliberateness. I imagined myself an Indian girl, lean, lithe, strong, and silent, perfectly at home in the woods. I could read all the forest signs, I knew where the animals slept and what they ate, I could find food or fresh water whenever I needed it, I was filled with the wisdom of the natural world, was one with nature. Disney Studios' cartoon version of Pocahontas was still decades in the future; if I had seen it, their Pocahontas would have certainly fed my fantasy, though I lacked her fleetness of foot—not to mention her tiny waist, blooming breasts, and sloe-eyed seductiveness. And I never was able to walk through the forest in perfect silence, like a real Indian.

Memories such as these are anything but remarkable for white Americans who were children during the mid-twentieth century. And ironically, not for white children alone; the African American writer Alice Walker, who also claims Indian ancestry, tells, in her essay "Beauty: When the Other Dancer Is the Self," of being accidentally blinded in one eye when she was a child, the victim of one of her brothers' BB guns in their own game of cowboys and Indians. Walker's story is a deft analysis of how race and gender converged in this ubiquitous children's game as well as in the mythic history that gave rise to it:

I am eight years old and a tomboy. I have a cowboy hat, cowboy boots, checkered shirt and pants, all red. My playmates are my brothers, two and four years older than I. Their colors are black and green, the only difference in the way we are dressed. On Saturday nights we all go to the picture show, even my mother; Westerns are her favorite kind of movie. Back home, "on the ranch," we pretend we are Tom Mix, Hopalong Cassidy, Lash LaRue (we've even named one of our dogs Lash LaRue); we chase each other for hours rustling cattle, being outlaws, delivering damsels from distress. Then my parents decide to buy my brothers guns. These are not "real" guns. They shoot "BBs," copper pellets my brothers say will kill birds. *Because I am a girl, I do not get a gun. Instantly I am relegated to the position of Indian.* ("Beauty" 386; emphasis mine)

Nor did Native children, even those growing up on reservations, escape the myth's pervasive influence. James Welch, in his book *Killing Custer*, tells of his childhood replaying of the battle at the Little Bighorn:

I can't think of a hero who has taught kids more about dying in mock battles than General George Armstrong Custer. I had even been Custer myself once, standing on a small sandy hill in the backyard when I was six or seven, suddenly clutching my chest when one of the "Indians" shot me, falling and tumbling down the hill to lie motionless while the battle raged on about me. . . . What made this particular reenactment different was that it was played out in the town of Browning on the Blackfeet Reservation in Montana and the "Indians" *were* Indians. I, Custer, was an Indian too, a member of the Blackfeet tribe. We also played cowboys and Indians, no particular cowboys and no particular Indians, just a lot of galloping around on make-believe horses, dodging from house to tree, shooting our cap pistols from behind garbage cans. The fact that I was a "breed," part Indian and part white, did not determine which role I would play. Or maybe it did. I suppose I could play either role with validity. But nobody seemed to find it strange that a little "full-blood" kid could play a cowboy emptying his cap gun at an advancing wave of Indians. (96–97)

I offer my own memories, then, not because they are unique, but on the contrary, precisely because of how typical such events and experiences were. They demonstrate the pervasiveness of a mythology of frontier and conquest, of the mythic contest between cowboys and Indians and of the ways race and gender were called forth and played out in that contest, well more than half a century after the "West" was "won." Doubtless like countless other children, I had no reason to believe women had played any significant role in the drama of westward expansion, except perhaps as victims. I was born and raised in the strictly segregated South, so from my earliest years I knew intimately, if unconsciously, about racial divisions and hierarchies. But I was a white girl, so those divisions and hierarchies were invisible to me, because Black people themselves were all but invisible, even though they were everywhere in my daily life. I saw Black people, but didn't really see them; I never saw Indians at all except in the movies I watched and the books I read. African Americans were there but not there; Indians dwelt in a mythic "elsewhere." That there might be some connection between the presence of African Americans in my world and the absence, as far as I knew, of Indians never occurred to me. I had not yet read Hawthorne, but like Young Goodman Brown, I could sometimes imagine an Indian lurking in every dark knoll, behind every tree in the woods behind my house. I feared Indians as representing some nameless, invisible threat to everything that made me secure, fed an insatiable curiosity about them with mass-marketed "information," and still, at times, wanted more than anything to be one.

Nor was such mythic lore confined to the experiences of those growing up in the United States; the "cowboy and Indian" drama, replete with all its stereotypes of machismo and savagery, is one familiar around the globe. In the popular-culture history of the United States, conflicts between Indians and whites have acquired epic and archetypal dimensions and have served as a universal definition of American identity and history. Michael Dorris, a writer of mixed American Indian and European ancestry, tells of a visit to the Cook Islands in the South Pacific, where he found in a gift shop for tourists "a tribe of plush monkeys, each wearing a turkey-feather imitation of a Sioux war bonnet and clasping a plywood tomahawk. The Rarotongan salesperson replied to my startled question that, yes, indeed, these simian braves were a hot-selling item. She herself, she added with a broad smile, had played cowboys and Indians as a child" ("Indians on the Shelf" 122).

Dorris continues with the story of the visit to his home of a young African man from Zaire:

> He was homesick for his tiny radioless, roadless, remote village on the west shore of Lake Tanganyika, and the Santa Clara pueblo chili I served reminded him of the spicy stews he had eaten in Africa as a child. He listened with rare appreciation to recordings of southwestern Indian music. He had never met "real" Indians before, he reported, and was interested and curious about every detail. But it was not until I brought out a nineteenth-century eagle-feather headdress, a family heirloom, that his eyes lit up with true recognition. Sweeping it out of my hand, and with an innocent and ingenuous laugh, he plopped it on his head, assumed a fierce expression and, patting his hand over his mouth, said "Woo woo woo." (123)

Myths do, however, have material consequences, and the "cowboys and Indians" story is no exception. Though it usually appears as an element of nineteenth- and early twentieth-century U.S. history in films and popular literature, the genre of the Western has its beginnings in the seventeenth century, the earliest period of Anglo settlement of eastern North America, in the tales of Indian captivity that accompanied and helped to foster that settlement and to define the nation that ultimately emerged.

Houston Baker has written that "A history may be conceptualized as an ideologically or imaginatively governed catalog of figurative elements. The catalog is inconceivable in the absence of ideology, and a shift, or rupture, in ideological premises promotes strikingly new figurations" (165; quoted in Kolodny, "Letting Go," 9). That Baker's observations are as true of a national history as of any other hardly needs to be said. In the work that follows, I focus on a couple of the "figurative elements" that have played central roles in the "ideologically governed catalog" of significant figures in the racial and cultural history of the United States: the white woman captive among Indians, initiated by the 1682 narrative of Mary Rowlandson's captivity among the Narragansetts in New England, and the "Indian princess," or Pocahontas, figure, introduced in the chronicles of the Virginia colony in the early seventeenth century.

The frequency with which stories and visual representations of white women's Indian captivity and of Pocahontas figures have appeared in American literature and cultural history prompts the question of why such stories have been told so many times for so long—of what "cultural work," to borrow Jane Tompkins's useful phrase, such representations have been asked to do. That question has motivated the work that follows. My purpose is to explore how this couple, and the narratives elaborating the two figures through the succeeding three centuries, have articulated cooperating ideologies of race and gender to construct and defend a privileged, protected version of white American identity, subjectivity, and nationhood throughout the history of the United States. I am indebted to Tompkins for the assertion that texts are "agents of cultural formation" (*Sensational Designs* xvii), "bearers of a set of national, social, [and] economic . . . interests" (xii) with "designs upon their audiences, in the sense of wanting to make people think and act in a particular way" (xi). That both the white woman captive and the "Indian princess" had their beginnings in histories but moved rapidly into more evidently fictional or fictionalized popular narrative forms demonstrates both "the textuality of history and the historicity of texts" (Montrose, "Professing the Renaissance," 20), another theoretical insight that informs my work.

I use the word "couple" above deliberately. The figures of the white woman captive and the young Native woman who welcomes and sustains colonial intruders into her country occupy opposite sides of the same discursive coin and have been partners in the ongoing constructions of race, sex, and national identity in the United States. Both figures were initially the products of colonialist discourses, and both were securely installed in the discursive process of nation building and in its concomitant mythologies by the end of the seventeenth century. Both have been repeatedly positioned on the dividing lines of race and deployed at self-defining moments in the evolution of an American nation since the earliest period of North American colonization; the effects of their stories are still evident today in the racial and sexual politics of the United States. Stories of the white woman captive and of the welcoming Indian maiden are "foundational fictions" (Schaffer 114) in U.S. cultural history, early and persistent features of the Euro-American mappings of colonial and national spaces in North America.

Stories of whites captured by Indians, especially those involving women, helped in significant ways to produce the difference, at first cultural but eventually racial, in which the stories of contending "red" men and "white" men were grounded and which became the rationale for European conquest and the emergence of a nation founded on white male supremacy. These stories, then, were a significant element in the construction of discourses of racial difference and racial categories of "red," "white," and "black" that have been so central a part of American social history from the colonial era to the present day. Furthermore, they initiated what would become a persistent trope in articulations of racial difference in the United States: white women, their bodies and their sexuality, positioned as guardians of the boundaries of race to serve the territorial and political purposes of white men and their claim to dominance. Stories of Indian captivity are witness to the construction and operation of discourses of race in America—and witness as well to the ways women and their sexuality have been conscripted to serve those discourses.

As Henry Louis Gates, Jr., has written, "Race is a text (an array of discursive practices), not an essence. It must be *read* with painstaking care and suspicion, not imbibed" (*Loose Canons* 79). Captivity tales, I will argue, have been part of the "text" of race in its peculiarly American character and have occupied an important place in that "array of discursive practices" that have constituted race and that Gates urges us to read with both "care and suspicion." Ruth Frankenberg points out that "the articulation and deployment of essentialist racism approximately five hundred years ago marks the moment when, so to speak, *race was made into a difference* and simultaneously into a rationale for racial inequality" (139). Racial difference as we know it in the United States today, then, as a discursive practice—and as a social and political reality—arose as a product of colonialism, especially in the encounters between English colonizers and their racialized "others" in the New World. And, as the captivity stories make clear, the female body was made into a crucial engineer of that difference, demonstrating the historical as well as contemporary accuracy of bell hooks's claim that "racism and sexism are interlocking systems of domination which uphold and sustain one another" (196).

At the same time that English colonizers generated and circulated the "array of discursive practices" that evoked and constructed the racialized, dark "other," their own whiteness emerged as a product of those same discourses of difference. As Frankenberg writes, "[O]ne effect of colonial discourse is the production of an unmarked, apparently autonomous white/Western self, in contrast with the marked, Other racial and cultural categories with which the racially and culturally dominant category is coconstructed" (17). Whiteness as a category of identity did not exist any more than did darkness until political expediencies called forth both terms, most dramatically in the North American colonies, as English colonists, along with other European settlers, laid claim to land, displacing the original inhabitants and importing African labor for plantation.

James Baldwin has written poignantly and repeatedly of the time when his ancestors were brought to this continent and *became black*; and, he insisted, whites in America also had to *become white*: "The time has come to realize that the interracial drama acted out on the American continent has not only created a new black man, it has created a new white man, too" ("Stranger" 89). In a similar vein, but focusing specifically on the cultural work of writing in America, Toni Morrison asserts in *Playing in the Dark: Whiteness and the Literary Imagination* that "cultural identities are formed and informed by a nation's literature, and . . . what seemed to be in the 'mind' of the literature of the United States was the self-conscious but highly problematic construction of the American as a new white man" (39). Further, she writes, race "is inextricable from the definition of Americanness—from its origins on through its integrated or disintegrating twentieth-century self" (65).

Morrison argues for the recognition of an "Africanist presence" underwriting all of American literature and culture. My purposes require that I extend Morrison's term "Africanism" to include the Native "other." That is, I believe an "Indianist presence" is also part of the "dark other" underwriting American history and culture—a presence that the spectre of "a devilish Indian behind every tree" in Hawthorne's "Young Goodman Brown" could be seen to signify. Lucy Maddox's analysis of canonical texts in *Removals: Nineteenth-Century American Literature and the Politics of Indian Affairs* would contribute to supporting the claim of such an Indianist presence; so too, I believe, would scrutiny of the tradition of the captivity tale, a project to which I hope to contribute here.

Drawing on the work of such scholars of the history of race in America as Alden T. Vaughan, Winthrop Jordan, Lerone Bennett Jr., Yehudi Webster, Theodore W. Allen, and Charles W. Mills, I argue that the Indian captivity tale, that uniquely American genre, appeared and evolved more or less simultaneously with the discourses that constituted the uniquely American version of racial difference. And as I will argue, the historical coincidence was no accident; rather, captivity narratives were very quickly recognized as useful instruments in the process of evoking "race" and asserting racial hierarchy. The captivity story was a crucial vehicle for Anglo-Americans to become white, as well as for the construction of a "dark" and supposedly inferior category that finally included both Indians and Africans, an "other" whom whites had to displace, discipline, and control in order to achieve their colonial aims. As captivity narratives proliferated, their own textual "other," stories of Pocahontas and other similar Indian "maidens," also moved toward and finally into the forefront of writing that took on a public character in the process of building and defining a nation.

I have not attempted here to construct or to extend the full history or catalog of stories of white women's Indian captivities or of the Pocahontas figure. Such a task would be daunting indeed, since, as Kathryn Zabelle Derounian-Stodola and James Arthur Levernier note, stories of Indian captivity alone "are so numerous that the full corpus of texts has yet to be identified" (8). Other scholars have recently made significant contributions in the direction of developing a more complete history of both figures: June Namias in *White Captives: Gender and Ethnicity on the American Frontier*, Derounian-Stodola and Levernier in *The Indian Captivity Narrative 1550–1900*, and Robert S. Tilton in *Pocahontas: The Evolution of an American Narrative*. Instead of furthering that project, I have made use of the work of these and many other scholars in trying to discern the motives for some of the representations and readings of white women captives and Indian "princesses" at particular moments in U.S. history and to elaborate on the significant coupling of these two specific figures. In that effort, I offer my own readings of both text and context of Mary Rowlandson's seventeenth-century captivity narrative, the Pocahontas legend in the seventeenth century, and selected instances of the deployment of both figures in literary and visual forms at various moments in American history in the late-eighteenth, nineteenth, and twentieth centuries.

Other critics have written about white women captives, and still others about Pocahontas; my contribution is to see the two figures as connected in the cultural work they have been made to do and to consider the ways the two figures have cooperated and intersected in the work of producing an evolving racially inflected and gendered American nationalism. My specific purpose is to explore the politics of race and gender, national identity and subjectivity, representation and reading that have clustered around these connected figures throughout U.S. history.

Kay Schaffer, writing about a nineteenth-century Australian captivity story, describes it as a "liminal narrative . . . arising from first contact between Europeans and the indigenous people": "These liminal stories of first contact . . . could be said to have several important, although discontinuous, effects. Through [written documents], oral histories, and local legends they incite the popular imagination and provide initial constructions of racial, class, and gender differences in and for the colony. . . . they make possible the *first mappings of the land*, producing *a new Western geography*, a social production of space" (114; emphasis mine).

I treat American accounts of white women's captivity and of self-sacrificing Indian women as "liminal narratives" in just that sense, arising in what Mary Louise Pratt has termed the "contact zone," where cultures meet and are mutually transformed. Annette Kolodny describes such narratives as unavoidably dialogic, "multilingual, polyvocal, and . . . multicultural" ("Letting Go" 19), informed as they are by the encounters between cultures and with landscapes that are themselves transformed by cultural exchange. The appeal of such a paradigm, Kolodny claims, "is that English texts, by themselves, could never constitute a sufficient history" (13). And yet the history of captivity narratives and Pocahontas legends in English shows little evidence of any acknowledgement of that inevitable multiplicity.

In the first chapter, "Mary Rowlandson Maps New Worlds," I argue that Rowlandson's narrative is indeed a profoundly dialogic text in which conventional Puritan ideologies contend with experiences that Puritanism could not accommodate. And while a number of scholars in recent years have noted the "double-voiced" quality of her narrative, most responses to the text from the time of its publication to the present have stressed its Puritan piety and its conventional English attitudes toward indigenous people, ignoring or rigorously suppressing the elements of the text that could destabilize the racial and sexual politics that supported first the Puritan errand in the New World and later a hegemonic discourse of white-male-dominated nationhood. In my reading, I have tried to retrieve and highlight the illicit or disqualified knowledges in Rowlandson's narrative that have been obscured by the dominant readings, passages that challenge the colonizing discourses of power her text has most often been used to support. I conclude the chapter with a reading of a poem by Louise Erdrich, a writer of Native American heritage, in which she rereads Rowlandson's narrative, also reinscribing its elements to place into question the ways it has traditionally been read.

Pocahontas, at least so far as we know, left no text of her own, no voice to be controlled; all we know of her is what other writers have made of her, and to retrieve the polyvocal possibilities of her story requires both resistant reading and imaginative reconstruction. In the second chapter, "Close Encounters of the First Kind," I return to the colonizing discourses that accompanied European exploration and "discovery" of the Americas to develop a resistant reading of the ways race, gender, and sexuality were constructed to consolidate and secure the inherently unstable subjectivity of the masculinized white European explorer-conqueror. Pocahontas was a crucial figure in that process in the histories of English settlement in Virginia, and I review the ways her story initially took shape, keeping at the center of my reading the fact that has usually been occluded in renderings in subsequent centuries: that Pocahontas was herself captured by the English and held hostage in Jamestown to protect the settlement from attack by her father, Powhatan, and his warriors. Pocahontas therefore assuredly belongs in a history of captive women in the struggle between Indians and English colonists; in fact, the story of her imprisonment in Jamestown is the first story of a woman's captivity to be written into that long history, and she herself becomes a kind of precursor and Native counterpart to Rowlandson, though a more thoroughly silenced one. I conclude that chapter with readings of some texts by contemporary Native women writers who have worked to decolonize Pocahontas, speaking to or through or for her to address issues of voice and voicelessness, agency and powerlessness, for Native women in American history and contemporary culture.

In the final chapter, "Making a History, Shaping a Nation," I consider some of the texts, both written and visual, in which the white woman captive and the Pocahontas figure have been resurrected for ideological purposes from the late eighteenth century through the nineteenth and twentieth centuries. Such representations in the post-Revolutionary period, I argue, supported the quest of the newly independent republic for a "suitable" national history and identity, one that placed whiteness and masculinity in a superior position to other categories of identity; in the nineteenth century, accompanied and engaged national policies and politics of Indian removal as well as the crisis over slavery; and in the twentieth century, were replayed in the wake of the two world wars, accompanied the civil rights movement, and have been enlisted in the current debates over multiculturalism as once again issues of race and national identity needed to be reshaped and reasserted.

"Myth," says Richard Slotkin, "is the language in which a society remembers its history" (*Gunfighter Nation* 655). Certainly representations and replications of captive women and of welcoming Indian maidens have made innumerable appearances in the "remembered" history of the United States and have become inextricable from our national mythology. Because myths are one of the ways a society *creates* the history it chooses to inscribe and perpetuate, the captive white woman and the Pocahontas figure have been manipulated and put to work to help create, and to serve, a history of the United States as a domain ruled by white Anglo-American men, even as the labor and contributions, both voluntary and coerced, of women, other immigrant groups, and people of color helped to underwrite the establishment of an Anglo-American nation on this continent.

Such a process of selection in the interest of promoting the "remembering" of particular versions of "history" is clear when we consider the typical omission of Pocahontas's captivity in most popular versions of her legend, including the recent animated Disney feature film *Pocahontas*. To admit her captivity would cloud the versions that strove to emphasize her embrace of Englishmen, English culture, and Christianity as symbolizing England's legitimate right to colonize North America. It is, after all, images of Pocahontas's "rescue" of John Smith and her baptism in Jamestown that decorate the U.S. Capitol building in Washington. (See Fryd 22, 48, 146.)

It is important also to recognize that the story of Pocahontas's captivity recorded in the chronicles of the Jamestown colony, with all its lapses and silences, must stand in for other missing narratives—those of the many other Native women who were taken captive by conquerors and colonists but whose stories were never written at all. As June Namias writes, "From the European perspective, the white captive was a centerpiece in history and literature from the earliest days of European and Native American contact. Although many natives, including Pocahontas, were kidnapped by the British, captivity by Indians made celebrities of John Smith, Mary Rowlandson, John and Eunice Williams, and Daniel Boone and his daugher Jemima" (8), among many others. The story of Pocahontas's capture perhaps was seen as worthy of recording not only because of her significance as a symbolic representative of her country, but also because her subsequent baptism and marriage to an Englishman "justified," from the English point of view, the act of their having taken her hostage.

Narratives of white women's captivities rest, therefore, on precursor narratives of Native women's captivities, which either were not written at all or, as in the case of Pocahontas, were written not by the captive herself but by those with vested interests very different from hers. White women's captivity narratives, including Rowlandson's, are thus hybridized not only by what they could and could not say about their contact with Indians, but because they rest on the suppressed and silenced record of Native women's captivity among white colonists. The later proliferations of both narratives continued to ensure the erasure of the indigenous woman's subjectivity while reproducing the constraints on the subjectivity of white women.

Of course, no study of women's captivities and their place in the histories of colonization in the Americas can claim to be definitive when confined to the written record of one colonizing group. This study is thus unavoidably partial. I have limited my investigation to texts in English and grounded my argument in those texts, in part because my field is American literature and culture in English and in part because English has been the dominant language and textual record in the evolution of the United States as a nation. An analysis of the ways representations of women's captivity have served the colonization of the Americas would be complete only if it included representations of women's captivities in colonizing discourses in Spanish and in French.

And even the record in those colonial languages, as I have indicated, could not be complete; because so many of the languages spoken by indigenous groups at the time of contact have been obliterated along with their speakers, a full colonial history of the Americas is irretrievable. We must therefore read the texts produced by the colonizing powers, as I do here those in English, fully aware that they tell only part of the story and fully aware of all that is missing—human beings and cultures along with their stories—because destroyed.

My interest in studying stories and legends of captive women and Indian "princesses" began precisely because of the ways race and gender emerge from these narratives, converging and cooperating in and through them to construct a particular version of "American-ness," one which has claimed power over other possible versions and obscured, erased, or co-opted them. My title, *Cartographies of Desire*, reflects my conviction that stories about white women's captivities and welcoming Indian maidens have repeatedly helped to construct the map of the United States, both geographic and ideological, of contested territory as well as of the ideologies of race and sex that have informed the evolution of an American nation on this continent. The desire of the colonizers for land was conflated with desire for a Native woman who was a representative or stand-in for the land itself; likewise, the effort to "protect" white women from the presumed desire of dark men, both Indian and African, was a coded insistence on the right of the colonists to territory already taken or not yet taken but desired. The history of Anglo-America, then, is a map of confluent desires, sexual and territorial, that over time produced and consolidated the map of America as we know it today.

Captivity narratives attracted my attention not only because of the ways they inscribe the subjugated woman and the convergences of race and gender in the construction of America, but also because I believe them to be a productive place from which to assert the intersections of textuality and materiality, of what is written and what is lived as experience. In the work that follows, conventional passages of textual analysis—the traditional form of literary scholarship—are supplemented with passages of personal narrative, stories thematically or imagistically related to the texts I consider. In reading texts and landscapes by way of both conventional textual analysis and personal narrative, my intention is to insist on the relevance of textuality to our daily lived experience. We know ourselves because of what cultural histories tell us about who we are; we occupy landscapes marked with the ideologies that produce those histories. I hope my narratives of memories and journeys to emblematic landscapes and cultural sites will invite readers to reflect on how texts such as the ones I consider have shaped the nation and ourselves as its subjects and citizens and will contribute to a more accurate understanding of U.S. history and culture as profoundly polycentric and polyvocal, multiracial and multicultural.

I have benefitted in ways I hope are obvious from the "shift, or rupture, in ideological premises" that Houston Baker describes and that has been taking place in recent years in the development of new historicist, feminist, African American and Native studies, and cultural-studies approaches to understanding the broadly defined "text" of American literary and cultural history, and I look forward to the "striking new figurations" of that history that will emerge from the collective effort of scholars in those fields. I see my work as both informed by and situated within that collective effort of "looking across the categories of race and gender . . . [to] see the ways in which definitions of race, gender, and sexuality have been inextricably interlinked with definitions of what is or is not 'American'" (Moon and Davidson 6).

Here, then, a cartography of America, and of some of the desires that brought it into being.

CHAPTER 1

Mary Rowlandson Maps New Worlds

The socially and historically produced concerns of women writers . . . help to form a map of the possible subject positions open to women, what they could say or not from within the discursive field of femininity in which they were located.

—CHRIS WEEDON, *Feminist Practice and Poststructuralist Theory*

To Lancaster: February 1991

Mid-February in Massachusetts is a liminal season: full winter, or flashes of early spring, or anything in between. Lancaster at shortly after midday on this February Monday in 1991 is quiet, as I suppose it usually is, and a high winter sun contends with but fails to conquer the clouds that mask its brightness but let a little of its warmth through. It's a pleasant day, a taste of coming spring, though the pleasantness is promised for a few hours only: tonight it is to turn cold again, and the clouds will prevail, thickening and sprinkling New England with snow or freezing rain. I'm here to nose around just briefly; I want to be home safe and sound before the bad weather hits.

Earlier this morning, I listened to the weather forecast on the radio, sandwiched between news from the Persian Gulf, as I dressed for my foray: jeans, turtleneck, denim shirt with Native designs embroidered on the placket, heavy socks and hiking boots in case I had to do some trekking, and as a final touch, silver earrings, "Genuine Indian Hand Made," in honor of the occasion.

On the radio, someone was talking about the Gulf war, "Desert Shield" now metamorphosed into "Desert Storm," and about the army's Apache and Blackhawk helicopters. A meeting is going on in Moscow: Mikhail Gorbachev will confer with Iraq's foreign minister, Tariq Aziz, to discuss Iraq's conditional offer to withdraw from Kuwait. But a ground offensive seems imminent. There was a report on how satellites are, the woman's voice said, "playing a vital role in the prosecution of the war by allied forces." The satellites predict weather, pick out targets, and assist navigation. But they were apparently unable to detect the movement of civilians into a Baghdad building the United States bombed last week. Iraqi civilians don't count, so aren't counted in the toll of the war; they're "collateral damage." Once again we are seduced by technology, even unto death, even when the technology doesn't work.

So much of this war reminds me of Vietnam, echoes and reverberations in every news story. Different, but the same. The rhythmic whack-whack of chopper blades. The inability—or worse, the refusal—to see things from the point of view of others. In my most syncretic and cynical moods, all the wars of America's history seem like that to me: different, but the same. This one is eerie in a new way; though I mostly manage to avoid it by not turning on the television, this is a prime-time war, the first to have its own title logo, even its own theme music, no doubt its own marketing experts, as the networks participate in the information blackout by pretending to "cover" the "news." No, it's Public Radio for me. It's harder to censor the mind's eye, and, absent actual images like the ones that haunted my sleep during Vietnam, my imagination produces pictures of the Persian Gulf drama that equal those earlier ones in their horror, images that, paradoxically, the current television coverage would shield me from. Painful as it is, I want the reality, even if I have to imagine it for myself.

Last week I saw a billboard with a Desert Storm image. The photographic space was filled completely with sand—no horizon line, no blue sky to balance the gold of the sun-drenched sand. And no trees, no low bushes, no plants of any kind; no water either, or evidence of it, and no sign of animal life. The field of sand was not completely empty, however. Superimposed on its blankness in the lower-right-hand corner was a dense, dark object: an armored tank, artillery ready. It appeared small in the photograph against the immensity of sand, but I know enough about tanks, having been close to them enough times before, to know that in actuality it is massive. The tank in the photograph was making its way across the desert, its twin tracks scoring the sand in its wake. Beneath the photograph, in bold black letters, was the phrase "Business As Usual" and then "Support Your Friends in the National Guard and Reserve."

I knew exactly how I was meant to read that photograph. American tanks in great numbers are at the moment leaving twin tracks in the desert sand of Saudi Arabia, and American National Guard and Reserve troops in large numbers are deployed in this latest American imperial errand. And yes, taking the long view, it is business as usual. A Cherokee acquaintance told me a few days ago of having read in the newspaper a remark made by Gen. Colin Powell in Saudi Arabia, announcing the military's readiness to invade Iraq: "We're prepared to go into Indian Country if we have to." I remember the phrase "Indian Country" being used in Vietnam as well. Colin Powell, African American and Vietnam veteran, should know better. For that matter, so should we all.

This morning, listening to the Desert Storm news, I kept recalling, seeing inside my head, the scene in Louise Erdrich's novel *Love Medicine* where Henry Lamartine, the Ojibwa soldier from a reservation in North Dakota, has been assigned to guard and interrogate a Vietnamese woman prisoner. The woman points first to her own Asian eyefold, and then to his: "You, me, same," she says. Henry gets it, and the weight of the awareness eventually causes him to crack. Taino, Arawak, Carib, Pequod, Narragansett, Wampanoag, West African, Cherokee, Ojibwa, Lakota, Vietnamese, Cambodian, Panamanian, Iraqi—nodes in a long and painful history. Different, but the same. As a nation, we seem to be locked in the past, too often repeating our history without understanding it. Our "Indians" are everywhere.

After coffee, in the still-early morning, I climbed into the car and headed east, my destination a town that was, three centuries ago, at the western frontier of the English settlement encircling Boston. I left the Connecticut River behind, the western boundary of the terrain that Mary Rowlandson and her Indian captors traversed during her weeks in the wilderness. Moved by a desire to understand another of our wars, one of the early instances of armed conflict between English colonizers and Native people in American history, I have come to Lancaster to assess a moment in our national past, come in search of traces of the two cultures that clashed so violently here exactly 315 years ago. The Indians were the victors in the battle on that February day in 1676. I know, of course, who won the war.

A few miles from home, I picked up the Mass Turnpike, its green signs featuring the familiar tall, buckled Puritan hat, now minus the Indian arrow that, I'm told, until recently pierced it on signs throughout the state. I wondered again, as I have before, what prompted the erasure of what I can't help thinking of as a sign of colonial vulnerability, and of Indian force and fury, from highway signs across Massachusetts.

In the rural stretches, the stark white of birch bark and scattered patches of snow accented the ochres, umbers, russets, and piney greens of the late-winter landscape. I had mapped my travel: the turnpike east to Worcester, north on 190, east to Lancaster. It's a quick route; spared the circuitous foot travel that Rowlandson and her captors were forced into, I covered in less than two hours the distance that took them nearly two months.

Lancaster lies just to the west of Interstate 495, the outermost beltway around Boston, and north of Clinton, east of Sterling, south of Gate's Crossing, south and west of Fort Devens, which I know from a previous life was once, and for all I know may be still, the stateside headquarters of the U.S. Army's Special Forces troops, the Green Berets. The names of the counties that surround Boston and are in turn enclosed by I-495 are, in their aggregate effect, startlingly English: Essex, Middlesex, Norfolk, Plymouth. Apparently the colonists' organization of land for purposes of rule and governance—counties, townships, towns, and villages—

proceeded hand-in-hand with English naming. If I had been willing to wander and take more time en route, I could have passed through the villages of Nichewaug and Quinapoxet, but most of the town names on the map are of distinctly English origin: Wheelwright, Spencer, Brookfield. And Princeton, where Rowlandson's captivity ended at what is now called Redemption Rock, when she was ransomed for twenty English pounds, a substantial sum in those days. All around me in every direction, though, features of the natural landscape bore their ancient Native names: Lake Lashaway, Mount Wachuset, Wickaboag Pond, Quacumquasit Pond, Lake Chabunagungamaug. I crossed the Quaboag River and then headed toward the Wachuset Range. In the settlement days in this country, it seems, "nature" was Native, but "culture" was relentlessly English.

Sooner than I expected, I passed a familiar Massachusetts township line marker: "Lancaster, established 1653." The road widened at a crossroads; lawns and trees appeared, surrounding old homes and small-scale community buildings, and I found myself in the town where Mary Rowlandson's complex adventures began.

The Lancaster Fire Department is housed next to the town common in an impressive Victorian structure. I suppose a town that was once erased by fire, burned to the ground by Indians in its early days, thinks a fire department worthy of grand digs. I spot a historical marker, stop, and climb out of the car to read it:

ROWLANDSON ROCK

ON THE CREST OF GEORGE HILL, NEAR BY,

IS SITUATED ROWLANDSON ROCK WHERE THE CAPTIVES FROM

THE ROWLANDSON GARRISON HOUSE PASSED THEIR FIRST

NIGHT AFTER THE BURNING OF LANCASTER BY THE INDIANS

FEBRUARY 10, 1675–76.

MASSACHUSETTS BAY TERCENTENARY COMMISSION.

The sign is crested with the state seal bracketed by dates: 1630–1930. It celebrates the perseverance through three hundred years of the culture that was insistently inserting itself into this country in the seventeenth century but which was perched so precariously on this edge of Anglo settlement in 1676. Back in the car, I notice that a clutch of schoolchildren on the sidewalk stop, look up, and read the marker. My attention seems to have rendered it visible to them, maybe for the first time.

Though George Hill is supposed to be "near by," I look in all directions, but nowhere can I see anything I'd readily call a hill. A hundred yards to the east, a lovely, sprawling old white colonial building, in the typical paratactic New England style, cupola'd and green-roofed, announces itself as the "Southern New England Conference of the SDA." A large sign by the road says "Seventh Day Adventist Book Center." Off to the right a brick smokestack rises high above everything else in town, bearing the letters "AU." Atlantic Union College is the one thing I already knew was in Lancaster; its location is marked on my map with a red flag. I decide it must be an Adventist college, and I muse on how the name signifies what christianized this area in the first place—the "Atlantic union" of England and the New England colonies, bound by a common Christianity despite their differences. Christianity is still a dominant presence in the town; so far I see no trace of Native culture. But maybe I just don't know where—or how—to look. I start the car and, pausing a moment to decide on a direction, head off to find George Hill.

WRITING CAPTIVITY

Mary White Rowlandson wrote only one book, first published in both Boston and London in 1682, a narrative of her nearly three months' captivity among the Narragansetts in 1676 during Metacom's Rebellion, or "King Philip's War," waged in Massachusetts in 1675-76.[1] That book, though, was the first in prose written by an American woman, admitting all the difficulties of the designation "American" during the colonial period, and acknowledging too that it is a retrospective designation. Rowlandson would never have thought of herself as "American," as her narrative makes clear with its many references to things "English." That tension between English and American identity was then, and remains now, a source of her narrative's interest and persistent appeal; it became one of the first and most enduring best-sellers in American literary history and has remained almost continually in print during the more than three hundred years since its initial publication.

Furthermore, her narrative initiated and became the prototype for innumerable subsequent stories of the white woman captured by Indians, a figure that has been continually reinvoked in poems, novels, stories, pulp fiction, sculpture, and painting throughout the centuries of Euro-American efforts to claim and control the North American continent.[2] Renewed scrutiny of the colonial era prompted by the 1992 Columbus Quincentenary, combined with recent developments in the methodologies of literary criticism, including feminist, cultural-studies, Native studies, and new historicist approaches, has resulted in a resurgence of interest in captivity narratives, bringing Rowlandson's text once more to the attention of scholars of American literary and cultural history. Her narrative and the history of its reproductions offer compelling evidence that the figure of the white woman captive has been a primary site for the construction of race, gender, and national identity in U.S. culture.

Mary White was born in England sometime between 1635 and 1637, the daughter of John White and Joan West of Somerset.[3] The family immigrated to the Bay Colony in 1639, when Mary was still in her early childhood. In 1653, they moved west to Lancaster, a "plantation" on the outermost periphery of English settlement around Boston. The land had been purchased some ten years earlier from the Nashaways by a Boston trader.[4]

The Whites were among the first settlers in Lancaster—"settlers," as Alice Walker reminds us, being "a very benign euphemism for what they actually were" ("Blue" 5–6). Certainly most Puritan settlers saw themselves in benign terms: Bearers of the light of "human civilization" into a "New Eden," they believed themselves charged with installing their "godly" culture in this land which, as William Bradford wrote, they also saw as "a hideous and desolate wilderness, full of wild beasts and wild men" (70). They believed they were the tamers. Indeed, the indigenous peoples served as a convenient "other" against whom the Puritans could construct, and "prove" through difference, their colonial identities. As Richard Slotkin has written, "Looking at the culture of the New World in which they had come to live, the Puritans saw a darkened and inverted mirror image of their own culture, their own mind. For every Puritan institution, moral theory and practice, belief and ritual there existed an antithetical Indian counterpart" (*Regeneration* 57). Thus Puritans were "civilized" because Indians were "savage"; they were "human" because Indians were "beastlike"; they were "God's people" because Indians were "diabolical."[5] These oppositions served not only to secure Puritan identity, but also to justify the colonial exploitation of New England and the zealous attempts to eradicate Native Americans and their cultures from the region.

Joseph Rowlandson, the sole member of the Harvard class of 1652, was called to Lancaster as its first minister in 1654. He and Mary White married in 1656. They had four children: a daughter, Mary, born in 1658, who died in early childhood; a son, Joseph, born in 1662; another daughter, another Mary, born in 1665; and the baby, Sarah, born in 1669.

In 1675, a rebellion of the region's confederated Native peoples broke out, led by Metacom, leader of the Wampanoag. It was a violent and bitter last effort on the part of the region's indigenous people to rid their country of the English. By the late winter of 1676 rumors of an imminent attack on Lancaster circulated, and Joseph Rowlandson left home for Boston to petition the colonial council for reinforcements. While her husband was absent, Mary Rowlandson's long drama began, the sequence of events that would ultimately make her experience fuel for the ideological mill that would finally generate an American nation.

Before 1675, Puritan relations with Metacom's people had been for the most part less openly hostile. Massasoit, the Wampanoag sachem when the *Mayflower* landed at Cape Cod, treated with the English, "sold" them parcels of land, and before his death asked the governor of the colony, as a token of friendship, to give English names to his two sons, Wamsutta and Metacom,[6] thereafter known in English annals as Alexander and Philip. Wamsutta, he of that now most thoroughly domesticated name (appropriated by a company that manufactures "domestics," or sheets and towels), became the Wampanoag leader after Massasoit's death, but died suddenly and mysteriously en route home from a state visit to the English to settle a dispute; Metacom suspected, perhaps rightly, that the English had poisoned his brother (Abbot 171).

It was a major grievance in a long line of grievances. The proud Metacom, now King Philip to the English, became leader, or sachem, of the Wampanoag. Throughout his lifetime, he had watched the English encroachment with dismay. Resentful at the English appropriation of Wampanoag territory and the progressive debilitation of his people through the shrinking of land available for their sustenance as well as through the diseases imported from Europe to which they had no immunity, Metacom enlisted the Nipmucs and the Narragansetts in a confederacy to rise up against the English. He had a specific kinship alliance with the Narragansetts already: Wamsutta's widow, Weetamoo (also the sister of Metacom's wife Wootonekanuske), had after Wamsutta's death married a Narragansett, Quinnapin, Rowlandson's "master" in her narrative. Weetamoo[7] was the "mistress" Rowlandson served during captivity, and she reigned as a powerful squaw sachem over the Narragansetts. She harbored an especially fierce dislike for the English, no doubt in part because of the circumstances surrounding Wamsutta's death.[8]

Biding his time, Metacom planned an offensive that he hoped would wipe out the whites who occupied his country. In 1675, war erupted. The conflict, as Laurel Thatcher Ulrich characterizes it, was "one of the most destructive wars in proportion to population in American history" (173); by the time the war ended some six months later, "fifty-two of the ninety towns in the region had been attacked and twelve destroyed" (Ulrich 173).

The Rowlandson garrison house at Lancaster was a stockade, one of six in the town built for purposes of defense. At the time of the attack it sheltered an extended family that included two of Mary's sisters and their families. The garrison house, as a fortress, was clearly meant to keep things out—the seeming chaos of the "vast and howling wilderness" (132),[9] everything resident in the American landscape, especially its inhabitants, which was seen as a threat to English "civilization" and religious belief. But it was also meant to keep things in—to protect and sustain the Puritan theocratic worldview as well as the colonists' sense of their own Englishness, the foundation for preserving their identities and their sense of providential mission at what was for them the edge of the known world.

Of Rowlandson's narrative itself we can ask a similar question: what was it meant to keep in, and what was it meant to keep out?

"On the tenth of February 1675, Came the Indians with great numbers upon Lancaster" (118). So begins Rowlandson's narrative, a masterpiece of nonfiction prose told in language readers have described as "pure, idiomatic, sinewy English" (*Oxford Companion* 730), "vigorous" and "earthy" (Leach 201), "a powerful and deeply moving piece of writing" (Ulrich 227). The ensuing scene is gruesome, and Rowlandson plunges the reader into it with powerful immediacy. Death surrounds her. She sees a sister, a brother-in-law, nephews and neighbors fall. A bullet passes through the child she is holding in her arms—Sarah, age six—and into her own side. "Thus were we butchered by those merciless Heathen," she writes, "standing amazed, with the blood running down to our heels" (120). It is the end of life as Rowlandson has known it. Yet, in the first of a series of gestures the reader comes to know as characteristic of her, she chooses life, whatever its new terms may prove to be, and goes with her captors, carrying the mortally wounded Sarah in her arms: "I had often before this said, that if the Indians should come, I should chuse rather to be killed by them then taken alive but when it came to the tryal my mind changed; their glittering weapons so daunted my spirit, that I chose rather to go along with those (as I may say) ravenous Beasts, then that moment to end my dayes" (121).

Camped that first night on the crest of George Hill about a mile from Lancaster—she must have been able to look down and see the smoldering ruins of her own house and the rest of the town—Rowlandson, longing for the shelter of the familiar, asks her captors if she and Sarah might lodge in a vacant house "hard by"; their reply is "what will you love English men still?" (121). By implication, she must learn to love Indians, surely an unimaginable prospect to a woman heretofore securely contained within the walls of Puritan ideology. She is, and must stay, out-of-doors—is, in Susan Howe's wonderful phrase, "abducted from the structure of experience" (96). Out-of-doors, she occupies what is for her an unarticulated space, one that will require of her a new consciousness; she experiences the disintegration of the familiar world that anchors and gives substance to a remembered and recognized self. The security and predictability of the walled garrison gives way to the openness of the "wilderness," its utter unpredictability. With everything gone—husband, home, family, children scattered or destroyed or killed or captive—Rowlandson must structure experience anew. The next morning she must, as she so vividly puts it, "turn my back upon the Town, and travel with them into the vast and desolate Wilderness, I knew not whither" (122–23).

Rowlandson was one of twenty-four captives taken in the Lancaster attack, including her son and older daughter, from whom she was separated shortly after their capture. After a week of carrying Sarah in her arms, Rowlandson suffers the death of this beloved youngest child and is forced to leave her in an unmarked grave in the wilderness; once again she must "turn [her] back" on what is familiar and deeply loved, leave it behind, and move forward into the unknown. And once again, despite her desperate grief, she chooses life over death: "I have thought since of the wonderfull goodness of God to me, in preserving me in the use of my reason and senses, in that distressed time, that I did not use wicked and violent means to end my own miserable life" (125).

Mitchell Robert Breitwieser argues that Sarah's death, and the interrupted project of mourning that ensued, defined Rowlandson's experience in captivity. Her narrative, he asserts, is a record of the failure of Puritan theology to absorb all experience, and her grief was a sign of her radical separation from the Puritan community. It was a breach that Rowlandson's narrative in part records and in part attempts to elide; even her eventual ransom and return to that community failed to heal the breach fully, as the powerful closing passage of her narrative suggests. Sarah's death severed Rowlandson's last physical link to her former self except for rare meetings with her other two children; thus it dislocated her from her own history and identity in a way that could only have been terrifying in its profundity. The narrative is a record of Rowlandson's struggles to confront and accommodate that radical dislocation as, forced to accompany her captors as they flee the English militia, she is progressively removed from the world she had known.

Sarah's death, while the most devastating, was not the only affliction Rowlandson suffered in captivity. Displaced from her home and usual sources of sustenance, Rowlandson had to share her captors' dislocations as well, for they too were in constant danger of starvation and kept continually on the move by the pursuing colonial militia. During the twenty "Removes" that structure her narrative and signal her incremental distancing from the familiar world, she, like the Indians themselves, endured constant hunger, exhaustion, and cold. She suffered also from her separation from her surviving children, and from immediate, persistent anxiety: Would she be killed? Would she starve? Would her children survive? Would she be reunited with her family? And perhaps most deeply, what was the meaning of her experience? How was it to be comprehended?

Rowlandson's efforts to record and interpret her experience when she came to write the story of her captivity elicited two distinct narrative voices or registers. Both were required in order to represent that experience and all its contradictions, and yet readers become aware through repeated dissonances in the text that neither voice was adequate to account for all that she saw and for all that happened to her during her stay with the Indians.

Early in her captivity, one of the Narragansetts, returning from an attack on another English settlement, gives her a small Bible that had been taken as part of the plunder. The Bible is a source of spiritual sustenance for Rowlandson throughout her remaining time with her captors and in the narrative provides the sustained voice of the Christian soul living through her own trial in the wilderness. Citation of biblical passages is a primary interpretive strategy in the narrative as well as one of the structuring motifs of Rowlandson's text; it represents the conventional Puritan self to which she tries to cling as a way of explaining her captivity as well as a means of surviving and eventually escaping it. The interlacing of biblical texts into her own was doubtless also meant to give evidence to Puritan readers of her status as a member of the Elect, one who has been tried and found not wanting faith sufficient to guarantee salvation, and who, upon her ransom, or as the Puritans termed it, her "redemption," deserved to be welcomed back into the fold of the Puritan community with open arms. Thus the sustained Bible-quoting supports a typological reading of her experience as the journey of the soul, captive in time and mortal flesh, toward redemption and eternal salvation.[10]

Another voice, however, insinuates itself with that of the conventional, Bible-quoting Puritan woman and becomes progressively more evident as her time in captivity, and the text itself, increases. Robert Diebold has distinguished Rowlandson's two voices or narrative styles as "colloquial," the voice she uses to record and describe her experiences and observations, and "biblical," the voice she relies upon to interpret those experiences and observations (cvi). One way to figure the difference in the two registers is that the biblical is used to ensure and prove Rowlandson's spiritual survival in captivity, the colloquial to explain and defend her physical survival.

Puritan theology provided her with one way of reading the significance of her captivity, of seeing it as a test of faith, as a metaphor for the vulnerability of Christian settlers in a "heathen wilderness," as proof of God's favor in demonstrating her election among the saved. That theology, though, as an explanatory system, failed in the face of much of Rowlandson's experience; it could not accommodate such things as her captors' evident suffering at the hands of the English, their many gestures of solicitousness and generosity toward her, their always-respectful treatment of her person, her finding a place for herself within the Indian community. It is the colloquial voice within her text, then, the voice that records but cannot construct an interpretive schema, that remains compelling after the biblical interpretations are set aside as conventional. And it is the tension between these two narrative voices that invites scrutiny in any attempt to measure the cultural weight Rowlandson's text and others like it have had in the formation of a Euro-American nation and national identity.

Paradoxically, Indian captivity represented for Puritan women of New England an expansion of experience rather than what we might ordinarily think would be a contraction or restriction of experience. Captivity, as Laurel Thatcher Ulrich says, could open "new worlds both of terror and of possibility" (202).[11] The colloquial voice in Rowlandson's narrative is the one assigned to incorporate the expansion of her experience that captivity offered, to record what Puritan ideology could not contain. Rowlandson's text is one of the earliest ethnographies in English of Native American life, and the first written by a woman. Her colloquial voice is that of a woman who consumes Indian food, sleeps among Indians, learns some of their language—of a woman with the audacity to question God's providence in a number of passages in her text, once by "mention[ing] a few remarkable passages of providence" (158) in "pre-serving the heathen for farther affliction to our poor Countrey" (159) when the same circumstances confound the pursuing English army. It is the voice of a woman whose experience has given her evident authority outside the fold of the Puritan community, an authority based not on submission and cooperation, the prescribed modes for women in Puritan society, but on a new capacity—to refuse and to resist.

Puritan women of course played an important role in the project of colonization, often cooperating in the construction of an "other" that guaranteed and sustained Puritan identity, an "other" that was variously the wilderness, nature and its caprice, Indians—and also sometimes women themselves. Englishwomen and Indians in fact stood in a very similar relation to the patriarchal male Puritan: both were thought of as not fully adult; both were defined, in their benign aspects, by their presumed dependence on the Puritan "father" figure; both were thought to have a more intimate connection with the forces of "nature" (rather than "culture")—Indians because of their supposedly "uncivilized" or "precivilized" way of life, women because of their cyclic rhythms, reproductive function, and bodily experiences of childbirth, lactation, and nurturance—and thus to be more inclined to licentiousness and other kinds of unruliness. In the case of a woman captive, she was, through an act of violence, suddenly physically allied with those with whom she had been ideologically linked because of all that she and they were supposed to have in common. And while part of her dilemma was that precise connection, another was the requirement that she reverse her socially prescribed behavior: she must not cooperate but rather must resist, reject the passive subservience that had been required of her and that she had been socialized to, and repudiate the resemblances between herself and her captors that she had learned at home. Her capacity for resistance during captivity, her ability to fight back and to say no—essential to her survival and, upon "redemption," to her being accepted again into her home community—was also problematic and made her suspect within that community if she returned, because it signaled a transgression of her prescribed feminine role within the Puritan community.

The story of another captive, Hannah Dustan, provides a dramatic example of the difficulty that resistive behavior on the part of a returned captive woman presented to Puritan ideological constructions of gender and emerging constructions of race. Dustan, five days after giving birth, was captured during an attack on Haverill (Massachusetts) in 1697 along with her newborn infant and Mary Neff, who was attending her during her confinement. Her newborn child was killed, but eventually Dustan, with the help of Neff and a young captive English boy, Samuel Lennardson, escaped after murdering—and scalping—the family of Indians, which included six children, who were holding her captive. Dustan, along with Neff and Lennardson, returned to Boston with ten scalps and claimed the scalp bounty that the proof of the dead Indians earned her.

Dustan's story was problematic for the Puritans—and for later generations of Americans as well; Hawthorne, Thoreau, and Whittier all wrote about her[12]—because of the ways her behavior confounded both cultural and gender expectations and deconstructed differences in the oppositions masculine/feminine and English/Indian. On the one hand, she was viewed as heroic because she killed Indians, but on the other hand, her act of scalping her victims was so "Indian-like" and her aggression and capacity for violence so "masculine" that her story was deeply unsettling for the colonists, whose views of how Englishwomen ought to behave were rigidly codified. Laurel Thatcher Ulrich notes Cotton Mather's comparison of Dustan's act with that of Jael in the Old Testament, who slew an enemy of her people by "driving a tent peg through his head" (168), a method, as Ulrich observes, that is "a rude caricature" of the male role in the sexual act (170). Dustan's "heroism" was thus doubly transgressive: her behavior made her not only like an Indian, but, like Jael, also like a man.

The behavior required of a woman if she was to survive captivity, then, often required transgressing gender expectations in ways that would arouse suspicion of her once she returned to her home culture. Most often that suspicion located itself primarily in the question of her sexual integrity during captivity, a question situated, at the time of the first publication of Rowlandson's narrative, in the colonists' efforts to invoke and police racial distinctions between English and Native peoples.

RACE IN THE THEATRE OF COLONIALISM

Rowlandson's narrative appeared during the late seventeenth century, just at the time when discourses of racial difference were evolving in the colonies into the forms we would recognize today, as scholars of U.S. racial history have demonstrated. Alden T. Vaughan in *Roots of American Racism* traces the evolution of English attitudes toward Indians from the beginnings of colonization to the mid-nineteenth century; he argues that, at first, English colonists saw the differences between themselves and the indigenous people as cultural rather than racial. According to Vaughan, the process of racializing the Indians as utterly and irrevocably "other" took fully two centuries:

> English and American writers, and most likely the mass of their countrymen, believed at the outset of England's age of expansion that Africans were inherently and immutably black—a color fraught with pejorative implications—and that therefore Africans were fundamentally unassimilable even if they adopted English ways and beliefs. They were, as their color proclaimed, a separate branch of humankind. By contrast, Anglo-Americans believed that American Indians were inherently like themselves and that they were approximately as light-skinned as Europeans; they could—indeed would—be assimilated into colonial society as soon as they succumbed to English social norms and Christian theology. The basic beliefs about Africans held fast through - out the colonial period and beyond. The assumptions about Native Americans underwent a slow but drastic change in the late seventeenth century and throughout the eighteenth as Anglo-Americans shifted their perception of Indian character and, concomitantly, of Indian color from innately white to innately dark and eventually to red. . . . Although the Indians' position in British America was always precarious, not until they were thought of as inherently inferior "redmen" rather than unenlightened "whites" did their separate and unequal status become firmly fixed in the American mind. Only then could the bulk of American writers hold that Indians were prevented by nature— rather than by education or environment—from full participation in America's democracy and prosperity. (5)[13]

In *Before the Mayflower: A History of Black America*, Lerone Bennett Jr. uses class as another category for analyzing early colonial social arrangements when he notes that the institution of slavery itself evolved; that the first Africans brought to Virginia as laborers were owned by their masters only for a specified period of time, at the end of which they could become free; and that such indentured servants, both black and white, constituted "the majority of the colonial population" (40; see also Morgan 327 ff.). Bennett describes a cultural pattern in the seventeenth-century English colonies in which "race" typically took second place to the distinction between "bound"—indentured servants, both black and white—and "free"—landholders, largely of the white aristocratic class. Writing about the Virginia colony in the early seventeenth century, Bennett says,

> Working together in the same fields, sharing the same huts, the same situation, and the same grievances, the first black and white Americans, aristocrats excepted, developed strong bonds of sympathy and mutuality. . . . The basic division at that juncture was between servants and free people, and there were whites and blacks on both sides of the line.
>
> Of all the improbable aspects of this situation, the oddest—to modern blacks and whites—is that white people did not seem to know that they were white. It appears from surviving evidence that the first white colonists had no concept of themselves as white people. The legal documents identified whites as Englishmen and/or Christians. The word white, with its burden of arrogance and biological pride, developed late in the century, as a direct result of slavery and the organized debasement of blacks. (40)

Vaughan claims that when North American exploration and colonization began, most Europeans recognized the opposition white/black and believed that Africans were fundamentally different from themselves; Bennett, though, portrays that opposition as having been more unstable during the early years of colonization, at least among the subordinate class of indentured laborers, both black and white. Winthrop Jordan, situating the articulation of racial differences within the agendas of colonialism, says that Blacks and Indians presented Europeans with "distinctively different intellectual problems," and that "[b]y very reason of their own intention to plant themselves in America, Englishmen had from the first been under pressure to describe the Indian's complexion in terms which would render the prospect of settlement in the New World an attractive one"—that is, as more light than dark (239). The late seventeenth century, then—the time of the first publication of Rowlandson's narrative and its immediate immense popularity—was a period when transplanted English colonists were working out the racial differences among themselves as "white," Africans as "black," and American Natives as "red"—and the social practices those differences would underwrite.

Another scholar of U.S. racial history and theory, Yehudi Webster, also identifies the seventeenth century as the period when the philosophical foundations for racial differences were beginning to be constructed:

> Starting in the seventeenth century, certain eminent naturalists, ethnologists, and anthropologists initiated a systematic construction of different races within the human species. Nature was conceived as an intrinsically hierarchical order whose gradations culminated in a First Cause, or the Creator. Nonwhites were the last link in "a great chain of being." In some of these "scientific" writings, the black race was deemed inferior and derived from a separate biological tree. Its enslavement was a natural outcome caused by the unequal biological endowments of the races. (4)

That the cultural work of racializing the world and constructing a racial hierarchy was already underway by the early seventeenth century is indicated by these lines published in London in 1620 by the English poet Thomas Peyton contrasting the inhabitants of Africa with Europeans:

> The Libian dusky in his parched skin,
> The Moor all tawny both without and in,
> The Southern man, a black deformed Elfe,
> The Northern white like unto God himselfe.
> (quoted in Vaughan 6)

The poem not only places northern Europeans at the top of a racial pyramid with only God—a God who is white—above them and all Africans below, but it employs a descriptive color term, "tawny," which some early explorers used to describe the skin color of Native people of the Americas (Vaughan 8) and which eventually came to be used as a pejorative noun for Indians (as the Indian-hating servant Jennet uses it in Catharine Maria Sedgwick's *Hope Leslie* [1827]). The poem indicates that among English people at that time, a perception was already forming of a single racial demarcation, that between "white" and "dark," and thus predicts that the "tawny" North American Indians will eventually be enclosed with people of African descent within the category of "dark others."

The question for the English colonists in eastern North America, then, was whether the Indians were to be included in the "nonwhite" category; Vaughan's claim that their inclusion in that category was eventually accomplished is suggested by the dismal history of U.S. Indian policies during the period of Indian removal in the nineteenth century.

Throughout most of the seventeenth century, though, as Vaughan suggests, that enclosure was not yet fully accomplished, and Indians were usually discursively positioned somewhere between "white" and "Black." From the time Africans were first imported as labor into the English colonies (the first ship carrying African slaves arrived in Jamestown in 1619) Indians' ready acceptance of Blacks, some of them runaway slaves, into their communities and as sexual and marriage partners soon resulted in a sizable population of mixed Black and Indian ancestry.[14] The existence of that population, combined with the demands of political expediency to define "whiteness" as an exclusive, "pure," and superior racial category, prompted the eventual inclusion of both Indians and Africans in the category of "dark" and undesirable "others." The early collapsing of racial distinctions between Blacks, Indians, and persons of mixed parentage (Black-Indian, Black-white, Indian-white)—as well as the assumption that English colonists were a separate and distinct group—is evidenced in the antimiscegenation laws passed in the Maryland colony in 1661 (Frankenberg 72) and in the Virginia colony in 1691 (Smits, "Abominable Mixture," 158), both of which outlawed marriage or sexual partnership between English colonists and "negroes," Indians, and mulattoes.[15]

It is important to emphasize that "whites" as a racial category emerged in the nascent empire along with, and in contrast to, "nonwhites"—in other words that, as Theodore W. Allen puts it in *The Invention of the White Race*, whiteness was "invented" and established as a category of identity in the colonial setting of the New World (239-59). Ruth Frankenberg writes,

> Colonization . . . occasioned the reformulation of European selves. Central to colonial discourses is the notion of the colonized subject as irreducibly Other from the standpoint of a white "self." Equally significant, while discursively generating and marking a range of cultural and racial Others as different from an apparently stable Western or white self, the Western self is itself produced as an effect of the Western discursive production of its Others. This means that the Western self and the non-Western other are coconstructed as discursive products, both of whose "realness" stand in extremely complex relationships to the production of knowledge, and to the material violence to which [colonizing discourse] is intimately linked. (16–17)

In his recent book *The Racial Contract*, Charles W. Mills points out that the social contract has been always also a racial one since the beginnings of the period of European "discovery" and colonization, with whites allowed the status of full personhood and nonwhites relegated to the status of "subpersons" (16–17). The racial contract, Mills argues,

> [f]ar from being lost in the mists of the ages, is clearly historically locatable in the series of events marking the creation of the modern world by European colonialism and the voyages of "discovery" now increasingly and most appropriately called expeditions of conquest. The Columbian quincentenary a few years ago, with its accompanying debates, polemics, controversies, counterdemonstrations, and outpourings of revisionist literature, confronted many whites with the uncomfortable fact . . . that we live in a world which has been *foundationally shaped for the past five hundred years by the realities of European domination and the gradual consolidation of global white supremacy.* (20)

The construction and policing of racial dividing lines in the United States has, therefore, a long and complex history, one in which writing has of course played a significant role. Toni Morrison, in *Playing in the Dark*, cites a description by contemporary literary scholar James Snead (writing on Faulkner) of one of racism's primary rhetorical strategies as "fear of merging, or loss of identity through synergistic union with the other, [which] leads to the wish to use racial purification as a separating strategy against difference" (quoted in Morrison 67). In her own list of "common linguistic strategies employed in fiction to engage the serious consequences of blacks" (67), Morrison includes "fetishization": "This is especially useful in evoking erotic fears or desires and establishing fixed and major difference where difference does not exist or is minimal. Blood, for example, is a pervasive fetish: black blood, white blood, the purity of blood; the purity of white female sexuality, the pollution of African blood and sex. Fetishization is a strategy often used to assert the categorical absolutism of civilization and savagery" (68).

I would extend Morrison's observation to include not only fiction, but all forms of cultural expression, and to include as well (and in particular for my purposes here) the spectre of Indian/white as well as white/Black "mixing." That is, the fetishization of "blood" and "racial purity," with the sexuality of the white woman as its guardian, has been evident in numerous discursive forms and media, including representations of white women captured by Indians, as a white-supremacist Anglo-American culture and nation first took shape and then sustained itself. Ruth Frankenberg offers a similar critique of that strategy, placing it in a more explicitly political history: "In short, given male dominance within white culture, the 'protection' or 'salvation' of white women and their supposedly civilized sexuality from men of color and their 'primitive' sexuality has been the alibi for a range of atrocities from genocide and lynching to segregation and immigration control" (76).

Throughout their long history, then, Indian captivity narratives—historical, autobiographical, fictional or fictionalized, sensationalized, popular—have used the threat of racial "pollution," with white women's bodies as the contested sexual ground, to further the racial contract, to generate and enact the dramas of gender and race politics that underwrote the colonization of North America and that continue to shape U.S. culture.

For the early colonists, Indian captivity was an ideologically charged and ever-present possibility and discursive preoccupation. The circulation of captivity stories was motivated in part by the need to defend the colonists' own brutalities against the indigenous people and the injustices of their forceful occupation and takeover of the Indians' land and resources. Repeating and recirculating stories of captivity in such a way as to serve its own interests and purposes, the colonial culture used them to assert Native "savagery" and "diabolism," and thus difference from themselves; they rewrote in their own favor the indigenous peoples' efforts to defend themselves and their ways of life from the English who, as their behavior made clear, were quite apparently their enemies. In the process, the English began to write "difference" into the text of the colonial scene and to place Indians into a distinct racial rather than cultural category irrevocably separate from themselves. Captivity narratives were part of that discursive process and played a crucial role in the deployment of "race" as a difference that had particular social and political meanings, with effects that were devastating for the groups racialized as "other."

EXPLOITING CAPTIVITY

Those endlessly circulating tales of captivity, however, not only helped to construct Indians as a distinct racial group, with the bodies and sexuality of white women captives as the contested border zone, they also served a larger purpose: the narratives contained epic elements, in that the captive's story became the story of the colonial, and later national, culture itself. As Richard Slotkin and James Folsom have said, "These narratives formed the archetype of a kind of official [and protonational] mythology in which the colonial experience was symbolized by the peril of a white Christian woman in the Indian-haunted wilderness" (302). Puritan anxiety over what the woman captive's plight suggested about the colonists' situation was pronounced. She was a highly charged figure for the colonists because, as a representative of the colonial culture, she quite literally embodied its vulnerability; she raised the spectre of the deconstruction of the "integrity" of whiteness, of the colonial culture itself being in turn penetrated, reduced to a savage state, and separated from the God who supposedly vouchsafed the success of the colonial enterprise. Such a calamity would symbolically signal the failure of the colonial experiment in North America.

In the war for territorial dominance, then, the captive woman was made into a metaphor: she was herself the emblematic territory for control of which the two sides fought. The conflict between colonial and Native cultures contracted, during the time of her captivity, into the space she herself occupied; her body, both actual and textual, was a border zone, a mediating space between emergent races and cultures in conflict, a terrain for which and on which the ideological struggle between the two cultures took place. As both a captive and a woman, she symbolically represented the presence of white Europeans surrounded by or in the midst of Indians as well as the capacity of white colonial culture to define, protect, and reproduce itself. She was the site and sign of the colonists' vulnerability to the "wilderness" realm of the flesh and the devil, home of those they characterized as lustful and devil-worshiping; she was a locus of the contesting and conflicting desires of two distinctly different peoples and cultures.[16]

The sexual history of a woman who survived captivity, therefore, because of all it symbolically represented, was a matter of considerable concern to the whole Puritan community upon her return; the fetishizing of "the purity of white female sexuality," as Morrison observes, became a crucial strategy "to assert the categorical absolutism of civilization and savagery" (68). The challenge to the Puritan community was to respond to what they saw as the sexualized threat to the project of colonization embodied in the captive woman's situation, but at the same time to turn the captive's story into a parable of Puritan godliness and the Christian soul's struggle against the devil in its quest for salvation.

When Rowlandson's narrative was published, its potential as either an instrument of Puritan colonialism or a subversive threat to that mission was so great that masculine voices literally surrounded it: a preface, usually attributed to Increase Mather,[17] introduced the narrative, and Rowlandson's husband's final sermon, preached just days before his death in 1678, followed it in early editions.[18] The inclusion of both men's writing represented Puritanism's necessary effort to control Rowlandson's text, to insist that it be read in ways that supported the colonial project and confirmed Puritan theocracy. The voices of the two men, both of them divines deeply embedded in the gender, religious, and emergent racial hierarchies of Puritanism, literally bracket Rowlandson's story of captivity, in which expressions of conventional religious feeling vie with decidedly secular perceptions for the reader's attention. Rowlandson's narrative was thus enclosed by appropriative masculine voices, directive and exhortatory, in order to foreclose the possibility of its being read in ways that would open the Puritan colonial endeavor, and its accompanying politics of gender and race, to critique.

The preface, signed "Per Amicum"[19]—"By a Friend"—makes clear why this tale written by a returned woman captive had to be enclosed by authoritative male voices. The preface writer's rhetorical purpose is to highlight and protect the biblical voice in Rowlandson's story and to try to suppress the colloquial voice that records what Puritan ideology cannot accommodate, the voice of an isolate, individual Englishwoman who lives among Indians and suffers, but survives and gains new knowledge from her experience, knowledge that has the capacity to destabilize Puritan representations of Indians and relations with them and thus to challenge the founding ideologies of the colonizing mission in North America.

Situating his reading securely within the belief system that underwrote the Puritan errand to claim and conquer the "wilderness" and transform it into "New England," the preface writer characterizes the Indians as "atheisticall, proud, wild, cruel, barbarous, bruitish (in one word) diabolicall creatures" (116). He describes Rowlandson as a "Gentlewoman [whose] modesty would not thrust [her narrative] into the Press, yet her gratitude unto God made her not hardly perswadable to let it pass, that God might have his due glory, and others benefit by it as well as her self" (115). He begs the reader to forgive Rowlandson's appearance of unseemliness in coming forward and hopes that "none will cast any reflection upon this Gentlewoman, on the score of this publication of her affliction and deliverance" (115). Addressing the reader, he issues a directive of how the text is to be read and suggests that if it has some effect other than spiritual edification, the reader, and not the experience or its textual representation, is to blame: "Hear Reader, you may see an instance of the Soveraignty of God . . . Reader, if thou gettest no good by such a Declaration as this, the fault must needs be thine own" (117). The preface thus strives to incorporate the narrative into its own project of justifying the colonial enterprise.[20]

The motives of the Puritan divines for bringing Rowlandson's story to a public readership are plain: ostensibly intending to create an approved place from which Rowlandson can speak of her experience in this text "penned by the Gentlewoman her self" (115), they in fact mean to marshal her text into the service of Puritan theocracy, belief in gender and racial hierarchies, and providential sanction for English colonialism, from which the American nation would eventually emerge. In order to make use of the narrative for their own purposes, they must be at pains to emphasize its congruence with Puritan orthodoxy. In highlighting Rowlandson's "modesty" and in asking readers to "Excuse her then if she come thus into publick" (116), the preface writer foregrounds Rowlandson's gender and the implicit questions about her sexual history and propriety, not only in thus speaking out but, implicitly, in surviving captivity.

Patricia Bizzell has remarked the historical persistence of accusations of unchastity that have been aimed at women who dared to speak in public. The suggestion of sexual impropriety connected with a woman's entering the realm of public discourse, according to Bizzell, dates at least from the story of the Roman matron Lucretia, who argued publicly at her rapist's trial that not only he but also she should be executed in order to preserve the ideal of chastity; the suggestion is that she could speak in public only because she was already "defiled" by the rape, or even that in choosing to come forth with a public address, her defilement was doubled. In a thoroughgoing terminus to her convention-defying public address, Lucretia answered her own argument by taking her own life, plunging a dagger into her breast in a symbolic repetition of her rape, the actual and original cause of her death.

The story's moral is that a woman's chastity is coterminous with her life; once proved to be unchaste, she is as good as dead, might as well be dead, ought to be dead. Bizzell reports that "the woman speaking in public was almost obsessively condemned in Renaissance culture, and . . . the condemnation usually took the form of branding her as unchaste"

(52). In the Renaissance, Bizzell says, the Lucretia story was frequently repeated in writing and reproduced in painting, especially on "the Renaissance equivalent of hope chests, trunks in which young girls collected clothes and linens for their marriage" (52), both to instruct them in the cultural expectations of married women and to warn them of the results of transgression, even when, as in the case of rape (or capture), they were victims and not initiators. Given that the historical backdrop for the English colonization of North America was the high Renaissance, it is not surprising to find threats of appearing to violate the rules governing women's chastity continuing to police women's containment within the domestic sphere in the English colonies and to prohibit their entry into public discourse.

An entry from the journal of John Winthrop, then governor of Massachusetts, indicates just how powerfully regulated were gender divisions and the restrictions against women's occupying the gendered-masculine place of reader and writer in the Massachusetts colony. The journal entry is from April 1645, some thirty years before Rowlandson was captured:

> Mr. Hopkins, the governor of Hartford upon Connecticut, came to Boston, and brought his wife with him, (a godly young woman, and of special parts,) who was fallen into a sad infirmity, the loss of her understanding and reason, which had been growing upon her divers years, by occasion of her giving herself wholly to reading and writing, and had written many books. Her husband, being very loving and tender of her, was loath to grieve her; but he saw his errour, when it was too late. For if she had attended her household affairs, and such things as belong to women, and not gone out of her way and calling to meddle in such things as are proper for men, whose minds are stronger &c. she had kept her wits, and might have improved them usefully and honorably in the place God had set her. (2:216–17; quoted in Howe 108)

The "many books" that Winthrop reports Mrs. Hopkins wrote are a poignant reminder that many of the silences in the textual history of Anglo-America were created by suppressing or destroying the work of writers who were among America's "others"—women and people of color. "Mrs. Hopkins's books," Howe notes, "if they were ever published, are still a blank in American literary history" (109). Hopkins's vanished books, like the silence of Pocahontas and American Natives generally, point to the selectivity that is always at work to invest particular texts, voices, and versions of history with power, privileging particular histories over others that are excluded from the textual record.

Therefore, for Rowlandson to publish her text without the coverture of masculine Puritan authorities—the priestly sanction of the preface and the postscript of her husband's sermon—would have meant that, in violating the dictum against women speaking in public, she had stepped outside the chaste enclosure of domestic space defined for Puritan women. Her narrative was published only a little more than forty years after the 1638 trial and banishment of Anne Hutchinson from the Massachusetts colony for her public intellectual and spiritual independence— surely a legacy that encouraged and helped enforce women's public silence. If Rowlandson's text had not had the imprimatur of the Puritan clergy that both masculine voices provide, then, her story in her own words could most likely never have been published at all. The bracketing texts thus ironically made possible the publication of a narrative that renders visible the very ideological limitations and blindnesses within Puritanism that the preface and appended sermon attempted to elide.

Joseph Rowlandson's last sermon, preached on a Fast Day two days before he died (Diebold xcvii), also raises the question of Rowlandson's chastity, if more obliquely. The title, "The Possibility of Gods Forsaking a People, that have been visibly near & dear to him Together, with the Misery of a People thus forsaken," immediately suggests that the minister's concern, at least in part, is to understand his personal experience in the context of the tenets of Puritan faith and to offer a public apologia for the destruction of his home and the captivity of his wife and children, the death of his youngest child, and the inevitable questions about his wife's sexual integrity. And while he does not mention the experience directly, it is difficult to read the sermon without seeing it as his effort to make sense of what happened to his family and to construct some plausible explanation for it. Here is how he illustrates why God's anger is visited on apparently righteous people: "He will not spare them that have been near him, if they will not spare their sin for him. He is a holy God, and if they will have their sins, and their lusts, and their ways, and their lovers, he will vindicate his holiness, by inflicting his judgment on them" (40).

Elsewhere he uses a sexual metaphor, that of the faithful and the faithless wife, to represent the behavior of the righteous soul and the sinful soul when God withdraws: the "faithfull Wife" is contrasted to "the Adultress" who will "in her Husbands Absence . . . seek after other lovers" (35). The language of the sermon suggests that Rowlandson himself may have had doubts about his wife's having remained chaste during her captivity and implies that, while perhaps ostensibly attempting to defend her reputation, he might still have been troubled by the questions it raised. And as Slotkin and Folsom observe, "Rowlandson is tantalizingly silent about her reunion with her husband. We may only speculate upon their conversations after her return from captivity" (307).

That the Indians always "defiled" their female captives was (and long remained) a commonplace of colonialist rhetoric, part of the demonizing discourse the Puritans used to construct essentialist versions of Indian identity and to justify their expansionist politics, despite the evidence, including Rowlandson's, that rape was not a usual practice among the Algonkian peoples of the eastern woodlands.[21] The preface to Rowlandson's narrative, for example, notes God's providence in "curbing the lusts of the most filthy" (117) and thus asserts the belief that Indians are "naturally" inclined to sexual violence and that it is Rowlandson's faith, not her captors' willingness to treat her respectfully, that prevents her rape.

Polemicists of the period routinely employed the supposed threat of Indian rape of white women. William Hubbard in *The Present State of New-England* (1677) addresses the issue of whether Rowlandson and the other women taken in the Lancaster attack were raped during their captivity:

And such was the goodness of God to those poor Captive Women, and Children, that they found so much favour in the sight of their Enemies, that they offered no wrong to any of their persons, save what they could not help, being in many wants themselves. Neither did they offer any uncivil Carriage to any of the Females, nor ever attempted the chastity of any of them, either being restrained of God, as was Abimelech of old; or by some other accidental cause, which held them from doing any wrong in that kind. (61)

Like the writer of the preface to Rowlandson's text, Hubbard credits the "preservation" of the women to providence or accident, and thus the inclination to rape is figured as inherent in the Native character.

A letter by "N.S." (presumably Nathaniel Saltonstall) published in 1676 (the year of Rowlandson's captivity and ransom) was more sensational. It recounts Rowlandson's capture and tells a gruesome tale of the Indians seizing her along with two of her sisters. They immediately murder one of the sisters, who is pregnant: "As they were leading them away in this lamentable Condition, one of the Sisters being big with Childe, going into the Woods to be privately delivered, the Indians followed and in a jeering Manner, they would help her, and be her Midwives, and thereupon they barbarously ript up her Body, and burnt the Child before her Face, and then in a merciful Cruelty, to put her out of her Pain, knockt her o'th Head" (83). The anecdote is apparently an invention, since it is not told in Rowlandson's or any other account of the Lancaster captives.[22] The story not only highlights the Indians' supposed capacity for cruelty and disregard of "feminine delicacy" but raises as well the spectres of their visual "violation" of women captives and, concomitantly, of their intimate knowledge of their colonizers' sexual "property."

The threat of Indians serving a white woman as "Midwives" recalls a passage in a seduction poem by John Donne, "Elegie: Going to Bed," in which the speaker's mistress is his "America" but America is also his "mistress": pleading for the woman he desires—and by implication, the American continent—to discard her last vestiges of modest self-concealment, he urges, "As liberally, as to a Midwife shew / Thy self" (58). The territorial power struggle between colonists and Natives is in N.S.'s letter reduced to the question of who will get an intimate look at the "secret" sexual anatomy/geography of whose "terrain"; possessing the woman is conflated with possessing the land itself. The English clearly understood, and wanted to reserve to themselves, the power inhering in the penetrating male gaze.

In the same letter, N.S. says this about Rowlandson's sexual history during captivity: "There was a Report that they had forced Mrs. Rowlinson to marry the one eyed Sachem, but it was soon contradicted; for being a very pious Woman and of great Faith, the Lord wonderfully supported her under this Affliction, so that she appeared and behaved her self amongst them with so much Courage and majestick Gravity, that none durst offer any Violence to her, but on the contrary (in their rude Manner) seemed to show her great Respect" (83).[23] The suggestion of "forced marriage" is meant to be inflammatory, containing as it does the implication of repeated rape, and thus is intended to promote the Puritan project of ridding "New England" of its Native inhabitants. Like Hubbard, N.S. also attributes the fact that Rowlandson was not raped or forced to "marry" the Nashaway leader not to the Indians' inherent respect for her integrity but solely to her own character and piety.

Benjamin Tompson's propagandistic poem about the war, "New-Englands Crisis" (1676), also makes use of the myth of Indians' desire to violate white women in order to incite the colonists' outrage, racial animosity, and enthusiasm for war against the Indians. His contrasting descriptions of Indians and of English colonists are evidence of the emerging belief in racial difference between the two groups. To accentuate the supposedly appalling prospect of interracial sex, of the "polluting" of the "purity" of whiteness by "darkness," Tompson refers to Metacom (Philip) as "this greazy Lout" with "bacon-rine-like looks" (99) and imagines Metacom's speech inciting the Indian warriors to take up arms against the English:

Now if you'le fight Ile get you english coats,
And wine to drink out of their Captains throats.
The richest merchants houses shall be ours,
Wee'l ly no more on matts or dwell in bowers.
Wee'l have their silken wives take they our Squaws. . . .
(100)[24]

Like Hubbard, who ascribes the rebellion to "the instigation of Satan, ... no cause of provocation being given by the English" (10–11), Tompson nowhere registers the real reason for the Indian uprising—the colonists' appropriation of Native homelands and their unjust dealings with Native people. Rather, in a classic gesture of projection, he masks the colonizers' lust for Indian land and resources by portraying the Indians as coveting, and plotting to take by force, all that Englishmen possess and enjoy, including "their" women. Tompson's Indians, of course, do not refrain from raping English women whenever the opportunity presents itself:

Will she or nill the chastest turtle must
Tast of the pangs of their unbridled lust.
(100)

These and other similar texts helped create and perpetuate the climate of suspicion of women who returned from captivity and surely contributed to Rowlandson's desire to have her own say about her experience. In such a climate, she could hardly have failed to address the question of her sexual history. And yet in so doing she confronted a paradox. Here is what she says:

I have been in the midst of those roaring Lyons, and Salvage Bears, that feared neither God, nor Man, nor the Devil, by night and day, alone and in company: sleeping all sorts together, and yet not one of them ever offered me the least abuse of unchastity to me, in word or action. Though some are ready to say, I speak it for my own credit; But I speak it in the presence of God, and to his Glory. (161)

The passage is a microcosm of the contradictions that lace Rowlandson's text: Puritanism is right, the Indians are savage beasts; but Puritanism is wrong, the Indians are not bestial, can in fact be thoroughly humane and respectful toward a captive Englishwoman. As a survivor of captivity, Rowlandson must defend her sexual reputation or risk becoming an outcast among her people. So, on the one hand, she supports the colonizers' projection of Indian bestiality that masks their own forcible appropriation of Indian land. And yet by describing the dignity with which her captors treated her person, she destabilizes those oppositions on which the Puritan mandate to claim and conquer was founded. If she succeeds in making herself invulnerable to criticism, she renders vulnerable and begins to undo the founding mythologies of Puritan culture in New England.

Rowlandson remained a captive from February 10 until May 2, when she was ransomed and returned to Boston to be reunited with her husband. Both her son and daughter were also subsequently released. The family never returned to Lancaster, which had been Mary's home since her girlhood but which was now abandoned; they remained in Boston until April 1677, when Joseph Rowlandson was installed as pastor of the church he had been called to as minister, in Wethersfield, Connecticut. He died suddenly in November 1678; the town of Wethersfield voted his widow an annual pension of thirty pounds.

Until very recently, historians have assumed that Mary herself died not long after her husband, and many sources, including the Library of Congress classification, list "ca. 1678" as the date of her death. But David Greene demonstrated in a 1985 essay that she did not die until 1711, when the Wethersfield Vital Records report her age at death as "about seventy-three" (Greene 31). Rather, she remarried in August of 1679, the year after Joseph's death. Her second husband was Samuel Talcott of Wethersfield, an officer in the colonial militia during King Philip's War (see Bodge) and one of the counselors appointed by the Hartford County Court to assist Rowlandson in administering her first husband's estate. The fact that she chose as her second husband a man whose public reputation was due to his military leadership during King Philip's War invites speculation that, aside from considerations of personal attraction and affection, Rowlandson may still have felt the need, three years after her ransom, to heal the rifts in her consciousness that her captivity had opened, to reassert her allegiance to English colonialism and refute any suggestions of sympathy with Indians. If so, it was a gesture of forgetting.

The Lucretia story discussed by Bizzell provides an interesting way to view the longevity of the assumption that "despite the heroism both of her conduct and her narrative," Rowlandson "survived the horrendous experience [of captivity] by only two years" (Brooks, Lewis, and Warren 1:45; quoted in D. Greene 25). "Tainted" by her extended stay and intimate contact, however involuntary, with the Indians, she was, like Lucretia, supposed to die. Instead, she lived for thirty-five more years. Rowlandson's long life in itself stands as a challenge and rebuke to popular figurations of white women captives who are devastated or destroyed by their encounter with Indians, especially to the nineteenth-century sentimental versions of the returned white captive who expires, apparently of a combination of grief and shame over her assumed or evident sexual "contamination," upon her return to white society.[25]

Probably Rowlandson composed her narrative sometime between her ransom in May 1676 and her husband's death late in 1678 (Diebold c), since neither the narrative itself nor the preface says anything about his death. Nor does Rowlandson mention the family's relocation to Connecticut; the closing passage of the narrative suggests that the family was still in Boston at the time of her writing. The likelihood is, then, that she wrote it sometime within ten months of her release, prior to the move to Wethersfield in the spring of 1677.

The six years' delay between her ransom and the narrative's first publication would confirm my suspicions about why Rowlandson might have been finally persuaded to risk the usual prohibitions against women speaking in public in order to present her own view of her experience. Probably, as I have suggested earlier, the narrative was her attempt to rewrite herself back into the Puritan community by addressing the chief question leveled at a woman who survived captivity: whether her intimate contact with Indians had shaken her Christian faith or "tainted" her sexually, either by rape or by seduction. Perhaps during those years she was subjected to enough suspicion about the precise nature of her intimacy with the Indians that she was persuaded to override the usual Puritan injunctions against women entering the public realm in print and allowed her story to be published to defend her reputation. Perhaps she also needed to protect or defend her second husband's reputation by proving herself worthy of having entered her second marriage. It is worth remarking that during her long life as a Puritan wife and mother following her public role as the writer of the story of her captivity,

Rowlandson kept the retired demeanor, out of the public's attention, that that role urged upon her; the woman who wrote the first American best-seller never again, so far as we know, took up the pen.

Whatever the reasons for the delay in publication, though, the central importance given to the vexed question of Rowlandson's sexual history in the narrative itself, the preface, and at least by implication in the appended sermon by her husband must be taken into account in any effort to weigh the significance of Rowlandson's narrative as well as of the innumerable representations of women's captivities and the cultural work they have been made to perform throughout the centuries of European conquest and settlement of the Americas. Those represen-tations, textual and visual, are pointedly revealing of the ways "the threat and practice of rape" have functioned in colonial settings "as a form of political, discursive control over entire populations—not simply indi-viduals" (Athey and Alarcon 30). Moreover, and specifically to my pur-poses in my reading of Rowlandson and subsequent captivity narratives, those repeated and recirculated stories of white women's captivities, complete with their constructions of race, gender, and sexuality, which included "the threat and [presumed] practice of rape," are crucial to the effort of tracing the emergence of American nationhood and the ways it employed and deployed white women's bodies and sexuality in con-structing its founding discourses of "race."

READING ROWLANDSON

So much has been made for so long of Rowlandson's interpretive biblical voice, of her structuring use of the Bible and conventional Puritan theology to comprehend her experience, one is tempted to believe that the preface writer's directive to read the narrative as a defense of English Christian superiority over the "heathen" Indians is irresistible and that his occlusion of the colloquial elements in her text, passages that provide a view of Indians and Indian life to some extent divergent from Puritan orthodoxy, must prevail. It is certainly true that readings of Rowlandson emphasizing her narrative's racism, conventionality, adherence to a reductive typological Christianity, and evident belief that God himself supported the Puritan colonial endeavor have been conventional through the nineteenth century and even into the present.

In a 1985 essay, for example, Jane Tompkins claims that "captivity narratives [are] a poor source of evidence for the nature of European-Indian relations in early New England because they were so relentlessly pietistic" ("Indians" 71) and that Rowlandson only "saw what her seventeenth-century English Separatist background made visible" (70–71). Another recent instance is the publication in 1988 of an edition of Rowlandson's narrative by an evangelical Christian editor, Mark Ludwig, who describes it as "a story of amazing faith and perseverence [sic] in the face of adversity, and a great testimony to the faithfulness of God towards those who love him" (Ludwig v).[26] A text, however, is no more unified than is a culture—which is to say, not unified at all. Both Tompkins's and Ludwig's readings, though motivated by dramatically differing agendas, flatten Rowlandson's text and fail to acknowledge its complexities, the ways it undermines the ideologies that Tompkins herself wants to question and Ludwig wants to preserve and uphold.

There is, though, a reason other than the preface writer's rhetorical power or the convention of reading in certain ways to explain the continuing emphasis on Rowlandson as a representative of traditional patriarchal Puritanism. A much more persuasive explanation for such readings becomes clear when we see them as politically motivated—that is, when we consider her text's continuing usefulness in the ongoing process, both textual and political, of creating an American nation founded on white male supremacy, rigid race and gender hierarchies, and the exploitation and abuse of subordinated and racialized "others," both Indians and African slaves.

To understand Rowlandson's narrative and others like it as an important site for producing and articulating ideologies of race helps to explain the reappearance of her text at various pivotal moments in American history. Greg Sieminski has pointed out the "enormous popularity of Puritan [captivity] accounts during the Revolutionary era" (35), including Rowlandson's. After its popularity at the time of its publication in 1682, her narrative was republished only once (in 1720) in the years between its initial appearance and 1770, when it "was republished three times" in Boston (37); three more editions followed in the next two years—one in

1771, two in 1773—and five of those six editions between 1770 and 1773 were printed in Boston, which was "occupied by British troops" during that period (37). Sieminski argues that in the years just before the American Revolution, it was the colonists' growing sense of themselves as captives of the British crown that prompted their harking back to a genre that was by then familiar, the narrative of captivity, to represent to themselves their dilemma as "hostages" to Britain.

Another interpretive layer can be added to Sieminski's, however, one that focuses on the question of national identity. That question was a pressing one for a "new nation . . . unsure of its identity," as Sieminski himself describes it (51). Sieminski concludes the national identity question by saying, "In a pluralistic society, perhaps the most representative American is the one with the greatest plurality of selves" (51). I would say instead that the nation's historical pluralism has been a thorn in the dominant culture's flesh more than it has ever been a genuinely welcome characteristic. That pluralism has in fact elicited stringent and steady efforts from one segment of the American population, those of northern European descent, to remain on top. Perhaps the recurrent popularity of the Puritan captivity narrative during the years just before the Revolution can be best explained by reading it as a gesture that not only called upon captivity tropes to describe the colonies' relations with England but also recalled the narratives' earlier usefulness in constructing racial identities and placing them in a hierarchy with whites at the top of the racial pyramid. This was a function the narratives had served well before and would be called upon to serve again and again.

The woodcut illustration that accompanied the 1770 Boston edition of Rowlandson's narrative (figure 1) invites a reading of just that sort. In that woodcut, Rowlandson is depicted not only as naked—that is, divested of the clothing that would have marked her with a cultural identity—but indeed as flayed, lacking any skin whatever. She is, therefore, divested not only of culture but also of race; the illustration underscores the risks of loss of racial identity and privilege by white women who were captured by Indians. Furthermore, the dark child who follows this figure of a woman without culture and without racial identity makes vivid white culture's preoccupation with the captive woman's sexuality during

FIGURE 1. From a 1770 Boston edition of Mary Rowlandson's narrative. By permission of the Houghton Library, Harvard University.

captivity; it once again raises the spectre of the racial boundary being crossed and thus of the deconstruction of "whiteness."

But why would this issue become a pressing one again on the threshold of the war for independence? Precisely because it was a pivotal moment for Anglo-Americans in terms of identity; considering the possibility of separating themselves from the Old World anchor of their identity as white, Christian, and "civilized," they may well have felt considerable fear of losing that identity along with their allegiance to England. Their task was to separate without losing their identity as white Christian Anglo-Americans. One way to secure that identity would have been to recall and rehearse the old oppositions between themselves and their Native "others" so well invoked and articulated in the captivity narratives and responses to them. In that light, the woodcut in the 1770 edition of Rowlandson's narrative would have been a reminder of all that was at stake in the movement for independence, of all the colonies risked losing in the struggle to define themselves as an independent nation. The woodcut could be read as a visual plea to preserve their protected identities and not succumb to the "savagery" of the Indians as they prepared to sever the cords that bound them to England.[27]

By the early decades of the nineteenth century, the contest for land that had begun when the Atlantic coast colonies were established in the seventeenth century was continuing, and in the 1820s, Indian tribes remaining in state territories east of the Mississippi were being subjected to increasing pressure to move farther and farther west. That pressure was to culminate in 1830 in the passage of the Indian Removal Act, the result of which was that Indians in the eastern states had to remove themselves to designated territories west of the Mississippi, exchanging their sovereign lands for land they had never seen in the West.

During the decade of pressure on Indians to move westward that preceded the Indian Removal Act, a loosely excerpted version of Rowlandson's narrative, edited and with commentary by Joseph Willard, appeared in the April and May 1824 issues of the magazine *Collections Historical and Miscellaneous*. Willard's revival of Rowlandson's narrative was a timely effort to participate in generating anti-Indian sentiment among white Americans. His comments that accompanied the excerpts he selected from her narrative indicate his intention to use her experience and what she wrote about it to vilify Indians, to represent them as being still a terrifying threat to the peace and security of white Americans, to assert Euro-American "rights" to the American continent, and to figure the American national subject as white:[28]

> Even in a time of peace, [the colonists'] security was often more fancied than real, for their savage enemy, like some nations, high in the scale of civilization, regarded treaties only as a fit opportunity to gather up their strength, and ripen their plans, in order to strike a more effectual and deadly blow. Their approach was noiseless, like the pestilence that walketh in darkness; and a dwelling wrapt in flames, or a family barbarously murdered and scalped, were usually the first intimation of their appearance. (105–6)

Willard's observation on the disregard of treaties is especially ironic given the long history of U.S. betrayal of treaty agreements with Indian nations. The Indian Removal Act, for example, asserted in one fell swoop that "existing Indian treaties did not constitute federal recognition of Indian sovereign rights to the soil of their homelands" (Thomas et al. 293).

Even more important to understanding how Rowlandson's narrative was being put to use for contemporary purposes is the explicit way Willard uses his commentary to assert a genealogy of the American national character: "The attention that, within the few last years, has been bestowed on the more minute parts of our early history, is highly commendable. It has a higher and better purpose, than merely to satisfy a vain curiosity; it connects itself with the best feelings of our nature, and serves to raise in our estimation the character of those from whom we are descended" (105). There can be no doubt that Willard is referring specifically to white Euro-Americans when he speaks of "our early history" and "our nature," or when he invokes a "we" descended from early colonists. Willard goes on to say that "It is the historian's duty to describe national character in the aggregate," but his own purpose, while "more humble," is "to treasure up for the use of the future historian, and to set forth in detail whatever may illustrate the peculiarities of character, situation and conduct, that so strongly marked our ancestors" (105). Rowlandson's captivity history, in other words, is here made into a detailed instance and illustration of the traits Willard is at pains to celebrate and preserve in the American national character of the 1820s, traits that include courage, perseverance, unshakable faith in the rightness of the Euro-American colonial and later national project—and the supremacy of whiteness as a racial category, grounded here in fear and hatred of Indians, as it was elsewhere in the nineteenth century grounded in the politics of racial difference between white Euro-Americans and people of African descent, especially slaves. Willard's text, in its intersections with Rowlandson's narrative and with the racial politics of the era of its publication, is an instance where we can discern what Stephanie Athey and Daniel Cooper Alarcon have described as "the (at least) three-way mediation of racial exploitation in the Americas as European peoples negotiate domination via both African and [indigenous] American populations" (29).

A number of recent critics have addressed the ways captivity narratives, especially women's, performed cultural work like that Willard assigned to Rowlandson's text: by serving as sites for producing an emergent American identity and subjectivity, what Tara Fitzpatrick describes as "that peculiar amalgam of contradictions: the self-conscious and self-described American individual" (2–3). Fitzpatrick locates the transition in Puritan culture from communal to individual in the tensions between the returned woman captive's voice and that of her "ministerial sponsors" (2) who "vied with the returned captives for authorial control of their narratives": "Thus, these Puritan captivity narratives chart a double shift in colonial New England's conceptions of individual identity and national destiny, insofar as a rhetoric of the corporate covenant comes to be eclipsed by an emergent emphasis on personal agency" (3). Fitzpatrick focuses on the ways the captives' forced removal from home culture and their encounters with Indians fracture the communal ideal of the Puritan settlement in New England, and rather than centering her reading on the tensions between the competing cultures in colonial New England, she ascribes the "multiple and ambiguous" (5) quality of captivity narratives to gender-inflected tensions within the colonial culture of New England between the community and the emerging individual.

As a number of other scholars have argued in recent years, texts produced in that "contact zone" between cultures that is the colonial setting are inescapably fractured or hybrid. Readings that open up rather than erase those textual fractures or splits are most productive in terms of clarifying how power operated in colonial settings in the registers of race, gender, sexuality, spirituality, and relations to the land. Fitzpatrick's is one such reading, with its particular emphasis on gender and its role in eliciting and constructing an ideological American individualism within and around narratives of Indian captivity.

Nancy Armstrong and Leonard Tennenhouse have traced the specifically textual influences of captivity narratives, investigating "what happened when colonial writing flowed back across the Atlantic to England" (387), and they too read in captivity narratives the emergence of the American individual. Their exploration of the textual links between captivity narratives, especially Rowlandson's, and the emergent middle-class narrative subject in the English novel leads them to draw interesting parallels between Samuel Richardson's *Pamela* and Rowlandson's text and thus to assert the significant influence of the Rowlandson narrative and similar others on what became possible for subsequent writers in English. They argue that the sexual vulnerability and the isolation from home culture of both the captive Rowlandson and the hostage Pamela created the "detached—and thereby individuated—individual" (399), source of a narrative subjectivity new to English writing that gave rise to the novel. Armstrong and Tennenhouse's work suggests interesting connections between such an individualized narrative subjectivity and the obsessive preoccupation with the issue of sexual "virtue" common to both captivity narratives and eighteenth-century English novels.

Benedict Anderson has also written about the effects of the textualized Atlantic union, but with a focus more explicitly politicized than that of Armstrong and Tennenhouse. Anderson writes, "It was also through print moving back and forth across the ocean that the unstable, imagined [world] of Englishnesses . . . [was] created" (316). Unlike Armstrong and Tennenhouse, Anderson is interested less in the textual influences of captivity narratives on subsequent forms of literary writing than in the role such texts played in the emergence of nationalist sentiment. Anderson suggests, I think rightly, that nationalism emerges from the "hybridity" captivity texts displayed. Remarking the popularity of captivity narratives such as Rowlandson's among the reading public in

England and noting the "thoroughly creole crosscurrents" (314) in Rowlandson's text, he says, "A rapidly growing reading public in the recently united kingdom—Mary was captured two decades before Scotland—was becoming aware of anomalous English-writing women who had never been to England but who could be dragged through English fields by "savages." What were they? Were they really English? The photographic negative of "the colonial," the non-English English-woman, was coming into view" (315).[29]

Anderson's essay makes clear the connections between the instabilities of identity in Rowlandson's captivity narrative and those in the colonial setting generally. One hundred years before the English colonies declared their independence from the English crown, Rowlandson's narrative indicates the colonists' passionate desire to cling to their Englishness; but it indicates too the inevitability that their English identity will be eroded by their American experiences.

Precisely how the emerging "American individual" was to be articu-lated was a task on which captivity tales were also put to work. Carroll Smith-Rosenberg has claimed that captivity narratives, both historical and fictional (she offers readings of two late-eighteenth-century novels, Charles Brockden Brown's *Edgar Huntly* and Susanna Rowson's *Reuben and Rachel*), played a central role in the process of displacing the Indians' identity as "Americans" and allowing European colonists to occupy a refigured American identity and subjectivity. Thus narratives of women's captivity, for which Rowlandson's was the prototype and persistent model, were proto-epic in scope in the founding of a national identity (and literature). Depicting at close range a savage and unpredictable (because not understood) enemy against whom Europeans in America could consolidate their own identity and sense of themselves, captivity narra-tives were crucial to the process by which the colonizers came eventually to see themselves as the colonized and through which the colonists' identity as American subjects was constituted, a process preliminary to the colonies' declaring their independence from England and estab-lishing a new nation. Nor did this discursive process end with the war for independence; on the contrary, in the late eighteenth and nineteenth centuries that process accelerated as the infant nation strove to define itself: "In the years immediately following the American Revolution,

Euro-American subjectivity quite self-consciously fused two subject positions: the victorious postcolonial and the colonizer, heir to Britain's imperial venture in North America. Facing east, Euro-Americans positioned themselves as Sons of Liberty; facing west, they were the progenitors of a vast new empire" (Smith-Rosenberg 494–95).

Not surprisingly, the task of consolidating a national identity across such discursive splits produced a subjectivity "as decentered and fragmented as the discourses that constituted it" (Smith-Rosenberg 485). The task for this newly arrayed American subject was to locate a ground against which his only apparently coherent figure could become visible:

Contested and decentered subjectivities assume a coherence they have not in opposition to a series of others—especially negative others. The more contradictory and unstable the ideologies that construct subjectivities, the more insistent the mechanisms constructing these others become. Crowding the pages of political pamphlets, broadsides, sermons, even dictionaries and geographies, a host of negative others worked to solidify the new American subject[:] . . . sybaritic British aristocrats, wild European revolutionaries, deceitful men of credit and commerce, seductive and extravagant women. . . . Shadowing all these negative others, however, was a still more sinister, primeval figure—the savage American Indian warrior. (Smith-Rosenberg 485)

The connections between the issues of a woman captive's sexuality and a developing white Euro-American subjectivity and nationality can best be understood, I believe, by scrutinizing the tensions and the ambiguities in Rowlandson's text—its "hybridity," as Anderson describes it, or, as I have already suggested, the related frictions between the two narrative registers Rowlandson employs to represent her experience of captivity. The biblical voice, requiring as it does that she remain closed to the Indians, impervious to any possibility of influence or attraction, became for the Puritan community a means of consolidating and protecting English colonial identity. The colloquial voice, on the contrary, displays all the ways that Rowlandson was open to connections and intimacies with her captors and thus opens the way to the birth and development of a new American identity and subjectivity. I would argue that it is the inadequacy of both Rowlandson's voices together, their inability to constitute a coherent narrative to account for her experience, that, in the spaces left between those voices or narrative registers and in all the questions the narrative is unwilling or unable to answer, precipitates the emergence of a new subjectivity, the writing Anglo-American woman, and, concomitantly, of the ideological "American individual."

Fitzpatrick notes the irony in this gendered subjectivity, in American individualism's having emerged in texts written by women: "If part of the 'cultural work' of these captivity narratives was to accommodate a changing relation between the New England colonists and the wilderness—between the community's demands and the individual's desires— it is striking that women were among the leading creators of a mythology that has since had so resonantly masculine a voice" (20).

But if we situate the woman captive within that cluster of "negative others" against whom the emerging white male American subject defined himself and his identity, the fact of her gender becomes not surprising or ironic, but essential. Her femininity evoked and assured his masculinity; her captive status ensured his belief in his agency; her passivity and sexual vulnerability evoked and justified his aggressiveness—just as Indians' savagery confirmed his superior status as civilized, and Indians' darkness, or what was eventually constructed as their racial difference, rendered him white. Captivity narratives, beginning with Rowlandson's, conveniently brought together these two essential negative others, and thus offered a particularly useful vehicle for consolidating and asserting the identity and dominance of white American men, not only during the colonial era when that identity began to take shape, but, as we shall see, at many subsequent moments in American history, whenever that identity has been most aware of its own instability or felt itself threatened.

REREADING ROWLANDSON

Even readers ordinarily sympathetic to Indian rights have often found it difficult to locate instances in Rowlandson's narrative where Puritan ideology wavers. When the writer Mary Austin reviewed an edition of Rowlandson published on the occasion of the tercentenary of the Massachusetts Bay Colony in 1930, she wrote, "As the forerunner of a long line of narratives of Indian captivities among vanished tribes, it . . . constitutes itself one long shudder of the mingled terror and contempt in which the Indians were held by the English settlers" (1150). Austin concludes with a perceptive question: "In 'The Captivity and Restoration of Mary Rowlandson,' may not the American gather the roots of all he likes least in today's report of existing racial conflicts?" (1151).

The racism Rowlandson gives voice to in her narrative is, however, not as monolithic as Austin's review would indicate; Carroll Smith-Rosenberg points out that Rowlandson "inscribed a self-contradictory subject," and that "Rowlandson's subjectivity, fused with demonic Indians, continually divides, multiplies, and fragments" (487). Susan Howe, too, concludes her essay on Rowlandson with a succinct comment on the text's multiplicity: "Mary Rowlandson saw what she did not see said what she did not say" (128). There is, in other words, more than one Rowlandson in the text, expressing more than one attitude toward cultural and emerging racial difference as toward other aspects of her captivity.

Other twentieth-century readers, though, have experienced Rowlandson's text in ways similar to Austin's, also being sufficiently persuaded by the expressions Austin mentions of evident racism in the text to ignore the ways that Rowlandson takes up other narrative subject positions and relates to her captors and their culture in ways that undermine emergent Puritan racist attitudes and beliefs.

Laurel Thatcher Ulrich, for example, calls Rowlandson a "God-fearing Puritan" and "a transplanted Englishwoman thrown into an alien American world" (176). Ulrich, disregarding the fact that Rowlandson was only a small child when "transplanted" and had spent her entire adult life on the fringe of English settlement, reads the narrative as "giv[ing] constant evidence of resistance to what might be described as 'frontier' ways" (176) and cites Rowlandson's initial disgust at the prospect of eating bear meat as evidence. While I would not deny that numerous strategies of resistance, ideological and rhetorical, are in evidence throughout the text, I would argue instead that the bear-eating incident, like others in Rowlandson's narrative, demonstrates the extent to which identity was a fluid entity in the colonial setting, a contest between

"Englishness" and what it might mean to be "an American." Rowlandson does, after all, eat her piece of bear with relish (137).

Certainly I agree too with Mary Austin that, as I have already indicated, the foundations of American racism are in clear evidence in Rowlandson's text. What I also find there, though, is other evidence, admittedly tremulous and intermittent, of how her intimate contact with Indians offered a challenge to the Puritan characterizations of Indians and produced in Rowlandson some recognition, however reluctant, of their common humanity with her—perhaps even of the arbitrariness of racial categories and of the possibility of crossing them. I would argue that the long tradition of characterizing Rowlandson's text as an unproblematic, univocal exemplum and defense of colonial racism or of Puritan religiosity (Leslie Fiedler referred in 1968 to "the insufferably dull and pious journal of Mrs. Mary Rowlandson" [51]) results not from attending closely to the text itself and its many dissonances, but from the tyranny of the long history of racist and imperialist attitudes and practices that captivity stories, including Rowlandson's, have been made to support and serve in the history of the developing Euro-American nation.

Annette Kolodny, who has devoted two books, *The Lay of the Land* and *The Land Before Her*, to exploring the environmental effects of the discursive process that feminized the New World landscape and to the resulting difficulties for Euro-American women in finding a place and a voice within the feminized American landscape, says this about the Puritan captivity stories: "[I]n the earliest captivity narratives, Indian and forest alike functioned as symbolic props in a preconceived cultural script, the central focus of which was always the spiritual drama of affliction and redemption" (*Land Before Her* 28). That undisputed "spiritual drama," though, I would argue, clothed another accompanying drama that was equally, perhaps even predominantly, the focus of colonial concern: the contest for control of the land and its resources, along with the related desire to assert the dominance of white men in the emerging American culture.

In terms of those discourses of gender imported with the earliest European exploration of the Americas—the discourses Kolodny traces in *The Lay of the Land* that established the equation, still persistent in the twentieth century, of women with the very soil of the American continent—Rowlandson was supposed to be not the mapper, but the mapped. Her narrative, however, in its tracing of the twenty "removes" of the group through the wilderness, is not only a literal cartography of the contested landscape Rowlandson traversed during her time with the Narragansetts; it also maps the multiple ways she experienced captivity, and as such is a cartography of competing ideologies, including both the shifts in her views of Indians and their way of life and the resulting dissonances in her identity as a Puritan Englishwoman.

As Rowlandson attempts to make sense of her experience, she invokes and displays Puritan beliefs in divine sanction for English colonization and in the "savagery" of Native people. At the same time, however, the narrative continually reminds us of the experiences excluded from it and uncontained within its contradictory voices; it makes clear that Rowlandson's experience of captivity breached those governing ideologies the text often invokes, that her intimacy with her captors rent her Puritan worldview, perhaps beyond repair.

As conventional readings of Rowlandson demonstrate, her text is laced with protestations of how captivity tried and proved her faith and confirmed her Puritan identity. To prove how she learned to repudiate all things Indian, for one example, she relates how captivity prompted her to give up her use of tobacco:

> Then I went to see King Philip, he bade me come in and sit down, and asked me whether I woold smoke it (a usual Complement nowadayes amongst Saints and Sinners) but this no way suited me. For though I had formerly used Tobacco, yet I had left it ever since I was first taken. It seems to be a Bait, the Devil layes to make men loose their precious time: I remember with shame, how formerly, when I had taken two or three pipes, I was presently ready for another, such a bewitching thing it is: But I thank God, he has now given me power over it; surely there are many who may be better imployed than to ly sucking a stinking Tobacco-pipe. (134)

Recurring tensions in the text reveal too, however, that Rowlandson did adapt in many ways to the culture of her captors; survival would have required that of her. Her dislocation from the familiar world renders vividly visible the culturally constructed nature of her Puritan consciousness and identity; the narrative represents the destabilizing effects of captivity on her subjectivity and constructs a threshold or intercultural space from which she comes to view both cultures, as well as her own self, differently. Her view of her captors moves from a reductive constellation of attributes—"savage," "diabolical," "bestial"—in early passages of the narrative to later passages that accommodate her experience of them as complex and fully human people, capable, like her own people, of both cruelty and kindness. And Rowlandson is careful to record the many occasions when they do show her great kindness, as she also shows in many subtle ways her admiration for their bravery and endurance.

Rowlandson does not remain only a sideline observer and reporter of Indian life; she reveals in a number of ways her own integration into the Indian community. During the course of her captivity she meets Metacom himself, and, as in her descriptions of Quinnapin, she portrays Metacom as gentle, courteous, dignified, and kind. On one occasion he invites her to dine with him in exchange for her having made "a Cap for his boy"; she describes being served "a Pancake, about as big as two fingers; it was made of parched wheat, beaten, and fryed in bears grease, but I thought I never tasted pleasanter meat in my life" (135). She enters the Indian gift-and-barter economy by trading her sewing and knitting skills for food, and on one occasion, having received "a piece of Bear" and "a quart of Pease" in exchange for her needlework, she invites her "master and mistriss to dinner" (135). On another occasion, she receives a knife for having made shirts for an Indian's children and in turn gives the knife to Quinnapin as a gift; she describes herself as "not a little glad that I had any thing that they would accept of, and be pleased with" (136).

Even when she is unable to decipher the meaning of something that happens to her, she implicitly challenges colonial characterizations of Indian life as "precivilized" or "savage" by acknowledging Indian customs and social arrangements to be complex and intricate—even at times exceeding a colonial Englishwoman's ability to comprehend them. The narrative records a number of such instances. On one occasion, she reports that "they were so nice [fastidious] in other things, that when I had fetch water, and had put the Dish I dipt the water with, into the kettle of water which I brought, they would say, they would knock me down; for they said, it was a sluttish trick" (146). On another occasion, Rowlandson invites Quinnapin and Weetamoo to dinner, and she unwittingly commits some gaffe: "I boyled my Pease and Bear together, and invited my master and mistriss to dinner, but the proud Gossip [Weetamoo], because I served them both in one Dish, would eat nothing, except one bit that he gave her on the point of his knife" (135). The phrase about "serv[ing] them both in one Dish" is ambiguous because of the unclear pronoun reference; we can't know whether the transgression is that the bear and peas have been cooked together, or that she serves the food in one dish for both of her guests. In any case, by openly representing her perplexity about the Indian social system, she also represents, and reveals for her readers' reflection, her own and her fellow colonists' culpable ignorance of Indian life.

Near the end of her captivity and of the narrative, Rowlandson demonstrates that her months of embeddedness in Indian culture have given her new eyes with which to observe the people she has lived with and their ways, typically so foreign to the English. She describes in careful detail a "Powaw," a precombat ritual, that some of the Indians perform before they leave the camp to stage an ambush of a group of English soldiers near Sudbury (152–53). Her description is not only careful and attentive, but nonjudgmental and even interested. I quote it at length to demonstrate how precise was her memory of sequence and detail—especially remarkable given that the account was written some months after the event—a degree of attention that clearly signals her desire to discern the meaning of the ritual she observes:

> Before they went to that fight, they got a company together to Powaw; the manner was as followeth. There was one that kneeled upon a Deerskin, with the company round him in a ring who kneeled, and stricking upon the ground with their hands, and with sticks, and muttering or humming with their mouths; besides him who kneeled in the ring, there also stood one with a Gun in his hand: Then he on the Deer-skin made a speech, and all manifested assent to it: and so they did many times together. Then they bade him with the Gun go out of the ring, which he did, but when he was out, they called him in again;

but he seemed to make a stand, then they called the more earnestly, till he returned again: Then they all sang. Then they gave him two Guns, in either hand one: And so he on the Deer-skin began again; and at the end of every sentence in his speaking, they all assented, humming or muttering with their mouthes, and striking upon the ground with their hands. Then they bade him with the two Guns go out of the ring again, which he did, a little way. Then they called him in again, but he made a stand; so they called him with greater earnestness; but he stood reeling and wavering as if he knew not whither he should stand or fall, or which way to go. Then they called him with exceeding great vehemency, all of them, one and another: after a little while he turned in, staggering as he went, with his Armes stretched out, in either hand a Gun. As soon as he came in, they all sang and rejoyced exceedingly a while. And then he upon the Deer-skin, made another speech unto which they all assented in a rejoicing manner: and so they ended their business, and forthwith went to Sudbury fight. (152–53)

Rowlandson is obviously motivated here by curiosity and the acknowl-edgement, however unspoken, that Narragansett culture is structurally intricate, bound together by practices that, though she cannot decipher their significance, have meanings that exceed her ability to understand them. I read the passage as registering the dramatic change that has occurred in Rowlandson since she first was taken; it is unimaginable that the woman she represents herself as being when the narrative opens—a woman who can only describe her captors as a faceless and collective "they"—could observe and record the "Powaw" as she does.

Her descriptions of Weetamoo's and Quinnapin's habits of dress and adornment also register her growing ability to read the social setting of her captivity, even if not always to understand it. Of Weetamoo she says, "A severe and proud Dame she was, bestowing every day in dressing her self neat as much time as any of the Gentry of the land: powdering her hair, and painting her face, going with Neck-laces, with Jewels in her ears, and Bracelets upon her hands: When she had dressed her self, her work was to make Girdles of Wampom and Beads" (150). Rowlandson's comparing Weetamoo with a "Dame" of the English "Gentry" could perhaps be read as ridiculing Weetamoo's toilet and self-adornment as pretentious; her description is, however, the result of careful and attentive observation that could as easily be motivated by her curiosity about a Native world that is beginning to open itself up to her understanding. I find in the passage a hint of admiration and even envy on the part of the captive and bedraggled Englishwoman toward the regal dress and demeanor of the Indian "queen."

On the eve of Rowlandson's ransom, the Indians perform an elaborate dance to celebrate their victory at Sudbury. Rowlandson describes both the dancers and the dance in some detail, again evidencing both interest and admiration:

> [T]hey ate very little, they being so busie in dressing themselves, and getting ready for their Dance: which was carried on by eight of them, four Men and four Squaws: My master and mistress being two. He was dressed in his Holland shirt, with great Laces sewed at the tail of it, he had his silver Buttons, his white Stockins, his Garters were hung round with Shillings, and he had Girdles of Wampom upon his head and shoulders. She had a Kersey Coat, and covered with Girdles of Wampom from the Loins upward: her armes from her elbows to her hands were covered with Bracelets; there were hand-fulls of Necklaces about her neck, and severall sorts of Jewels in her ears. She had fine red Stokins, and white Shoos, her hair powdered and face painted Red, that was alwayes before Black. And all the Dancers were after the same manner. There were two other singing and knocking on a Kettle for their musick. They keept hopping up and down one after another, with a Kettle of water in the midst, standing warm upon some Embers, to drink of when they were dry. They held on till it was almost night, throwing out Wampom to the standers by. (156–57)[30]

These and other similar passages in the narrative provide evidence of the shifting and precarious nature of Rowlandson's identity and thus her attitudes toward Indians during captivity. But they beg the larger and persistent question, itself a potent metaphor for a possible shift of identity and allegiance: Did she or didn't she?

Rowlandson's report that the Indians were never sexually aggressive toward her does not mean that her story altogether lacks an erotic element. To accept the representations of her as a chastely restored Puritan wife requires that we ignore passages in the text that are indeed erotically charged. Her attachment to Quinnapin becomes intense in the course of the weeks she spends in his charge, and her frankness in expressing her closeness with him is striking. When Quinnapin leaves the group for a period of weeks, she misses him acutely: she writes, "my master himself was gone and I left behind, so that my Spirit was now quite ready to sink" (140). Upon being reunited with him after his long absence, she confesses "and glad I was to see him" (150).

The night before she is ransomed and released to return to her own community, Quinnapin, drunk from the whiskey that is part of her ransom payment,[31] summons her to his wigwam. The passage is charged with the possibilities of what might transpire between the two, for a few more hours still technically master and slave. Rowlandson goes with expressed trepidation, combined perhaps with an unacknowledged (indeed unacknowledgable) desire, but the moment of sexual reckoning is evaded when after all Quinnapin only drinks to her, "shewing no incivility" (157), and settles down for the night with one of his wives (158).

Rowlandson's narrative, though, in fact depicts many ways "Indian-ness" does literally penetrate or enter her, just as she enters to some extent into the Indian community—with the food she consumes, the language she learns and uses, her accommodation to Native social arrangements. She evidently becomes comfortable referring to Quinnapin and Weetamoo as "my master" and "my mistress." She reaches a point where she refers easily to herself and her captors as "we" (e.g., 133) and to the encampment as "home" (e.g., 143). Furthermore, she uses a number of Indian words in the text—Wigwam, Sannup, Sachem, Squaw, Papoose, Saggamore, Matchit, Powaw, Wampom, Nux—indicating that she acquired some ability and willingness to understand and converse in her captors' tongue.

The ways Rowlandson represents herself as "Indian-like" in the negative senses typical of Puritan descriptions of Native people are even more significant in understanding how captivity rewrites her identity. The persistent and acute hunger she suffers throughout her captivity produces a kind of obsessive and animal-like ferocity about getting sufficient food. (The Narragansetts as well as their captives were suffering from starvation during this time because of the war and their enforced flight from their pursuers.) In the opening pages of the narrative, we see Rowlandson as a victim, enduring the horror of the Indians' attack, "standing amazed, with the blood running down to [her] heels" (120). In a few short pages, though, we find her with "blood about [her] mouth" (133). Grief over her predicament and the death of her child combine with acute hunger to transform her into an icon of savagery, eagerly devouring a half-cooked piece of horse liver she has begged from one of the Indians: "What, sayes he, can you eat horse liver? I told him, I would try, if he would give me a piece, which he did, and I laid it on the coals to rost; but before it was half ready they got half of it away from me, so that I was fain to take the rest and eat it as it was, with the blood about my mouth, and yet a savoury bit it was to me" (132–33).

Nor is this an isolated incident. She repeatedly and eagerly eats things that she previously would have thought, as she says, "would turn the stomach of a bruit creature" (137)—horse's guts, hooves, and ears, even the bark of trees. Scenes abound in which Rowlandson consumes with relish what she at first calls "their filthy trash" but what soon becomes "sweet and savoury" (131) to her. She quickly becomes what she has initially and very conventionally described her captors as being: a "ravenous beast," even able on one occasion literally to take food out of the mouth of a captive English child in her fierce determination to preserve her own life:

> Then I went to another Wigwam, where there were two of the English Children; the Squaw was boyling Horses feet, then she cut me off a little piece, and gave one of the English Children a piece also. Being very hungry I had quickly eat up mine, but the Child could not bite it, it was so tough and sinewy, but lay sucking, gnawing, chewing and slabbering of it in the mouth and hand, then I took it of the Child, and eat it myself, and savoury it was to my taste. (149)

But in some profound sense, one is what one eats. Rowlandson's report of her eager consumption of Indian food, even food taken out of the mouth of an English child, along with the suggestion that she learns something of their language, recognizes and even admires the intricacy of some of their customs, and adapts to some of their ways, would surely have rendered her vulnerable to suspicions after she was ransomed of having "gone native," suspicions closely related to the question of her sexual history during captivity.

One incident that takes place shortly before Rowlandson is ransomed serves to illustrate that she did sympathize and identify with the Indians to a degree that permanently unsettled her identity as a Puritan Englishwoman. It is a vivid metaphor for the way her captivity rewrites how she sees herself:

> Going along, having indeed my life, but little spirit, Philip, who was in the Company, came up and took me by the hand, and said, Two weeks more and you shal be Mistress again. I asked him, if he spake true? he answered, Yes, and quickly you shal come to your master again; who had been gone from us three weeks. After many weary steps we came to Wachuset, where he [Quinnapin] was: and glad I was to see him. He asked me, When I washt me? I told him not this month, then he fetcht me some water himself, and bid me wash, and gave me the Glass to see how I lookt; and bid his Squaw give me something to eat: so she gave me a mess of Beans and meat, and a little Ground-nut Cake. I was wonderfully revived with this favour shewed me. (150)

The incident reveals Rowlandson's "savage" or "bestial" self that arises from the deprivations of captivity—she is dirty, weary, starving, anxious, and dispirited because of the absence of the master to whom she is very attached, separated from her son and daughter and thus from her maternal identity as well as from her home culture. But as I read the passage, it is Quinnapin who gives her a new "self"—a self that has arisen specifically from the complexities of captivity. When he gives her the mirror, the woman she sees cannot be the same woman who was taken captive in the winter. Instead, she must see herself as she is among the Indians, see herself as they see her, and through their eyes, see herself as she has become. The late April afternoon on which she is recalled to herself—*re-vived*, given new life—through Quinnapin's urgings and ministrations marks the spring of her rebirth; we can read her washing as a ritual baptism that discards the old self and asserts the new and her subsequent meal as a feast of communion between herself and the people who now surround and sustain her.

But that image of herself, regardless of how "wonderfully" it has "revived" her in captivity, was surely a persistently unsettling presence in her life after her return to the Puritan community.[32] Reunited with her husband and her surviving children in Boston, Rowlandson writes in the narrative's closing passage of how her experience continues to haunt her:

> I can remember the time, when I used to sleep quietly without workings in my thoughts, whole nights together, but now it is other wayes with me. When all are fast about me, and no eye open, but his who ever waketh, my thoughts are upon things past. . . . The portion of some is to have their afflictions by drops, now one drop and then another; but the dregs of the Cup, the Wine of astonishment, like a sweeping rain that leaveth no food, did the Lord prepare to be my portion. (166)

I am reminded here of another haunting passage, a stanza in Adrienne Rich's poem, "Song":

> If I'm lonely
> it must be the loneliness
> of waking first, of breathing
> dawn's first cold breath on the city
> of being the one awake
> in a house wrapped in sleep
>
> (20)

A metaphoric reading of Rowlandson's wakefulness is irresistible: her familiarity with Native people, the Native way of life, her recognition of the suffering her people were inflicting on them, of their being not so much radically other but much like her own people, and herself like them—all this must have left Rowlandson feeling at times that she was the only one "awake" in the "house wrapped in sleep" that was Puritan colonialism. Her desire to return to the serene security of her former unquestioned identity must have been perpetually thwarted by the residues of her experience with the Indians.

REWRITING CAPTIVITY

If Rowlandson's narrative was meant to secure her passage back into the Puritan community, its heritage, as I have pointed out, has long been to be read as a defense of that community and its history. Such a reading requires obedience to the Puritan fathers who ask readers to suppress the other voice weaving itself into and through her narrative. The narrative, though, however much it reveals through all its tensions and contradictions how Rowlandson's captivity unsettled her identity—and implicitly that of the Puritan community—also masks a text that is missing. If the narrative we have is Rowlandson's map of her captivity that was meant to purchase her reentry into the Puritan community, we lack the map she constructed for herself during captivity as an entry into the Indian community.

That absence, one that parallels the absent text of Pocahontas's own narrative and that of other silenced Native women, has attracted the attention of Louise Erdrich, a contemporary poet and novelist of mixed European and Ojibwa descent. Erdrich refuses to obey the directive of the Puritan fathers on how to read Rowlandson's narrative and returns to the text to construct a counter-narrative, retrieving the colloquial voice that Puritan orthodoxy obscured. In her poem "Captivity," Erdrich gleans from Rowlandson's narrative a constellation of incidents and images that allow her to recover possibilities in Rowlandson's experience that Puritanism exercised its power to suppress. The opening lines of the poem signal the threat that captivity will pose to the coherence of Rowlandson's Puritan identity:

The stream was swift, and so cold
I thought I would be sliced in two . . .
(26)

Erdrich too, like the early Puritan readers, sexualizes Rowlandson's experience, but Erdrich's gesture is not an imperialist or exploitive one; rather, it is an effort to rewrite and so to recover the sexual—thus *connective*—possibilities in the scene of captivity, a scene that for so many years was used as a motive force for racial and cultural division. The poem makes clear that an erotic bond with her master is precisely what saves Rowlandson from being destroyed by this splitting of her consciousness:

> There were times I feared I understood
> his language, which was not human,
> and I knelt to pray for strength.
> . . . .
> I told myself that I would starve
> before I took food from his hands
> but I did not starve.
> One night
> he killed a deer with a young one in her
> and gave me to eat of the fawn.
> It was so tender,
> the bones like the stems of flowers,
> that I followed where he took me.
> The night was thick. He cut the cord
> that bound me to the tree.
>
> (26–27)

In Erdrich's poem, the food Rowlandson consumes during captivity is not "filthy trash," as Rowlandson has called it, but is instead celestial and redemptive, food for the spirit as much as for the body. If "the tree" in the poem is a reference to the cross of Christianity, the emblem of suffering and sacrifice on which rest repressive Christian codes of sexual morality, especially for women, then her master's cutting the cord that has bound Rowlandson to that tree suggests that Puritan doctrine has enslaved her in many ways, including both spiritually and sexually, long before she was taken captive. With the image of "cut[ting] the cord,"

Erdrich frees Rowlandson from her bondage to the cross of Christianity, and her sojourn with the Indians is figured as a site not of enslavement but of release, indeed of rebirth. Erdrich's poem reconstructs Rowlandson's seduction by the sensual and spiritual beauty of Indian life and rewrites her captivity as captivation. To the question "Did she or didn't she?" Erdrich offers an answer: That Rowlandson "followed where [her master] took [her]" is both irresistible and inevitable, even though it opens a terrifying inner space where "birds mocked. / Shadows gaped and roared / and the trees flung down their sharpened lashes" (27). It is a space, the poem insists, that can never be closed, that memory sustains, even after Rowlandson's return to her people.

Just as Rowlandson's experience seems to have permanently unsettled her perceptions of her own and her community's identity, so together her narrative and Erdrich's poem unsettle and revise traditional representations of Native culture and of Puritan encounters with Indians. Together they challenge the traditional histories of white colonists in the world that was "new" to them, but "home" to those from whom they wrested it.

Rowlandson's assertion that captivity did not threaten either her chastity or her Christianity, her observations of the chaste demeanor of her captors and her recognition of the sophisticated complexity of their social arrangements, proved to have a tenuous hold on the colonial, and later national, imagination. Again and again, the figure of the white woman captive among Indians that Rowlandson for so long represented or shadowed has been used to create and enforce racial boundaries, to impugn Native people, and to justify a brutal national politics of Indian removal and extermination. And because that figure has historically been called upon to serve ideologies of white dominance, it is important to return to Rowlandson's text to recover the "colloquial" voice within it that has so often been occluded—the voice of a woman whose experience allowed her to move from characterizing Indians early in her narrative as indistinguishable and unreadable "black creatures in the night" (121) to seeing them as individuals with names, distinguishing features, characters, and habits and an intricate network of social customs and conventions—to know them, in other words, to be as fully human as herself.

If Rowlandson's writing has been for much of our own century less well known than it deserves, the figure of the white woman captive whom her experience and her text established has certainly been familiar, long-lived, and culturally powerful from the period of colonial settlement to the present. In our continuing efforts to reckon the ideological consequences—political, racial, sexual, textual, and ecological—of our colonialist history, narratives of Indian captivity and readings of them remain important sources for understanding how those ideologies took shape and voice.

Beginning with Rowlandson's narrative, captivity stories have repeatedly positioned a woman—her body, spirituality, sexuality, and reproductive capacity—as a border zone where cultures in conflict meet and contend and where discourses of race and gender are generated and played out. Especially throughout the nineteenth and into the twentieth centuries, representations of white women captured by Indians have been recirculated in fiction, poetry, painting, sculpture, and film as a site for reasserting and legitimating racial hierarchies and white Euro-Americans' claim to the continent. As we shall see, it remained only for the newly created white-dominant nation to retrieve from the history of English settlement the companion figure to the white woman captive: Pocahontas, the welcoming Indian "princess" whose "love" for the English colonists could be invoked to complete the task of heroizing them and their desire to establish an Anglo-American republic on the American continent.

LEAVING LANCASTER

In Lancaster, George Hill Lane crosses gentle George Hill. I find it without trouble, at the end of Narrow Lane. Comfortable houses with wide lawns line the road; the mailboxes bear names like Kilbourn and Ward. In the woods, the snow is still solid and deep. I find myself wondering what sort of shoes Mary wore during captivity. Did she walk some of those many miles in moccasins? I'm certain now that this is ground she must have covered. Rowlandson Rock is probably somewhere in these woods to my left, near the crest of the hill. But it would be in somebody's backyard now, and I don't want to trespass.

From the crest of the hill, I follow Sterling Road back toward Lancaster Center, passing more houses, open fields, a dairy barn with twin silos, a run-down split-level house behind a low New-England-style stone wall with a hand-lettered sign posted on a tree at roadside: "Whats Nu Gifts."

At the bottom of the hill the lane merges with a two-lane country highway. To my surprise, to my left are enormous stone pillars supporting a large iron-grillwork gate across a long driveway that winds up the hill into the trees. The gateposts carry a brass plaque: "Maharishi Ayurvedic Health Center." So. My own voyage of discovery ends with this trace, not of the people Columbus and his ilk found in the "new world," but of the people they sought and for whom the inhabitants here were mistaken and misnamed.

The afternoon sun is low, and a chill is in the air. It's time to turn my back on the town and head home. Halfway, I stop at a turnpike rest area for coffee and to stretch the stiffness from my spine and legs. I browse in the small shop featuring souvenir gifts of Massachusetts: Bruins, Patriots, Celtics mugs and banners, refrigerator magnets in the shape of the state, playing cards with scenes of Boston or the colonial stars and stripes. A felt banner proclaims "Massachusetts" in progressively shrinking letters against a background of representative vignettes: a beach, a leaping fish, a gull, Old North Church, the state capitol, a Minuteman, a Pilgrim. Not a sign of an Indian. I spot a harmonica in the shape of a lobster claw and almost give in, but I resist and climb back in the car.

As I drive through the fading light, I listen with a heavy heart to the evening NPR news of the war in the Persian Gulf and meditate on the persistence of self-deception, nationalist arrogance, avarice, and loss: Shortly after Rowlandson was ransomed, Weetamoo, her "mistress," drowned while trying to escape capture; her pursuers cut off her head and exhibited it on a pole in Taunton. Quinnapin was captured and executed by the English. On August 1, 1676, just as the war was drawing to its bitter close, Metacom's wife Wootonekanuske and their nine-year-old son, the boy for whom Rowlandson had sewn a cap, were captured and, like countless other Indians of the Northeast, were sent to the West Indies to be sold into slavery and lost to history. Chroniclers of the war reported that Metacom's heart and spirit were broken by their capture. About ten days later "Philip," having retreated in defeat into a swamp just south of his homeland of Montaup (ironically renamed by the English "Mount Hope"), was shot by an Indian traitor accompanying the English who were hunting him down. Increase Mather, in *A Brief History of the War with the Indians in New England*, says this about Metacom's death: "And in that very place where he first contrived and began his mischief, was he taken and destroyed, and there was he . . . cut into four quarters, and is now hanged up as a monument of revenging Justice, his head being cut off and carried away to Plymouth, his hands were brought to Boston" (139).

By the time the snow starts to spit I'm almost home. Night has fallen, I am sad and weary, but my feet are warm and dry inside my boots.

CHAPTER 2

Close Encounters of the First Kind

The bright girl knelt, bathed in repentant tears—
connecting link between two hemispheres.
         —MARY MOSBY WEBSTER, *Pocahontas: A Legend*

When I think of Pocahontas, I am ready to love Indians.
         —HERMAN MELVILLE, *The Confidence Man*

TO GRAVESEND: APRIL 1992

I begin where Pocahontas ended: at Gravesend, at the mouth of the Thames.

I'm not familiar enough with trains. Somehow, on a car with facing seats, I always sit in such a way that I travel backward. I realize I've done it again as soon as our train starts to pull out of the Charing Cross station. But we're ensconced: I, facing where I've been instead of where I'm going; Mary Lou, in London because she's teaching there for the semester, and her small daughter Claire in the seat opposite. Maybe it's appropriate after all, this traveling backwards to Gravesend, in search of Pocahontas.

Claire at four is excited about a day trip to find an Indian princess. She looks like a little princess herself, in her purple plush coat with its big gold buttons. She's just learned to skip, and she skipped springily, if a little unpredictably, down the hill on our way to the tube station this morning. No cartwheels yet, though no doubt it won't be long. Pocahontas was, by most reckonings, about ten when she would come into the Jamestown settlement and cartwheel, "naked as she was, all the fort over," as William Strachey wrote.

Mary Lou, with motherly foresight, has brought along books, drawing paper and crayons, snacks to amuse and divert Claire on the journey. I think of Pocahontas's small boy, with his English name, Thomas: the divided child, with an Indian mother, an English father. What did she bring along to amuse him on their travels? He would have been about two, only half Claire's age, when he lost his mother at Gravesend, just before they were to set sail to return to Virginia. Home. She would have been, at the most, twenty-two. I wonder if she gave him an Algonkian name too, a term of endearment she would have used when no English people were around. My newest children's book on Pocahontas, William Accorsi's *My Name Is Pocahontas*, says she did—in Accorsi's story, she called him Hoko. And surely she spoke to him in the language of her people, taught him the names of things, how to call them, and used those words when she told him about Virginia, or as variously reported, in Algonkian *Attanoughkomouck*, *Wingandacoa*, or *Tsenacommacah*—home; his too. If so, he didn't listen, or he was too little, and he lost them, his name and the other words, the bright notes that would have held the memory of his mother's voice. Her voice is lost to us as well. Even the language she spoke is now extinct.

That I'm off to find Pocahontas's final resting place is something of a surprise, even to me. During this five-hundredth anniversary year of the "discovery" of America, I've come to England to find out what was being written and read here in the seventeenth century about early English colonial women who were captured by Indians, especially Mary Rowlandson, whose captivity narrative was published here as well as in Boston in 1682. I've been spending my days in bliss in the vast, high-domed

Reading Room of the British Museum Library, that history-encrusted repository of Western culture that Virginia Woolf described so perfectly when she said one felt, when there, like an idea in a giant cranium.

Day after day I order up and devour the beautiful ancient books, occasionally rest my eyes and neck by bending my head back to look up at the pigeons flying in and out a broken window at the top of the dome, and, like the other scholars, mostly ignore the occasional warnings to gather up my belongings and evacuate the building because of suspected IRA bomb threats. Somehow, somewhere among all those tomes, Pocahontas presented herself to me and wouldn't let go. Of course I'd known her story: saving John Smith, bringing corn, welcoming the strangers, even marrying one of them. Virginia's equivalent to Squanto, only better, because of the romance. It's a story familiar to every school-child in America. But now I read another story: Pocahontas was a captive too, held hostage in Jamestown for three years to protect the settlement from attack by the warriors who served her father, Wahunsonacock, leader of the Powhatan confederacy, known as "the Powhatan," or simply "Powhatan." He especially loved this daughter, whose birthname was Matoaka but whom he nicknamed "the playful one." Ralph Hamor in his *True Discourse of the present Estate of Virginia* (1615) calls her "Pow-hatans delight and darling . . . whose fame hath even bin spred in England by the title of *Nonparella of Virginia*" (4). A small rift opens within me when I read of her capture, of her pleas to be released, of Powhatan's refusal to ransom her by returning the English men and guns he is holding—it's like what I felt when I read, months ago, about how Squanto had learned English, which the Plymouth Pilgrims found so surprising, and so valuable, when he came among them and taught them how to plant maize, Indian corn. He too had been a captive, taken by force to England in 1614 by an English adventurer and very likely put on exhibit as a curiosity, as other Indian captives before him had been. When he escaped and contrived passage back to his own country, he found his village, Patuxet, empty except for bones and skulls, his entire people dead of a plague that Europeans had brought to the New World (Calloway 27; see also Salisbury). Now Pocahontas. Given all this information, I have to wonder what her "love" for the English must have been like.

When I called the British Tourist Office in London to ask about where she might have been buried, no one there knew whom I was talking about. The British, I guess, haven't as many reasons to make hay of her as Americans have had, or as the English themselves had, centuries ago. The next day I found the information I needed in a book at the Museum Library. To find Pocahontas, I would have to go to Gravesend.

And so today we're off. After an hour's train ride, we arrive in Gravesend. It's a grey, chilly, drizzly, English April Sunday. It was March when Pocahontas died here in 1617, so the weather might have been not very different from this, certainly not good for an exhausted and probably consumptive, certainly desperately ill young woman. Gravesend seems an appropriate place to visit on such a dreary day as this. Gulls soar and squawk overhead as we wander up and down and along the steep cobbled streets leading to the waterfront, looking out at ships in the river channel and thinking of Pocahontas, wondering if it was in one of these ancient pierside inns that her illness claimed her and she drew her last breath.

We make our way to St. George's Church, where she was buried. It's now a memorial chapel dedicated to Pocahontas. At the back of the chapel, we point out the portrait of the "Indian princess" to Claire, who seems unimpressed and says, but she doesn't *look* like a princess. True enough; no crown, and no happy smile. It is a reproduction of the famous Van de Passe engraving of 1616, labeled *Matoaka als Rebecka, Daughter to the mighty Prince Powhatan*—Matoaka *as*, or as I choose to read it, *disguised as*, Rebecca. She looks stern, as well she might, and she's decked out in English ruff and hat, wearing the same style gold-and-pearl earrings worn by Venus in a famous painting by Rubens done in 1616—the same year as Van de Passe's engraving. In the Rubens painting, Venus's pearls are different—one is white and one, reflected in a mirror held out to the goddess by the boyish god Amor, is black. A sign, perhaps, of love's dark side, as well as of its tendency to lose its lustre. I wonder if the Rubens painting was exhibited in London during the time of Pocahontas's visit. Is the earring in her portrait yet another indication that the English thought of her as a New World Venus, a goddess of love? Love for themselves, of course. In the Pocahontas portrait, only one earring is visible; its pearl is white. What color, I wonder, would the other be, if we could see it?

I move to get a closer look at the stained-glass windows on either side of the altar. On the left is the "Rebecca" window. "Rebecca" is the name Pocahontas was given when she was baptized in Jamestown in April of 1613. I had wondered why that particular name; then I remembered Rebecca was the woman at the well in the Bible, giving the strangers all they needed—water, food, shelter. My curiosity piqued, I looked up her story and found the passage in Genesis; after a long period of infertility, Rebekah, the wife of Isaac, conceives:

> And the children struggled together within her; and she said, if it be so, why am I thus? And she went to enquire of the Lord.
>
> And the Lord said unto her, Two nations are in thy womb, and two manner of people shall be separated from thy bowels; and the one people shall be stronger than the other people; and the elder shall serve the younger.
>
> And when her days to be delivered were fulfilled, behold, there were twins in her womb.
>
> And the first came out red . . . .
>
> (Genesis 26:22–25)

Esau, that "red" son of Rebekah and Isaac, was the one who sold his birthright to his brother Jacob. Rebecca was, then, a painfully appropriate name for Pocahontas, given the English determination to engineer another genesis—of English colonial control of her country and her "red" people. And given also that she would be the subject of a legend that made her the representative of the "elder" people of Virginia who should serve the later comers, and made her also one who "sold" her birthright.

The window in St. George's shows a figure of the biblical Rebecca with a water jar on her shoulder. Banners to the left and right of the figure carry the words "Faith" and "Hope." A small scene in a window below the main figure is inscribed "The Baptism of Pocahontas at the Church of Delawarre." The arrangement of the figures resembles that in the Chapman painting of the baptism of Pocahontas hanging in the Rotunda of the U.S. Capitol in Washington (figure 2). Pocahontas is kneeling, her long dark hair tied at her nape and streaming down her back; she wears a flowing white dress. An oval portrait of her in the lower right of this

FIGURE 2. John Gadsby Chapman, *The Baptism of Pocahontas at Jamestown, Virginia, 1613.* The painting was placed in the U.S. Capitol Rotunda in 1840. Courtesy of the Office of the Architect of the U.S. Capitol and the National Archives.

window is of the Native woman romanticized—and anglicized: Her hair is loose and crowned with some sort of circlet. Again she wears a white gown; its pallor cloaks her Native skin.

To the right of the altar is the "Ruth" window, again celebrating a biblical figure, the woman who, like Pocahontas of the legend, adopted her husband's people and religion as her own. The banners here say "Love" and "Constancy." The scene below the large figure of Ruth is of Ruth and Naomi at the moment of the pledge, with an inscription: "Thy people shall be my people, and thy God my GOD." Another inscription says that the window was presented in 1914 by the Colonial Dames of America in Virginia "as a token of gratitude for services rendered to that colony by Princess Pocahontas." The small oval portrait in this window is a replica of the famous Van de Passe engraving of Pocahontas in an English hat.

It comes to me as I stand there that the windows are meant to be read, left to right, as a history: First she is baptized, renamed Rebecca, and given a new identity; then she declares her loyalty to her "new people" and her new God and proves her love and constancy by appearing in seventeenth-century English dress. I wonder, as I've wondered so often in thinking about this woman, the life lived and the legend so remarkably long-lived, whose story this really is.

Claire, grown restless at our gentle urging that she should be a bit still in church, says it's time to go outside. So much quiet is too much to ask of a lively and playful girl. I drop my pence in the metal box and take copies of the brochures on Pocahontas at the back of the church. In the garden, Claire skips and romps in the drizzle and tries to climb the bronze statue of Pocahontas—like the legend, larger than life. Mary Lou and I stand quietly and stare for a long time at the statue, a replica of the Partridge sculpture at Jamestown. Her features are softened into a bland symmetry; the sculpted face looks nothing like the engraving, the only verified portrait of her drawn from life, and there is little about her face to suggest her identity as a Native woman of the American coastal wood- lands. Even her dress is like that of a Plains woman, a misprision typical of the nineteenth-century process that made Plains Indian culture repre- sent all Indian cultures. But of course it's not the historical Pocahontas we're looking at; it's Pocahontas idealized, mythologized, incorporated into and serving Anglo-American legend and culture. Predictably, I haven't found in Gravesend the Pocahontas I'm looking for—one with a voice and a mind of her own, one who might speak for herself.

It's time for tea, and after several futile efforts to find it in one of the pubs nearby (it being Sunday, they're serving only the usual roast pub lunches), we end up in a McDonald's, of all places, on the main street. Claire, the American child, is very pleased with our choice. At a table near us, a group of English youngsters is enjoying a McDonald's birthday party. I think with great amusement of how culture, so to speak, is now flowing west to east, across the blue Atlantic and back to England. Serves them—and us—right, I suppose.

Back through the drizzle to the train station; backwards, again, to London; then the tube to Great Percy Street and home. All three of us are tired to the bone. It's been a long day, and I'm left unsatisfied, unsettled by my quest. I know it's far from over. Pocahontas is everywhere in American culture—and at the same time nowhere to be found. Sleep overtakes me after a single chapter of Catharine Maria Sedgwick's nineteenth-century novel *Hope Leslie,* with its heroic Indian girl, Magawisca, modeled on the legendary Pocahontas in so many ways, not the least of which is her self-sacrificial impulse to save a captive English youth whom she loves from death at the hands of her people. She loses an arm in the process. Pocahontas lost her life. But America gained a legend.

ENGENDERING THE NEW WORLD

If Rowlandson's narrative provided first the colonizers and then the architects of the budding nation with a fruitful site for furthering their projects and purposes, the Pocahontas story, or stories, offered an even richer opportunity precisely because Pocahontas left no known text of her own, never represented herself or her point of view on her experience in any way we might read. Thus she never achieved the narrative subjectivity that, in Rowlandson's text, proved so troubling to the English colonizers in New England that it required intervention and efforts to control how the text was read. The absence of any self-representation by Pocahontas, unlike Rowlandson's written narrative, offered no resistances to the inscriptions of race, sex, and emergent nationhood that her legend has for centuries been made to serve in so many ways—unless we read her silence itself as a kind of resistance, a refusal to use the language of the colonizers in the way they valued, as written. She did, after all, learn English, so she might well have learned to write it too; but if Pocahontas did write her story, it is forever lost, and the many stories that have proliferated around her have depended upon her continued silence to ensure their perpetuation.[1]

Despite the significant difference in self-representation, though, Rowlandson's and Pocahontas's functions in cultural history have been more similar than not, especially in the ways both women and their stories have been repeatedly conscripted into the evolving dramas of colonialism and, later, of creating and defining a racialized nation and national identity. Both women were caught in the webs of violence resulting from the territorial and cultural contests of the early English colonial era, and both experienced cross-cultural captivity—the Englishwoman among

Indians, the Indian woman among the English. The bodies and sexuality of both were appropriated to serve the project of English colonialism: the body of the white woman captive was insistently "closed," controlled by patriarchal discourses of "protection" that served not her interests or desires but those of white hegemony; the body of the Native woman was made to symbolize the continent itself and so rendered insistently "open" to union, willing or not, with England. Both were positioned at the boundaries of evolving racial categories; while movement across racial dividing lines by white women captives like Rowlandson was feared and policed, Pocahontas figures moved, or were moved, readily back and forth across the borders separating "white" and "dark," "English" and "Indian," "civilized" and "savage." The positions depended upon the purposes of particular renderings of her legend, but they were consistently used toward the ends of articulating "race" and addressing the racial dominance of the "dark other" by whites. Likewise, the meanings given to the two figures' stories have functioned symbolically in divergent but also pro-foundly interconnected ways as a Euro-American nation evolved in North America. Like the proliferating stories of white women captured by Indians, the legend of Pocahontas—her "rescue" of John Smith, her conversion to Christianity, her marriage to an Englishman—also points vividly to the ways race, gender, and sexuality were deployed in concert in the ideological theatre of colonialism in the new world.[2]

Pocahontas may have been the first Native woman to be appropriated as a symbol to serve the project of colonization, but a great deal of ideo-logical work prefaced that instance of appropriation and made it possible, work that feminized and sexualized the "new world" as the object of the masculine colonizer's desire.[3] A sixteenth-century poem by John Donne, "Elegie: Going to Bed," is illustrative:

> License my roving hands, and let them go,
> Before, behind, between, above, below.
> O my America! my new-found-land,
> My kingdom, safeliest when with one man manned,
> My mine of precious stones, My empery,
> How blest am I in this discovering thee!
>
> (58)

When Donne penned these lines, probably in the closing years of the sixteenth century[4] and thus concurrent with the beginnings of English settlement in North America,[5] he was not being particularly inventive in using the metaphor of New World exploration to express his desire to uncover, explore, and possess his mistress's body; the figure of the New World as a sexualized female body had already become a commonplace in the discourses of discovery. And Donne, like so many other Englishmen of his class and era, was at least a peripheral actor in the national project of claiming and colonizing the "new" lands. He was acquainted with Sir Walter Ralegh, one of the engineers of English settlement in the New World, having sailed as a "gentleman adventurer" with Ralegh and Essex on an expedition from Plymouth to Cadiz in 1597. His interest in having a personal role in English colonization is indicated by his having sought, without success, the secretaryship of the Virginia Company in 1609 and in his having contributed a poem, "To His Friend Captaine John Smith, and His Worke," to Smith's *The Generall Historie of Virginia*, published in 1624 (Hubbell 180). These anecdotes of Donne's biography invite a reading of his seduction metaphor in the poem as doubly significant: not only is the speaker's mistress his "America" in the poem, but America is also his mistress, awaiting, perhaps even inviting, a sexualized process of "dis-covery," exploration, and conquest.

Ralegh had made his voyage to Guiana in 1595, two years before the expedition to Cadiz on which Donne accompanied him, and had used a similar metaphor to describe that country in his published report *The Discovery of the Large, Rich and Beautiful Empire of Guiana* in 1596: "To conclude, *Guiana* is a Country that hath yet her Maidenhead" (120). Of the description of America as "virgin," Peter Hulme has said, "probably no single word has had to bear so heavy a weight in the construction of American mythology from the moment when, in Samuel Eliot Morison's immortal words [written in 1942], 'the New World gracefully yielded her virginity to the conquering Castilians.' . . . To speak of the 'maidenhead' of Guiana or Virginia was to condense into one potent image the absence of significant native agriculture and the joyful masculine thrust of Elizabethan expansion" (158–59). The rhetorical figure of virginity represents an empty land, one not yet possessed, and so at once erases both the Native inhabitants and all traces of their cultures.

If Guiana is a "virgin," "she" is a blank page, awaiting inscription; thus "she" can be represented as either ripe for being raped or "sacked" (Ralegh 120), or as an appropriate "bride" for a masculinized England.[6] In the latter case, the metaphoric relation between the two worlds is rendered "sacred," like Christian marriage. The marriage metaphor, though, like actual marriage, artificially sacralized what was in fact essentially an economic enterprise. In the terms of the metaphor, a masculinized England would first convert and then marry this virginal and fecund new world, this "mine of precious stones," to the presumed greater honor and glory of God and, not at all incidentally, to the increased material wealth of the "bridegroom."

Ralegh too in representing Guiana as a ripe virgin ready for deflora-tion (the current deforestation of Central and South America comes hauntingly to mind with that term) was adding to what already had by the time of his writing become an established metaphor. From the earliest period of European contact with the New World, the metaphor of sexual uncovering and penetration was at work.

Theodore Galle's 1580 engraving of a drawing (ca. 1575) by Jan de Straet (sometimes latinized as Stradanus) depicts Vespucci "awakening a sleeping America out of repose" (figure 3; Glaser 190) and shows a fully clothed Vespucci, European symbols of cross and compass in hand, confronting a naked and startled "America" who is rising up from her hammock open-mouthed, extending her arm toward the explorer in an ambiguous gesture that can be read as greeting, alarm, or self-defense.[7] It is a prototypical scene of "discovery": Vespucci, robed and armed with European ideology and technology, claiming with his masculine gaze the metaphorically female continent that would later bear his name.[8]

Ralegh received from Elizabeth I in 1584 the letters patent authorizing his explorations in her name but in his own material interests; in that same year, coincidentally—or prophetically—on the fourth of July, Arthur Barlowe explored the outer banks of the Carolinas in Ralegh's name (Montrose, "Work of Gender," 7). The letters patent granted Ralegh "free liberty and licence" to "discover search fynde out and viewe such remote heathen and barbarous landes Contries and territories" (quoted in Montrose, "Work of Gender," 7) that had not been claimed by any other Christian monarch or were not inhabited by Christians. The

FIGURE 3. "Vespucci awakening a sleeping America out of repose" (Glaser 190). Engraving by Theodore Galle, ca. 1580, of a drawing by Jan de Straet (Stradanus), ca. 1575. Beinecke Rare Book and Manuscript Library, Yale University.

absence of Christianity masked the presence of any alternative spiritual system and served to classify such lands and peoples as "barbarous" and thus to justify invasion.

The "licence" Elizabeth gives Ralegh in the letters patent echoes the first line of the passage quoted from Donne's poem; the patent constituted a *mandate*—its root derived from the Latin *manus*, hand—and thus actually did "licence" Ralegh's "roving hands" to explore the enticing New World and to enjoy the pleasures of discovering and then owning "her." The permission to "discover search fynde out and viewe" emphasizes the specular quality of the colonizing gesture and, like "N.S." nearly a century later on Rowlandson's captivity in his letter about King Philip's War, invokes the gendered roles in the drama: the male gaze, a figural speculum, privileged to view, penetrate, possess, and claim the objectified female "America."

The colonial practice of renaming both the land and its inhabitants, a practice that began with the earliest European adventures into the Americas and continued for centuries, reenacts the politics of naming in patriarchal marriage traditions and illustrates the ideological alignment of colonization with marriage: Guanahani becomes "San Salvador" (Columbus log 76); Wingandacoa, or Tsenacommacah, becomes "Virginia" (De Bry 60); Shawmut becomes first "Tri-mountain" and then "Boston" (Sedgwick 129); Wamsutta and Metacom become "Alexander" and "Philip"; Montaup becomes, ironically, "Mount Hope"; Pocahontas, or Matoaka, becomes "Rebecca Rolfe"; Sacajawea becomes "Janey" (Fiedler 75); and so on. Likewise, the patent's phrase "to have [and] holde" echoes the words of the Christian marriage ceremony,[9] while the "licence" to "occupy and enjoye" certifies and legitimates the conjugal "right" of taking sexual pleasure at the same time that it grants the "right" of conquest and occupation.

The differences in the vows spoken by husbands and wives in the sixteenth-century marriage service (and even up to the present time) are worth noting here: they would almost certainly have been the vows exchanged by Pocahontas and John Rolfe in 1615. Unlike her husband's, the wife's vows required her to promise to "obey . . . and serve" the man she was marrying. The religious ideology of matrimony, then, with its hierarchical roles for the dominant husband and the subservient wife, meant that it was not only appropriate but essential that a metaphoric "bride" like the New World "obey and serve" her colonizer "husband"— all of which gives a particular resonance to fears of the husbands of white women captives that they might be "replaced" by Indian partners and also places romanticized versions of Pocahontas's marriage to Rolfe in a particularly ironic light.

In Ralegh's patent, as in other documents that licensed or reported discovery, conquest, and colonial settlement, we find traces of the conflating of the projects of conversion and capitalization. The mission of conversion was repeatedly used to disguise Europe's economic motives for expansion into the New World, just as romantic or courtly love conventions masked the essentially mercantile nature of the patriarchal marital relation: the courtier/suitor's posture as supplicant and "vassal" to his "mistress" was only that, a pose, and a woman's acceptance of his suit in marriage meant in fact that her person and her worldly goods belonged entirely to her husband.

The work of the metaphor of marriage, then, was to legitimize both the pleasure and profit that England—and Englishmen—would get from "marrying" the New World. Such was precisely the appeal made by Thomas Morton, the New England colonist and proprietor at "Merrymount" who was so troublesome and troubling to the Plymouth Pilgrims, in his *New English Canaan*, or *New Canaan* (first published in London in 1632), an encomium to the beauties of New England designed to recruit like-minded Englishmen—i.e., lusty and industrious planters and artisans rather than dour Puritans or Separatists—to join the project of New World "plantation." Even Morton's title carries an oblique threat: New England is certainly a paradise, "nothing inferior to Canaan of Israel, but a kind of paralell to it, in all points" (17), but whether it will be an *English* paradise, as Morton hopes, depends on how persuasive he and other writers can be and on how responsive his readers are to the seductiveness of the picture he paints. Here is Morton's "Author's Prologue":

> If art & industry should doe as much
> As Nature hath for Canaan, not such
> Another place, for benefit and rest,
> In all the universe can be possest,
> The more we proove it by discovery,
> The more delight each object to the eye
> Procures, as if the elements had here
> Bin reconcil'd, and pleas'd it should appeare,
> *Like a faire virgin, longing to be sped,*
> *And meete her lover in a Nuptiall bed,*
> Deck'd in rich ornaments t'advaunce her state
> And excellence, being most fortunate,
> When most enjoy'd, so would our Canaan be
> If well imploy'd by art & industry
> Whose offspring, now shewes that *her fruitfull Wombe*
> *Not being enjoy'd, is like a glorious tombe,*
> Admired things producing which there dye,
> And ly fast bound in darck obscurity,
> The worth of which in each particuler,
> Who list to know, this abstract will declare.
>
> (xx; emphasis mine)

Morton is a cavalier lover to his "faire virgin," waxing poetic in his description of the "bewty of the Country with her naturall indowements" (xx), as in this later prose passage with its climactic meter and rhyme:

> And whiles our howses were building, I did indeavour to take a survey of the Country: The more I looked, the more I liked it.
>
> And when I had more seriously considered, of the beauty of the place, with all her faire indowments, I did not thinke that in all the knowne world it could be paralel'd. . . .[These endowments] made the Land to mee seeme paradice, for in mine eie, t'was Nature's Masterpeece: Her chiefest Magazine of all, where lives her store: if this Land be not rich, then is the whole world poore. (59–60)

Morton is quite openly advertising for mail-order "husbands" for a virginal "New England," so eager to be led to bed and to turn over her "wombe" to production for English profit—a womb now to be rescued from its "darck obscurity" and opened to the colonizing male gaze as the body of this "faire virgin" is anatomized in the service of colonial enterprise.

The metaphor of the marriage of Old World and New did indeed prove irresistible to Europeans engaged in the takeover of the Americas. Pocahontas's conversion and then marriage to Rolfe, roughly twenty years after Ralegh's *Discovery of . . . Guiana* and twenty years before Morton's *New English Canaan*, was therefore a symbolic as well as actual fruition of the rhetoric that figured the connection of the Old World and the New as a marriage. As Annette Kolodny writes, "The excitement that greeted John Rolfe's marriage to Pocahontas . . . may have been due to the fact that it served, in some symbolic sense, as a kind of objective correlative for the possibility of Europeans' actually possessing the charms inherent in the virgin continent" (*Lay of the Land* 5). Rolfe himself seems to have seen things similarly; he gives at least a hint of that view in his *A True Relation of the State of Virginia* (1616) when he observes that if the colony were provided with "good and sufficient men" for exploration, defense, building, and farming, "then might triall be made, what lieth hidden in the womb of the Land" (3). It needs only to be added that

Rolfe's "possessing the charms" of Virginia as a result of his marriage to Pocahontas was indeed more than a symbolic possibility. Powhatan granted him, as a gift upon the marriage, a large tract of fertile land on the James River, and Thomas, the son of Rolfe and Pocahontas, inherited thousands of acres more through his maternal claim (Woodward 164).

But if the "marriage" of New World and Old was one of the figurative possibilities residing in the representation of the New World as a woman ripe for sexual address, a possibility the Pocahontas legends have helped to confirm, another more violent possibility lurked in that representation as well. What follows Ralegh's figure of a virgin Guiana in the *Discovery*, for example, is not at all ambiguous; Guiana's virgin status quite specifically invites her rape, with all its attendant violence: "Guiana is a country that hath yet her Maiden head, never sacked, turned, nor wrought, the face of the earth hath not been torn, nor the virtue and salt of the soil spent by manurance, the graves have not been opened for gold, the mines not broken with sledges, nor their Images pulled down out of their temples" (120).

Louis Montrose has called attention to the way this passage activates a "bawdy Elizabethan pun" in the figure of Guiana as a "*count*ry" that has a "Maidenhead" ("Work of Gender" 12). Ralegh's rhetoric too, like Donne's and Morton's, anatomizes the intimate sexual geography of Guiana's "body" and quite starkly promotes and sanctions the rape, plunder, and sacrilege of that "*count*ry"; it thus provokes and enlists masculine sexual desire in the service of English efforts to colonize the New World.

One clear effect of such rhetoric is to construct the explorer and conqueror of such a feminized "new-found-land" as masculine (see Montrose, "Work of Gender"). There was for Ralegh, furthermore, no room in this country for two "men," that is, for both England and Spain, or, for that matter and more ominously, no room for both explorer and Native; the country too, like Donne's mistress, is "safeliest when with one man manned." Ralegh's erection of "him" who will take "her" "Maidenhead" is a gesture that simultaneously erases both Spain as England's rival in colonization and the Native inhabitants who, in their own fashion very different from that of Europe, had themselves long been "husbanding" the land and its resources.[10]

Given the sexual and economic realities of patriarchal marriage practices, the two possibilities residing within the representation of the new world as feminine—a sexually receptive or vulnerable bride or a potential victim of rape—converge. Indeed, in the light of subsequent histories, including or even especially Pocahontas's, we can read the appropriation of the New World by the Old as a forced marriage that authorized and legitimized the rape of America, its land, its resources, and its people.

But the metaphor of a feminine New World was doubled in yet another way; the sexualized contact of old and new worlds was also represented as fraught with risk to the colonizers (despite the fact that the risk was actually much more often to the Native inhabitants), and from the beginning there was a dark undercurrent at work in the metaphor of a femininized New World that threatened the newly consolidated and thus precarious masculine subject of colonialism: Its intended object, the New-World-as-Woman, was sometimes represented as a terrifying Amazon, warlike, cannibalistic, and sexually voracious, fiercely independent and resistant to male control, a spectral figure who threatened literally to devour her would-be "suitors." In the background of the Galle engraving above (figure 3), for example, Native women are gathered around a fire over which a human haunch is being roasted.

This "unnatural" woman was part of a set of imaginary New World creatures whose representations fostered the construction of the newly discovered lands and their inhabitants as "other." Amazons, cannibals, and hermaphrodites, the three related morphologically or by reason of "unnatural custom" and often overlapping (as in the Galle engraving, which shows both cannibal women and an Amazon America), appeared in many visual and textual representations of the New World.[11] Such phantasmagoric figures represented a challenge not only to the project of conquest but also to the newly consolidated, and thus still unstable, European masculine "self" produced by emergent capitalism[12] and to the economies imbricated with the gender system from which the European adventurers came and within which they operated. But if we recall Carroll Smith-Rosenberg's claim that the unstable masculine subjectivity of the colonizer, as later of the American subject, was stabilized in insistent opposition to a set of "negative others" (485), we can see how these phantasms evoked in the masculine subject the terms of the identity he desired. The cannibal displaced onto Native populations the colonizers' own voracious appetite for and fierce consumption of New World lands; the hermaphrodite, with his/her ambiguous gender and sexuality, elicited and confirmed the colonizer's masculinity. The Amazon was a distinctly "unfeminine" figure and so, like the hermaphrodite, a transgressor of gender. If, consonant with the discovery tracts that feminized the New World landscape, we read their "territories" as representing their bodies, the Amazons are figured as women who will not only refuse marriage but also resist rape in kind, by violent means; thus they threaten to deflect and deter the masculine sexual desire that has been elicited to drive the colonial project. The discursive function of the Amazon was to elicit a hyper-masculinized explorer/colonizer powerful enough to invade, subdue, and claim her "territories."[13]

In the series of engravings that appeared in Theodore De Bry's fourteen-volume *Historia Americae* (1590–1624), drawn from many different records of New World exploration, as well as in Galle's engravings of de Straet's drawings of the New World, depictions of cannibals are numerous. Women typically figure prominently in both the visual representations of cannibalism and in the textual descriptions of cannibalistic customs in the New World (e.g., De Bry 110–11). In the engravings, the preparation of a cannibal feast is often part of a monstrous domesticity practiced by the women of the New World, as they slay the victims, butcher and cook them, eat them, and feed them to their children.

The text accompanying one of the De Bry engravings, for example, one drawn from Hans Staden's 1557 account of his long captivity among the Tupinamba of Brazil, draws attention to the action of a woman in the center foreground, thus the focal center, of the engraving: "[The women] . . . stop up his fundament with a piece of wood so that nothing of him may be lost" (De Bry 110). The woman's gesture of "stop[ping] up his fundament" is a figurative anal rape that dislocates the masculine explorer/captive into the feminine object position and the cannibal women into the masculine subject position; thus it contributes to an anxious confusion of gender. The monstrosity of the cannibal women, then—like that of the Amazons armed with phallic spears and javelins (and like that of Hannah Dustan in later colonial New England)—was accentuated by their supposed "unnatural" masculine capacity to "rape" their victims before consuming them.

Small wonder, then, that the work of many of the textual and visual representations of encounters between Europe and America was to domesticate this version of the female America, to disarm her and deconstruct her power, and thus to reassure Europeans that conquest was possible. In the 1580 engraving of Vespucci "awakening America" above (figure 3), for example, the woman representing America is taken by surprise and at a moment of great vulnerability: alone in her hammock, having just been awakened from sleep. Europe, represented here by Vespucci, is clearly the more powerful figure, though he is the stranger in a strange land. He is standing; she is seated, a bit off balance, having just risen from a reclining posture, and literally ungrounded: Her foot treads the air, seeking the support of solid earth. He, on the other hand, has both feet on the ground; he is fortified with knowledge, backed up with manned ships as well as with the sign of Christianity. This "America" is, then, a woman at a disadvantage. Despite the scene of cannibalism in the background, she is no monster of insatiable female desire, and it is evident that the contest between Europe and America prefigured here will be won by Europe. As Montrose points out ("Work of Gender" 6), America's state of having been "asleep" erases any past that precedes this vivid present moment; thus she lacks both a history and a community that might enable her resistance to Vespucci's intended conquest. In this configuration, the masculine explorer alone possesses subjectivity; America has none and is instead persistently rendered as the object of the male subject's desire and quest. Whether Europe sacks her or saves her, marries her or rapes her, converts her or cashes in on her, this America is a woman who lacks the wherewithal to resist.

The recurring figure of the woman cannibal, on the other hand, raises the spectre of a devouring female insatiability; it suggests that America has perhaps been awake all along, and that she may not be receptive to Europe's "roving hands," may not cooperate with European efforts to convert and settle her. The figure raises the possibility that the colonial effort will fail, that savagery will overcome and defeat European efforts to claim the New World in the name of civilization. In short, the figure offers the unsettling possibility that the New World does in fact possess a subjectivity that eludes European comprehension and control, is not merely a passively receptive object but has a point of view on the prospect of being invaded and colonized that is (understandably) decidedly unfriendly.

The threat the figure of the New World as a gigantic femme fatale posed to the masculine explorers, then, anticipating Freud, was not just decapitation, but castration[14]—she very specifically threatened the "joyful masculine thrust" of colonialism. Here is a passage from Vespucci's 1503 letter to Lorenzo de Medici: "Another custom among them is sufficiently shameful, and beyond all human credibility. Their women, being very libidinous, make the penis of their husbands swell to such a size as to appear deformed; and this is accomplished by a certain artifice, being the bite of some poisonous animal, and by reason of this many lose their virile organ and remain eunuchs" (quoted in Montrose, "Work of Gender," 5).

The passage is a compact network of significances. The "libidinous" native women both titillate and threaten; the women's sexual appetite arouses the desire of the male explorer/conqueror and at the same time threatens his emasculation, entices him to the New World only to destroy his manhood and his very identity. The dynamic of arousal-and-threat, like so much of the sexualized discourse of discovery, can be read both metaphorically and literally: the land itself as well as its female inhabitants are represented as open and eager for (sexual) contact—a perspective inviting to Europe and its envoys—but both the land and the Native women are possessed of a (sexualized) power that threatens to thwart the very desire they activate, the desire to possess, and to destroy its agency. Both the land and the women thus provoke the Europeans' passion to subdue and control, a passion founded not only on economic and political ambition but also on a deep-seated gender and sexual anxiety.

The ideological threat the gender and sexual differences of New World cultures posed to the precarious subjectivity of the colonizers was transposed into physical violence of many sorts inflicted on the people the Europeans found here. Peter Hulme argues that the reports of New World cannibals functioned to create the "boundaries of community" that held Europeans *inside* and New World peoples *outside*; the "outsiders" then became a projected threat against which the community had to defend itself, a process Hulme identifies as "the central regulating mechanism of colonial discourse" (85)—and its accompanying colonial practices of regulating the bodies as well as the territories under colonial rule. Arguing that there was no factual basis in indigenous social practices for constructing the image of the New World cannibal, Hulme locates the function of that figure within colonial discourse itself, where it "has gained its entire meaning" (86). It was the colonizers themselves, not the Native inhabitants of the New World, who were the real cannibals.[15] Similarly, I would argue, the figures of the Amazon and the hermaphrodite were also projections, extrapolations from Europe's rigid and artificial gender binarism, a psychosexual and representational excess that impelled the gender policing and sexual terrorism the Native population endured at the hands of the conquerers.

Amazons, cannibals, people of fluid and indeterminate gender, all more or less naked and living communally in a state of apparent sexual liberty—these figures clustered in the explorers' imagination around the precarious masculine desire to penetrate and possess what seemed to Europeans to be an untapped and inexhaustibly rich continent. These monstrous figures represented the simultaneous fascination and terror of both the men who ventured here and the people who consumed the reports of those ventures at home. They helped construct the image of the New World as an irresistibly desirable but at the same time hostile and dangerously different terrain that, if it did not offer itself willingly, had to be taken by force. These figures also paved the way for later constructions of the Pocahontas legend, a richly productive means of allaying English fears of America's potential ferocity. The legend became a persistent and popular means of domesticating the female America by rendering her as a docile and pliant woman, as beautiful and virginal as the continent she symbolized, one who welcomed, nurtured, and loved the English, fostered their toehold on the continent, and traded her Native identity and culture for an English name, an English husband, and an English God.

Ralegh's *Discovery*, Morton's *New English Canaan*, Columbus's records of his voyages, and indeed almost all the texts of discovery can be explicated similarly: the early records of the European encounter with the Americas are, with few exceptions, examples of what Michel de Certeau has called "writing that conquers,"[16] writing that constructed the legitimacy of invading and usurping territory and enslaving people. As the bishop of Avila wrote to Queen Isabel in 1492, "Language is the perfect instrument of empire" (Hulme 1), and as Lynn Glaser has phrased it, "The tide of discovery rose on an ocean of ink" (1). Such texts as the ones I have cited helped create the ideologies that enabled and structured European explorations of the New World: ideologies of race, gender, sexuality, religious belief, property, and statehood, which were often conflated in the writing that promoted and facilitated the conquest. It is clear how important to the colonial project was this sexualized act of penetration and implantation, of a figurative as well as literal intercourse between European cultures and the "dis-covered" lands, and why it was evoked repeatedly in the discourses that paved the way for empire building in the New World.

Louis Montrose has pointed out how representational instabilities or dissonances like those I have been tracing would have allowed the writing/colonizing subject to obtain "coordinates for the constant if often subliminal process by which he locates his shifting position in moral and social space" ("Work of Gender" 33). As the conflicting views of the inhabitants of the New World were erected and enacted in the moral, social, and textual spaces of the encounter, the romantic view would come to fruition in a literary genre especially popular in nineteenth-century America that heroized and sentimentalized the American "noble savage," while the bestialized view became, in Lynn Glaser's words, "a guide for practical politics" (190). Representing the New World as a "faire virgin" who was sexual fair game not only made possible and justified the plunder of the continents that were "new" to the Europeans who stumbled upon them; it also determined the roles European men and women would play in the colonial project, the treatment Native men and women were to receive at the hands of the colonizers, and the shape of the histories, stories, and legends that helped to engineer and define a nation of white European settlers in North America. Those that have clustered around the figure of Pocahontas are a pointed example.

COLONIZING POCAHONTAS

"Come, boyes, Virginia longs till we share the rest of her
maiden-head."
—GEORGE CHAPMAN, BEN JONSON, JOHN MARSTON,
"Eastward Hoe," 1605

Descriptions like those I have discussed above of the feminized New World
and its "savage" inhabitants were an important element in the discursive
context and backdrop for the establishment of the English colony at
Jamestown in 1607. E. McClung Fleming, tracing the iconography of
America as an "Indian princess," has shown how that image evolved from
the early figuration of America as a Native woman or "queen," one of the
four female continents in early maps of the world. Fleming asserts that by
1603 the iconography had a sufficiently long history, and was sufficiently
commonplace, to have become standardized (68).

When the Jamestown colonists made the acquaintance of the curious,
friendly, and lively young Powhatan girl, daughter of a "king," it would
have been easy for them to see her as their own local instance of the
image of princess, to turn her into the symbol they needed, to place her
in the already well established role of the "female America," icon of the
very continent that was her home, and to articulate her in ways that made
her the antithesis of the monstrous Amazonian America. Pocahontas's
role was to be made to welcome, not threaten, the colonists, and to feed,
not feed upon, them. In other words, she had to be made to confirm
rather than challenge the identity of the masculine English colonizers by
"loving" them; she thus became "the great alternative to those of her race
who would slow the settlement of the new nation" (Tilton 27). It was a
role for her that has persisted in American literature, art, and popular
culture through succeeding centuries. And it is still evident today, for
example in the Jamestown Settlement Museum where, above a reproduction of her portrait in English dress, are painted the words, "Pocahontas:
Symbol of a New World."

In order for Pocahontas to be made into a suitable symbol for an
America that loved Englishmen and was eager to be colonized, several
complex cultural and discursive operations had to be accomplished.

First, she had to be portrayed at the start as a naked, wild, and savage Native girl, a stand-in for both her people and the countryside they knew as home—one who had the potential to become a fierce threat to the infant colony. She had to be signified as virginal, not yet "taken" or "possessed" (whether or not she actually was), and then she herself had to be taken with, or taken by, the colonists—captivated, or captured, or, as proved to be necessary, both—and had to fall in love with English colonialism in the person of an Englishman who was its representative. She next had to be dislodged from her native culture by making her exceptional rather than typical and either made white like the English or profoundly and irrevocably allied through sympathy, allegiance, or resemblance with the English and their cause. She had also repeatedly to be *remade a woman*, as that role was understood within English or Anglo-American culture in the shifting historical settings for stories and legends about her. Finally, her Native identity had to be nearly erased, retained only in traces useful to the colonial project, as she was absorbed into and subsumed by white English culture via conversion, heterosexual romance, marriage, and mothering an "English" child.

The result of this diligent cultural work is that Pocahontas—her body, her history, and the stories that have collected around her—has served as a crucial site for resolving the tensions and oppositions in the two competing images of the New World as "other" woman: as terrifying Amazon cannibal-warrior or receptive virgin-bride. Images and stories of a welcoming, compassionate Indian woman who nurtured and sustained the English colony safely held in abeyance the spectral image of frenzied, cannibalistic, aggressively libidinous New-World-as-Woman. Pocahontas thus became a crucial means for domesticating and rendering docile the colonized body of the figurally feminine New World.

One of the early mentions of Pocahontas in the Jamestown annals is in William Strachey's *Historie of Travaile into Virginia Britannia* (1612). There we find Pocahontas as a playful Indian girl, unashamedly naked:

[T]heir younger women goe not shadowed [covered] amongst their owne companie until they be nigh eleaven or twelve returnes of the leafe old . . .; nor are they much ashamed thereof, and therefore would the before remembered Pochahuntas, a well featured, but wanton yong girle, Powhatan's daughter, sometymes resorting to our fort, of the age then of eleven or twelve yeares, get the boyes forth with her into the markett place, and make them wheele, falling on their hands, turning up their heeles upwards, whome she would followe and wheele so her self, naked as she was, all the fort over. (65)

This is Pocahontas from an English point of view, as a whirling figure of gender transgression or destabilization—a carnival figure, "Powhatan's tomboy," as the John Smith character calls her in Virgil Geddes's 1933 play *Pocahontas and the Elders* (24). The fact that she is on the threshold of sexual maturity, though, combines with her availability to the penetrating gaze of the colonists to enable them to fix her as indisputably female and so as an object of desire for the male colonial subject. Strachey has her both "well featured" or pleasing to look at, and "wanton,"[17] so perhaps willing to serve the colonists as a sexual symbol. The nakedness of young girls was something the English colonists were surely not accustomed to seeing, at least not displayed without shame in the marketplace. This image of Pocahontas, then, crystallizes her as a sexual object open to the penetrating gaze of Englishmen, and, in her youth and nakedness, conveniently represents the unresistant availability of "Virginia" to their concupiscent desires.[18]

In the same year as Strachey's writing, 1612, John Smith wrote in *The Proceedings of the English Colonie in Virginia* of rumors in the colony about Pocahontas as a prospective wife for himself (Smith typically wrote about himself in third person):

Some propheticall spirit calculated hee had the Salvages in such subjection, hee would have made himselfe a king, by marrying Pocahontas, Powhatans daughter. It is true she was the very nomparell of his kingdome, and at most not past 13 or 14 yeares of age. Very oft shee came to our fort, with what shee could get for Captaine Smith, that ever loved and used all the Countrie well, but her especially he ever much respected: and she so well requited it, that when her father intended to have surprized him, shee by stealth in the darke night came through the wild woods and told him of it. But her marriage could no way have intitled him by any right to the kingdome, nor was it ever suspected hee had ever such a thought, or more regarded her, or any of them, then in honest reason, and discreation he might. If he would he might have married her, or have done what him listed. For there was none that could have hindred his determination. (128)

The passage is plain in openly conflating marriage or sexual intimacy with Pocahontas and possession of the land, while simultaneously denying the conflation with Smith's rebuttal of such an intent. His declaration that he could have married her, or "done what him listed," signifies her openness to an intimate connection with Smith as the representative of English colonialism and so eroticizes her for colonial purposes, despite his own declared sexual reticence and in contrast to the rhapsodic sexual eagerness with which other colonial scribes responded to the voluptuous promise of the female America. Also, as Smith expresses it here, he locates agency exclusively with himself, reserving to himself the power to decide whether or no about sexual intimacy; Pocahontas is figured only as passively willing or as a potential rape victim, unlikely or unable to "hinder his determination."

Given what was reported of Algonkian sexual custom by English observers, though, Pocahontas may well have been possessed of more sexual self-determination than was typically the case among unmarried English girls, at least those with pretensions to class status or property. Roger Williams, in his *Key into the Language of America* (1643), says of the northeastern Algonkians whose language and customs he recorded, "Single fornication they count no sin, but after Marriage (which they solemnize by consent of Parents and publique approbation publiquely) then they count it hainous for either of them to be false" (138). And contemporary ethnohistorian Howard S. Russell says of seventeenth-century southern New England Indians, like the Powhatan Indians part of the Algonkian group, that "a woman was the unquestioned mistress of her body. If unmarried, she might without shame accept a bed companion or withhold her favor as she preferred" (97). Unmarried Indian girls, then, apparently had license to pursue sexual pleasure as they would; certainly the Judeo-Christian codes of chastity for women, with their ties to property and inheritance, were evidently very different from the customs of female sexuality among the indigenous tribes of eastern

North America, and adultery was no less grievous a transgression for a man than for a woman.

Such indications of Indian sexual customs made more difficult the project of making Pocahontas consonant with the "virginal" American continent and of incorporating her into English sexual ideologies. Strachey, in fact, reported in his *Historie* that in 1612 "younge Pocohunta, a daughter of [Powhatan's], using sometyme to our fort in tymes past, [is] now married to a private captaine, called Kocoum, some two yeares since" (54). That would make the approximate date of Pocahontas's marriage to Kocoum 1610, when she would have been between thirteen and fifteen, an appropriate age for marriage, as it was usual for Algonkian women to marry soon after they passed puberty. If Strachey's report is accurate, the Pocahontas who was taken captive in 1613 and held hostage at Jamestown, then, was not a pliant and innocent virgin, but a young woman already three years married. Nothing further is known about Kocoum or the marriage, so if Pocahontas and Kocoum had children, and if so, what became of them, and whether Kocoum was dead or the marriage was already dissolved by mutual consent when Pocahontas was captured, or whether the marriage was intact at the time of her capture but presumed dissolved by the length of time that passed during her captivity, can only be matters for speculation.

Not surprisingly, her marriage to Kocoum got little or no attention from the machinery of myth-making around Pocahontas because of its potential to unravel the constructed "pure maiden/virgin continent" Pocahontas of romantic legend in the nineteenth century and in twentieth-century reincarnations of that legend. Edson Kenny Odell, for example, in his poem *The Romance of Pocahontas* (1912), says in a footnote, "Some believe that Pocahontas was married to young Chief Kocoum before she became the wife of Master Rolfe; but this seems hardly probable" (99 n). The passage of more than eighty years has apparently made her marriage no more "probable" than it was when Odell wrote; in Disney Studios' 1995 animated feature film *Pocahontas*, Kocoum is the stern Powhatan suitor whom Pocahontas rejects in favor of a very blond and blue-eyed John Smith. Pocahontas was Rolfe's second wife, his first having died shortly after their arrival in Jamestown; his prior experience of marriage presented no obstacle to the mythic construction of his marriage to

Pocahontas, but the requirement that she, representing the continent, be virginal and thus easily able to be claimed by England makes her possible earlier marriage "hardly probable" and requires the suppression of her perhaps having had another husband before she married Rolfe.

Another passage from Smith's writings, this from the *Generall Historie* (1624), offers a picture of Pocahontas in an apparently erotic Native context seemingly indecipherable to the Englishman. On a visit to Werowocomoco, Powhatan's seat of governance, Smith awaits the arrival of Powhatan, who is some distance away when Smith arrives: "[I]n the meane time, Pocahontas and her women entertained Captaine Smith in this manner. In a fayre plaine field they made a fire, before which, he sitting upon a mat, suddainly amongst the woods was heard such a hydeous noise and shreeking, that the English betooke themselves to their armes, and seized on two or three old men by them, supposing Powhatan with all his power was come to surprise them" (167–68).

Pocahontas and the other "beholders, . . . men, women, and children" reassure Smith and his companions that no harm will come to them, and the "anticke" resumes, the young women, interestingly enough, decked out in a manner similar to common colonial-era representations of Amazons:

[T]hirtie young women came naked out of the woods, onely covered behind and before with a few greene leaves, their bodies all painted, some of one colour, some of another, but all differing, their leader [Pocahontas?] had a fayre payre of Bucks hornes on her head, and an Otters skinne at her girdle, and another at her arme, a quiver of arrowes at her backe, a bow and arrowes in her hand; the next had in her hand a sword, another a club, another a pot-sticke; all horned alike: the rest every one with their severall devises. These fiends with most hellish shouts and cryes, rushing from among the trees, cast themselves in a ring about the fire, singing and dauncing with most excellent ill varietie, oft falling into their infernall passions, and solemnly againe to sing and daunce; having spent neare an houre in this Mascarado, as they entred in like manner they departed. (168)

After the "Mascarado," the women "reaccommodate themselves" and lead Smith "to their lodgings, where he was no sooner within the house, but all these Nymphes more tormented him then ever, with crowding, pressing, and hanging about him, most tediously crying, Love you not me? love you not me? This salutation ended, the feast was set, consisting of all the Salvage dainties they could devise: some attending, others singing and dauncing about them; which mirth being ended, with fire-brands instead of Torches they conducted him to his lodging" (168).

Clearly Smith was confronted with a ritual of some kind, the contextual meaning of which he either failed to understand or was unable or unwilling to transcribe. Entertained with nearly naked young women singing and dancing, then crowding and pressing around him begging for declarations of love—how was an Englishman to respond, or even to read what was happening?—if indeed it happened as he reported it. The scene revives the image of the powerful and lustful New World Amazons with their phallic spears and arrows and so, understandably, unsettles Captain Smith. His response was to exploit the scene for his readers' titillation but also to report the scandal of a culture that so disregarded the ideals of female chastity, unlike the England of Christian allegiance and infant capitalism. And once more Native culture was incorporated into a narrative that rendered it a lascivious and diabolical other and the colonizing male subject as at once desirable and chaste.

Later contributors to the Pocahontas legend have likewise had difficulty in assimilating this incident into their protrayals of the virginal Indian girl who befriended the English and have often evaded the problem of its sexual implications altogether. The later repressions and rewritings of the incident provide an interesting example of how Pocahontas narratives have shaped her story to their own purposes. Most of the twentieth-century children's books on Pocahontas (of which there are many) omit the story altogether, doubtless because of the resistances it offers to incorporating Pocahontas as a founding heroine of Anglo-American culture in the benign history such books are usually at pains to serve. Others include the incident but edit it to conform to whatever version of the story of Pocahontas they are committed to telling.

Ingri and Edgar Parin d'Aulaire, in their 1946 picture storybook *Pocahontas*, revise the incident considerably by making Powhatan rather than Pocahontas the instigator of the masque, also emptying it of any erotic element and turning it into a simple entertainment, a merry rustic frolic intended to cement the friendship between Indians and whites:

> Out from the trees whirled Pocahontas, leading a band of young girls. The girls were painted in gleaming colors and each had a pair of antlers tied to her head. Leaping and yelling, they stormed up to the fire, and danced an Indian dance around it. As suddenly as they had come, they ran back into the woods. There they took off their antlers and paint, and gently walked back to the meadow.
>
> Now the Indians led the white men to the house where the food was prepared, and they made merry and feasted together. . . . Next day they parted as friends. (30)

Another 1946 book, *Pocahontas: Brave Girl*, a purported biography of Pocahontas by Flora Warren Seymour (one of the Bobbs-Merrill "Childhood of Famous Americans" series) treats the incident in a similar vein and turns the dance into an occasion for Pocahontas to express curiosity about English culture and a desire to see England for herself:

> "A strange sight, indeed!" said the Englishmen.
>
> "It is the custom of our people," said Pocahontas. "Before long we shall do this for our own villages. Do not your girls at home dance in this way?"
>
> Captain Smith smiled. "Well, I have seen many dances, but nothing like this one."
>
> "I wish I could see the girls in your country dance," said Playful Girl. (124)

Times of war typically produce crises of national identity and purpose; apparently the World War II era in which both Warren and the d'Aulaires were writing invited a renewal of the myth of Indian-English friendship to consolidate the initiating image of the nation, one it wanted to reclaim for itself at the time of a major war.

Jean Fritz, in one of the better children's books on the subject, *The Double Life of Pocahontas* (1983), makes the masque part of Powhatan religious observance (though with evident Judeo-Christian overlays in the masculine personification of "their god"): "[Pocahontas] was overjoyed to have John in her world. How she'd entertain him and his friends! And feast them. She'd gather her sisters and friends together to dance for them. She would let John see how enthusiastically her people worshiped their god, how they painted themselves and sang for His pleasure, how they opened their hearts and tired out their bodies for His sake" (35).

Writing in the 1980s, a period of renewed interest in Indian history and culture, Fritz registers the dissonance between the two cultures when she writes that Smith thought of the performance as "a kind of freak show," while "for Pocahontas, it must have been an ecstasy" (36). Fritz evades the eroticism of the scene, though, when she turns the young women's "Love you not me?" plaint into simple requests for compliments on their performance (36).

In a book for much younger readers, *Pocahontas: Daughter of a Chief*, also from the 1980s, Carol Greene too acknowledges Smith's inability to understand what he saw and represents the scene being read very differently by the representatives of the two cultures:

> Once Pocahontas and her friends danced for the strangers. They wore green leaves and painted their bodies. They put horns on their heads. Out of the woods they ran. Around the fire they danced.
>
> "I love this dance!" thought Pocahontas.
>
> But John Smith thought it was strange. He did not understand Indian dances. (22–23)

Smith's response, in Greene's prose, renders the women's dance merely "strange" and puzzling, removing any element of wild exoticism or the fearfulness Smith may have felt because he did not understand its import. By having the young women dancing simply because they "love" the dance likewise ignores any significance it may have had within Powhatan culture or any meaning Pocahontas and the other women may have intended for Smith to understand from it.

That books for children tend to erase or suppress the erotic element in the scene is perhaps not surprising, but accounts written for adult readers have not done much better in interpreting the incident. Philip Barbour, in a 1970 book, *Pocahontas and Her World*, does acknowledge the element of overt sexuality, though he fails to extrapolate its significance beyond the moment of its occurrence: "Surrounding Smith, the werowance [headman], they coaxed him into a large lodging where they offered themselves to him, as Indian courtesy demanded on such occasions. Smith, whose modesty verged on prudery, refused. But the girls, apparently thinking that it was a matter of personal preference rather than a blanket rejection, then threw themselves at him, one after the other, crying 'Love you not me?'" (39).

Barbour does not cite a source for his assertion that the women's offering themselves to Smith was a requirement of "Indian courtesy"; one passage from Smith's *Generall Historie*, though, reports the Powhatan custom of offering women to honored male guests as a gesture of hospitality: "[A]t night where [the guest's] lodging is appointed, they set a woman fresh painted red with *Pocones* and oyle, to be his bed-fellow" (148).[19] Barbour's reading, therefore, is a plausible one, though in both the Barbour and Smith passages (in contrast to what observers of Native customs had to say about women's sexual self-determination), sexual agency belongs only or primarily to the male, and the possibility that the women in the "Mascarado" were celebrating and attempting to enact their own dramas of desire and pleasure is not acknowledged. Barbour, like Smith himself, also does not mention whether Pocahontas was herself one of the "Nymphes" who pressed herself on Smith and begged for a declaration or demonstration of his love—and so whether he refused her directly. Nor does he raise the question of whether Smith's refusal— his "modesty" or "prudery"—was grounded in tenets of sexual propriety or in aversion to sexual contact with "savage" women, to heterosexual relations, or to sexual activity of any sort at all.

Smith's account of the entertainment, as well as later retellings, does little to dispel the mystery of its meaning, but it does demonstrate that Pocahontas was part of a culture whose customs—sexual, spiritual, and social—the English were more often than not at a loss to understand, rendering the descriptions themselves questionable. It suggests also that the erotic life Pocahontas might have had within her home culture was utterly different from the eroticization she underwent at the hands of Anglo mythmakers. The incident, like the story of Pocahontas's capture by Samuel Argall and her three years' imprisonment at Jamestown, is a lacuna of sorts in that it resists self-serving interpretations by the English of Native culture as lacking complexity and also resists easy incorporation into sentimental versions of the Pocahontas legend. That doubtless explains why both the masque and Pocahontas's captivity have been so often omitted in popular accounts of her encounters with the English colonists. Both elements of Pocahontas's story stand as traces of all that "American history" is at pains to forget and exclude in the stories the nation has so carefully constructed about its past.

One thing, though, is both clear and clearly self-serving in what Smith wrote of the event: in his account of the masque and its aftermath, he represents himself as an object of desire for the Indian women of Virginia. That representation, combined with his eroticizing claim that he could have married Pocahontas or "done what him listed" with her, became a foundation for the legend that Pocahontas was in love with John Smith—a version that has held remarkably tenacious sway in most of the stories, poems, and legends of Pocahontas for nearly four hundred years, including most recently the Disney film Pocahontas.

That she fell instantly in love with Smith is the usual explanation for the most famous of the Pocahontas legends, her "rescue" of Smith when he was a captive among her people. As Smith told the story in the *Generall Historie*, Powhatan concluded after "a long consultation" with his "grim Courtiers" that Smith must die:

> [T]wo great stones were brought before Powhatan: then as many as could layed hands on [Smith], dragged him to them, and thereon laid his head, and being ready with their clubs, to beate out his braines, Pocahontas the Kings dearest daughter, when no intreaty could prevaile, got his head in her armes, and laid her owne upon his to save him from death: whereat the Emperour was contented he should live to make him hatchets, and her bells, beads, and copper . . . (64–65)

Did Pocahontas indeed save John Smith from death, as he reported, and if so, why? The question remains an actively debated one. Whether Smith was telling the truth when he told the story has been a matter of impassioned dispute for well over a century, ever since 1860, when

Charles Deane, a scholar from Massachusetts, raised questions about the reliability of Smith's accounts, especially the one of being rescued by Pocahontas (Hubbell 181). Henry Adams, in an essay in *The North American Review* in 1867, echoes the charge Deane made that Smith's story is not to be believed. Adams's critique of the truth of the legend is based not only on its resemblance to heroic folk tales of many times and places in which a wandering soldier is captured by the ruthless enemy leader and then saved by the intervention of a beauteous woman, but also on the fact that Smith published the account for the first time in 1624 in the *Generall Historie*, by which time Pocahontas had been dead for seven years. Thus she was no longer alive to refute Smith's version of what transpired during his captivity. Hubbell, though, impugns Adams's motives in writing his "exposé," suggesting that it was a gesture of bald self-publicizing. He quotes Adams in *The Education of Henry Adams* as admitting that to revise the Smith-Pocahontas story "would attract as much attention, and probably break as much glass, as any other stone that could be thrown by a beginner" (in Hubbell 181–82). Adams's choice of target for his attack is a clear acknowledgement of the status of the rescue story as a founding myth of the nation, for only a story with that kind of status would create so much "broken glass" in being shattered.

Later writers like James Branch Cabell, writing an open "letter" to Pocahontas in 1934, and Philip Young, in a 1962 essay, took up Adams's cause in questioning the story's veracity. Addressing Pocahontas, Cabell writes of the rescue, "upon this ever-memorable occasion, your conduct was of a cast so noble as to evoke one's honest regret that you should never have heard of it" (201)—that, in short, "your entire legend is pure balderdash" (203). Young, remarking the story's resemblance "precisely in all essential parts" to "one of the oldest stories known"—that of the adventurer rescued by the daughter of the fierce king (409), traces the obsession of American poets, dramatists, and painters with Pocahontas, and calls her legend "a magical and moving explanation of our national origins" (392). Clearly dubious about the story's veracity, Young says that "Since the evidence is not decisive, perhaps everybody has a right to believe as he [sic] wishes," because "What counts more [than whether the story is true] is the truly extraordinary way in which the story . . . pervades our culture" (399). One explanation he offers for its popularity is that the Pocahontas story is "perfectly ideal propaganda for both church and state" (412).

The historian J. A. Leo Lemay has recently (1992) published a monograph on the question of the rescue story. He painstakingly musters a great deal of evidence, both historical and textual, that Smith was after all telling the truth in his account of Pocahontas saving his life. Lemay proceeds mostly by discrediting Adams's motives for attacking Smith and by arguing that Smith's 1616 letter to Queen Anne on Pocahontas's behalf, in which he reports the rescue, was indeed in circulation while Pocahontas was in London, therefore before her death as well as before the rescue story's publication in 1624 as part of Smith's *Generall Historie.* "Adams's attack on Smith," Lemay argues, "began as part of his anti-Southern campaign," written "in 1862 as war propaganda,"[20] an effort to tarnish not only the image of Smith as the prototype of the Virginia gentleman, but also all those Virginia aristocrats who claimed descent from Pocahontas (4).

Robert Tilton, in his thorough study of the evolution of the Pocahontas legend in the nineteenth century, also explores the many ways the rescue story became a discursive field of contention between North and South: "The Pocahontas narrative could be construed as a recollection of the founding moment of a particularly southern culture (as opposed to that of the United States as a whole), and so it became crucial to many southerners who were seeking to create an alternate history, and especially so to those who based their need to establish a separate, Confederate nation on the racial differences they perceived between themselves and citizens of the "Union" (149).

Both before and after the Civil War, then, Pocahontas was reactivated in another border zone, this time between the North and the South, deployed in Northern attacks against the secessionist states of the Southern Confederacy of which she had already been made something of a guardian angel,[21] and invoked in the South's claim to being the true site of the origins of English America.

About the rescue, Young is, of course, right that what happened is less important than what stories get told about events and by whom and what has been made of those stories. In the case of the story of the lovely and virginal Indian girl, a symbolic America who loves English colonialism so much that she's willing to sacrifice herself for its continuation, the crucial task is to uncouple it from the self-serving political use that white America has made of it and thus to deconstruct its power in the service of white Anglo-American histories of America. That task of separating fact from the fictions it generated can be accomplished, I think, even without accusing Smith of being a self-promoting liar. That is, the story of the "rescue" can be, and in fact has been, revised to serve other purposes than that of defending a heroic version of the history of English colonialism and the nation that arose in its wake.

Perhaps Pocahontas really did cover Smith's head with her own when her father's warriors were about to beat his brains out against the stones, thus moving Powhatan to spare his life. It is possible, as several scholars have suggested, that the events occurred much as Smith described them, but that he failed altogether to understand the meaning of what was happening.[22] Smith, all unawares, was perhaps being adopted into the Powhatan tribe, with Pocahontas as his sponsor. If Smith did report the events as they happened, if he did experience a ritual that was to accomplish what Peter Hulme terms "a 'kinning' of strangers" (150), what seemed an imminent execution would have been instead a staged death-and-rebirth ritual, marking Smith's symbolic demise as a stranger and his rebirth as a kinsman and thus an ally. Hulme notes that in prestate societies (or proto-state societies, as the Powhatan confederacy could be described), transactions with strangers were crucial and were centered on protocols of hospitality that "dissolved the category of stranger" (148) and determined whether the stranger would become an ally or an enemy. Arguing that "Powhatan acted in accordance with a set of established social and political practices," Hulme offers this reading of the rescue story:

> Powhatan's decision must have been that the English were too dangerous to be alienated: an alliance should be made, perhaps with a view to absorbing them into the confederacy. The appropriate ceremony was prepared. The *pawcorance* [ritual stone] was brought in, Smith laid upon it, and clubs raised above him. At a prearranged signal Pocahontas threw herself upon him and pleaded for his life. Powhatan granted her request. Smith—though he was obviously

unaware of it—had passed through an elaborate ritual of mock-execution whereby he allied himself with Powhatan. (150)

Hulme's reading accepts that Smith's account of the events is accurate, even if he did not understand their significance. Hulme explains Smith's omitting the story in earlier publications on his Virginia adventures by suggesting that only after the "massacre" engineered by Pocahontas's uncle, Opechancanough, in March 1622 (in which nearly a fourth of all English colonists in Virginia were killed) did the "rescue" become comprehensible as signifying a possible alternative, though now lost, history of "peaceful co-operation" between Indians and whites, a dream of intercultural harmony that Opechancanough's "viciousness . . . destroyed all hope of" (172).

Such a reading as Hulme's also renders events subsequent to the rescue more understandable. Smith reports in the *Generall Historie* that two days after the "rescue," Powhatan took him to "a great house in the woods," gave him an Algonkian name, made him the werowance of Capahowosick, another Indian town, and told him that he would "for ever esteeme him as his sonne" (65). Smith's failure to comprehend the ritual and its implications, if that is indeed what it was, is understandable, if tragic in light of later developments, given his relative ignorance of Powhatan custom and culture and of their language, of which his knowledge was then only minimal.

Interpreting the story as an adoption ritual that bound the adoptee to the family and tribe also helps to make comprehensible Smith's report in the *Generall Historie* of Pocahontas's behavior when she and Smith met for the last time, in England after many years apart. When he came to visit her, she at first turned her back on him and refused to speak; she was evidently hurt and angry that he had failed to understand and honor his kinship obligations to her and her people, that he had delayed for so many months visiting her once she was in England, and that she and Powhatan had not even known whether he was alive or dead until she landed in Plymouth, because, while she had been told he was dead, as Smith reports she said, "your Countriemen will lie much" (72). In that last interview, Pocahontas insisted on reestablishing the bond of kinship she felt Smith had failed to honor; by his account, she spoke to him these words:

> You did promise Powhatan what was yours should bee his, and he the like to you; you called him father being in his land a stranger, and by the same reason so must I doe you . . . Were you not afraid to come into my fathers Countrie, and caused feare in him and all his people (but mee) and feare you here I should call you father; I tell you then I will, and you shall call mee childe, and so I will bee for ever and ever your Countrieman. (72)

The adoption story is of course just that, a story, with no greater truth value than any other; it too is dependent upon Pocahontas's silence, and the facts of the events are forever and utterly inaccessible to us. The traditional story invites continued reinscription, though, because of the enormous cultural power it has wielded for centuries in support of European and Euro-American capture of the continent. The adoption story has an advantage over the Smith-Pocahontas romance version in that it grants the Powhatan culture a social and diplomatic complexity and sophistication that Smith's version, in which the Indians are brutal savages who mean simply to beat out his brains, lacks. It also situates Pocahontas *within* the sophisticated complexities of her culture rather than figuring her as a rebel or traitor against it, working in favor of the white colonist and of preserving the enterprise he represented. Perhaps Pocahontas was not after all what Leslie Fiedler called her, "our first [Uncle] Tom" (70).

And yet those revisionist versions have had little effect against the persistent mythic romance of Pocahontas and John Smith, perpetuated in so many versions over so long a time. The romance plot that enlisted Pocahontas and John Smith (or his stand-in, John Rolfe) in signifying a metaphorical love affair between a masculinized English colonialism and the feminized American continent was itself a revisionist myth, rewriting in order to make more tolerable the often violent colonial encounter between England and America. To support the colonial endeavor and to cover up the painful actual histories of settlement, Pocahontas had to be made to love John Smith, whether or not she did.

CAPTIVATING POCAHONTAS

> I asked myself,
> was I stolen or did I give myself?
> —PAMELA HADAS, "Pocahontas from
> Her New World"

To understand the longevity and persistent popularity of the story of Pocahontas's rescue of John Smith and the romantic love-and-marriage epic that arose in its wake requires that we consider whose interests the story has served. The answer becomes clear if we read Pocahontas's gesture as symbolizing the feminized and docile New World's welcoming "love" for the English colonists and her willingness to sacrifice herself for the survival and success of their colonial enterprise. That wistful hope and belief has underwritten most of the retellings of the Pocahontas legend in U.S. cultural history. In order to tolerate our history, white Americans have needed to believe that, as Philip Young says, "she loved us anyway," loved us so much she wanted to *be* us, or at least was willing to die herself in order to save us.

But what about loving her? From the beginning, in fact, sexual intimacy between the white colonists and the Native people was viewed with suspicion, even open hostility, by the English, as is evident in the letter John Rolfe wrote to the governor of the colony asking permission to wed Pocahontas. Declaring himself sensible of the "inconvenyences which maye thereby arrise," making him "looke aboute warely and with circuspection, into the grounde and principall agitacions wch thus shoulde provoke me to be in love wth one, whose education hath byn rude, her manners barbarous, her generacon Cursed, and soe discrepant in all nutriture from my selfe, that often tymes with feare and tremblinge I have ended my pryvate Controversie wth this, Surely theise are wicked instigations hatched by him whoe seeketh and delighteth in mans distruction"[23]—he means, of course, Satan. Rolfe must justify and mitigate his desire for a "savage" woman by declaring his desire to convert the savage; thus he reasserts her "savagery," in contrast to himself. Characterizing her as "blynde," "hungry," and "naked," Rolfe, sensitive to the "duetyes of a Christian," means to "leade" her, "gyve [her] breade," and "cover" her (347). By representing himself as the bringer of gifts into his union with a "naked" (and so uncultured) Pocahontas, Rolfe obscures the fact that it was she and her people who saved and sustained the colonists by giving them "breade" and obscures as well all that he stands to gain materially from the marriage, all that he will take in taking her as his wife. He denies that he is motivated by "unbridled desire of Carnall affection" (345) and of course omits any mention of possessing land as a result of the marriage.[24] To those who doubt the nobility of his purposes, he says, "Lett them knowe tis not my hungrye appetite to gorge my selfe with incontinencye" (347). Rolfe even goes so far as to say, in stressing that Pocahontas is not the best he could do for a wife, that he could get one "more pleasing to the eye" (348). His declarations that he wants to marry her to win her to Christianity "for the good of the Plantacon, the honor of our Countrye, for the glorye of God" (345) carried the day, and his petition was granted.

As Rolfe's letter demonstrates, Pocahontas's Indian identity had to be problematized and destabilized and her status as "exceptional," or at least potentially so, had to be asserted in order to qualify her for marriage to Rolfe. The marriage was celebrated by the English because it symbolically consolidated England's colonial presence and power in the New World. So enchanted was Gov. Thomas Dale, in fact, with the idea of an Englishman and a royal Indian bride, and with all the symbolic implications of such a union, that he later sent Ralph Hamor to ask Powhatan if Dale might have Pocahontas's younger sister for a wife ("*Pochahuntas* being already in our possession," writes Hamor [37])—notwithstanding that he already had a wife in England (Hamor 37 ff.). Powhatan refused.

Despite these exceptions, that the prospect of Anglo-Indian intermarriage or other sexual liaisons remained a troubling one to the Virginia colonists is demonstrated by their passing a law in 1691 aimed at preventing the "abominable mixture and spurious issue" of such unions by banishing from the colony any white person "intermarrying with" or "unlawfull accompanying with" a "negro, mulatto, or Indian man or woman bond or free" (statute quoted in Smits, "Abominable Mixture," 158 n). The colonists' legal collapsing of distinctions between Indians and persons of African descent acknowledges the historical connections and intermarriages between those two groups; it elicited from Philip Young a remark on the ironies of early-twentieth-century Virginians, still living under rigid antimiscegenation laws, who in proudly celebrating their descent from Pocahontas along with the three-hundredth anniversary in 1907 of the founding of the Jamestown colony, "appeared to have forgotten" that, according to their laws, "the girl was colored" (399).[25]

The issue of Pocahontas's "race" is related to another question: If it was John Rolfe she married, why has it so often been John Smith who figures as the love interest in the Pocahontas legend? Robert Tilton traces the evolution of the Pocahontas narrative from the late eighteenth century, when the marriage was typically highlighted as a crucial element in her story, to the nineteenth, when the marriage fades in importance or disappears altogether and Rolfe-as-husband is typically replaced by Smith-as-love-object in a romance that is never consummated. As Tilton demonstrates, eighteenth-century tellers of the tale, such as Robert Beverley (in *The History and Present State of Virginia*, 1705), often took the position of retrospective advocacy of English-Indian intermarriage as a solution to racial conflict, saw the Pocahontas-Rolfe union as "a foregone golden opportunity for a mixing of the two races into a single 'American' people" (Tilton 13), and criticized the early colonists' failure to adopt the practice as a means of "absorbing" the Indians and legitimizing English territorial claims. That failure produced, as Tilton observes, the "perceived need to carry out alternative, usually violent, strategies against the Indians" and, by "deflect[ing] the blame" for their contemporaries' more violent practices onto the early colonists, "alleviate[d] the guilt" for their own behavior (16–17).

The racial distinctions between whites and Indians, as Vaughan demonstrates (28 ff.), were nearly as widely acknowledged by the nineteenth century as those between whites and Blacks, and Tilton argues that the dilemma of Pocahontas's race was the central shaping force in the dominant nineteenth-century version of the Pocahontas legend. In that articulation of the story, produced by the frequent conflation of Indians and Blacks into a single group of racial others and so by "the sentiment against the portraying of successful interracial unions during the antebellum period" (Tilton 72), Pocahontas falls in love with Smith (and in some versions, he also with her) and rescues him from her father's wrath out of love. His injury from exploding gunpowder and subsequent forced return to England for treatment, however, prevent their marriage; frequently there is no mention in these texts of Rolfe or of his marrying Pocahontas. Such a version of the legend, as Tilton argues, allows its romantic and tragic possibilities to be fully exploited without an interracial union, or what would in the nineteenth century have been seen as a problematic instance of "miscegenation," having to be confronted or condoned.[26]

It is interesting to note, in light of Tilton's argument, that the 1995 Disney animated film *Pocahontas* repeats the typical nineteenth-century version in its entirety. Pocahontas falls in love with Smith the moment she lays eyes on him, and he likewise with her. Contrary to historical portraits, the Disney Smith is possessed of very light blond hair and pale blue eyes, features whose strangeness, instead of hindering the attraction, seem to help capture Pocahontas's heart. She rejects the husband her father has chosen for her, a resolute, square-jawed, and sombre Kocuom, who is soon conveniently dispatched by a trigger-happy English lad. Smith is captured in the ensuing fracas. The film enacts the conventional rescue scene; Pocahontas, in a fever of self-sacrificing love, declares that if Smith is to die, her father must kill her too in order to kill him. Disney's Powhatan quickly learns the lesson his daughter's gesture is here meant to teach him: that violence is wrong, and that the moral high road is to welcome the English and live peacefully with them. The fact that the film does not address the subsequent history—any part of which would demonstrate the tragic consequences of such a stance on the Indians' part—allows Powhatan's newfound open-heartedness to stand as heroic. When Smith is injured and sent back to England, Disney's Pocahontas, like her mythologized nineteenth-century predecessor, nobly sacrifices her desires to the cause of Indian and English coexistence and, as the film ends, commits herself to remaining in Virginia to work for peace rather than following her heart and accompanying Smith to England. The Disney film, then, repeats the nineteenth-century myth entire, a myth that articulated racial difference without posing the dangerous prospect of its being deconstructed via intermarriage. The film appears superficially to support current efforts for greater recognition of cultural pluralism in the United States; it actually undermines any real egalitarian pluralism, however, first by replicating the gesture in which Pocahontas "recognizes" the racial and cultural "superiority" of the English colonists by falling in love with Smith at first sight and working to sustain the presence of the English in her country, and then by ignoring the subsequent history of Indian-white relations.

One answer to the dilemma of Pocahontas's race for those who would make her into an American heroine was, as I have suggested, to make her both exceptional—different in significant ways from other Native people—and also to render her in some way white or to ally her inextricably with whiteness, a task her conversion, renaming, and marriage supposedly made secure. The process began early, with Smith's (and later Hamor's) descriptions of her as the "nomparell," or unequaled one, of Virginia, asserting that there were no other Natives quite like her, and it has continued in both historical reports and fictional re-creations through the centuries.

That English colonists so warmly welcomed into their ranks this young Indian woman whom they had been at such pains to represent as having so warmly welcomed and sustained them was made possible by her being made thus exceptional. The gateway for Indians into colonial English society ordinarily more closely resembled the proverbial eye of the needle and admitted only exceptional Indians, those who could be made to transcend the standard characterizations of Indians as savage, bestial, rude, uncivilized, and so on. (As we have already seen in Rolfe's letter, Pocahontas herself was sometimes subjected to such characterizations, indicating how her image oscillated across the racial dividing line; she was either white or dark as she needed to be to serve the varying purposes of the mythmakers.) Nor was the gateway from colonial culture into Indian life any easier for white colonists to negotiate; the passage from the almost unimaginable hardships of early colonial life to the relative ease and comfort of life among the Indians was rigidly and even brutally policed. Strachey, in his *Lawes Divine, Morall, and Martiall for the Colony in Virginia Brittania* (1612), included a prohibition against English colonists running away to live with the Indians: "No man or woman, (upon paine of death) shall runne away from the Colonie, to Powhathan, or any savage Weroance else whatsoever" (20). It was not an idle threat. Edmund S. Morgan, drawing on George Percy's *Trewe Relacyon*, relates this gruesome episode from the spring of 1612:

Governor Dale is supervising the building of a fort at Henrico, near the present site of Richmond. He pauses to deal with some of his men, Englishmen, who have committed a serious crime. In the words of George Percy, "Some he apointed to be hanged Some burned Some to be broken upon wheles, others to be staked and some to be shott to death." The reason for such extremities was the seriousness of the crime and the need to deter others from it: "all theis extreme and crewell tortures he used and inflicted upon them to terrify the reste for Attempting the Lyke." What, then, was the crime these men had committed? They had run away to live with the Indians and had been recaptured. (74)

Morgan's fascination is with what can only be termed the pathological behavior of the colonists. In the paragraph preceding the quotation above, Morgan relates an appalling story of the Jamestown colonists' capture in 1610 (three years before Pocahontas's capture) of another Native woman, the queen of the Paspaheghs, along with her children, in an unprovoked attack on their principal town, an act of revenge for Powhatan's reportedly "disdaynefull" treatment of the English on a recent occasion. In the boats as they returned to Jamestown, the men began to complain because the queen and her children had been spared; to placate them, Percy threw the children overboard and then "shote owtt their Braynes in the water"; the queen herself was stabbed to death once they reached Jamestown (74).

Morgan's study is an impressive effort to understand why "the English, unable or unwilling to feed themselves, continually demanding corn from the Indians, take pains to destroy both the Indians and their corn" (74)—and why, later, the most impassioned revolutionary rhetoric, borrowing its vocabulary from the institutions of slavery, came from people who themselves owned slaves but were determined not to be themselves enslaved by the English crown, but to be free.

Apparently the enslavement of Indians and Africans was one of the conditions of possibility for the freedom of Anglo-Americans. Certainly it is true that Indians in very large numbers as well as Africans were pressed or sold into slavery by English colonists in both Massachusetts and Virginia in the seventeenth century (see Vaughan 60; Morgan 328 ff.) and after.[27] And while Euro-Americans made much of the capture of white women by Indians throughout the history of settlement, it is also certainly true that Native women in considerable numbers were taken captive by Europeans, though that story was seldom and only minimally reported, and then only in the margins, as it were, of the records of discovery and settlement.[28]

Michele de Cuneo, for example, an Italian nobleman who sailed with Columbus on his second voyage, gave this account of the rape of a captive woman in the Caribbean in 1493:

> While I was in the boat I captured a very beautiful Carib woman, whom the said Lord Admiral [Columbus] gave to me, and with whom, having taken her into my cabin, she being naked according to the custom, I conceived desire to take pleasure. I wanted to put my desire into execution but she did not want it and treated me with her finger nails in such a manner that I wished I had never begun. But seeing that (to tell you the end of it all), I took a rope and thrashed her well, for which she raised such unheard of screams that you would not have believed your ears. Finally we came to an agreement in such manner that I can tell you that she seemed to have been brought up in a school of harlots. (quoted in Sale 140)

One can only imagine how the two "came to an agreement" and how the captive woman arrived at the decision to reflect her captor's behavior back to him by treating him as the whoremonger he so clearly was.[29]

Tzvetan Todorov dedicates *The Conquest of America* (1984) to another captive Native woman, a Mayan, who because of the dying request of her warrior husband, refuses sexual relations with the conquistadores; they then have her "thrown to the dogs," who devour her. And during Metacom's Rebellion (King Philip's War) in 1675 in Massachusetts, Maj. Samuel Mosely, in a letter to the governor of Massachusetts (his wife's uncle) dated at Hatfield, boasts of having taken an Indian woman captive at Springfield from whom he extracts information on the strength and whereabouts of the Indian forces. In a postscript "written in his hand on the margin of the letter" (Bodge 69), Mosely says, "'This aforesaid Indian was ordered to be torn in peeces by Doggs and she was soe dealt with all'" (quoted in Bodge 69).

Pocahontas, then, was by no means the first nor last Native woman to be taken against her will; her experience of captivity may be unusual only in the fact that she was not killed. And her historical captivity or enslavement, it must be remembered, underlies the long history of her supposed love for things English. Her experience of being deceived in order to be captured may well have been one of the motives for her observation to John Smith on the occasion of their last meeting that his "Countriemen will lie much." Ralph Hamor gives this report of her capture by Samuel Argall in the spring of 1613, when she would have been between sixteen and eighteen years old:

It chaunced *Powhatans* delight and darling, his daughter *Pocahuntas,* (whose name hath even bin spred in England by the title of *Nonparella of Virginia*) in her princely progresse, if I may so terme it, tooke some pleasure . . . to be among her friends at *Pataomecke* (as it seemeth by the relation I had) imploied thither, as shopkeepers to a *Fare,* to exchange some of her fathers commodities for theirs, where residing some three months or longer, it fortuned upon occasion either of promise or profit, Captaine *Argall* to arrive there, whome *Pocahuntas,* desirous to renue hir familiaritie with the English, and delighting to see them, as unknowne, fearefull perhaps to be surprised, would gladly visit, as she did, of whom no sooner had Captaine *Argall* intelligence, but he delt with an old friend, and adopted brother of his *Iapazeus,* how and by what meanes he might procure hir captive, assuring him, that now or never, was the time to pleasure him, if he entended indeede that love which he had made profession of, that in ransome of hir he might redeeme some of our English men and armes, now in the possession of her Father, promising to use her withall faire, and gentle entreaty: *Iapazeus* well assured that his brother, as he promised would use her curteously promised his best indevours and secresie to accomplish his desire, and thus wrought it, making his wife an instrument (which sex have ever bin most powerfull in beguiling inticements) to effect his plot which hee had thus laid, he agreed that himselfe, his wife, and *Pocahuntas,* would accompanie his brother to the water side, whether come, his wife should faine a great and longing desire to goe aboorde, and see the shippe, which being there three or foure times, before she had never seene, and should bee earnest with her husband to permit her: he seemed angry with her, making as he pretended so unnecessary a request, especially being without the company of women, which deniall she taking unkindely, must faine to weepe, (as who knows not that women can command teares), gave her leave to go aboord, so that it would please *Pocahuntas* to accompany her: now was the greatest labor to win her, guilty perhaps of her fathers wrongs . . . yet by her earnest perswasions, she assented: so forthwith aboord they went. (4–5)

As Hamor describes it, Iapazeus had been bribed "with a small Copper kettle, and some other les valuable toies so highly by him esteemed, that doubtlesse he would have betraied his owne father for them" (5). After a supper aboard the ship, "merry on all hands," as Hamor describes the gathering (5), the company retired for the night. Pocahontas, "being most possessed with feare, and desire of returne, was first up" (5) in the morning and tried to hasten the group's departure from Argall's ship; but Argall refused to let her go, "whereat she began to be exceeding pensive, and discontented, yet ignorant of the dealing of *Iapazeus*, who in outward appearance was no les discontented that he should be the meanes of her captivity, much a doe there was to perswade her to be patient, which with extraordinary curteous usage, by little and little was wrought in her, and so to *James* towne she was brought" (6). And in Jamestown she remained as a hostage for the next three years, because the English refused to come to terms with Powhatan for her ransom (Hamor 6).

It could be argued that in fact Pocahontas was a captive for all that remained of her life, a short four years. A year after her capture, the colonists used her as a decoy aboard a ship on a foray upriver; they wanted to lure Indians out of the woods by declaring that "the cause of our comming thither . . . was to deliver *Pocahuntas*" (Hamor 7). When the Indians "let their arrowes flie," the colonists, "thus justly provoked," as Hamor says, "manned our boates, went ashoare, and burned in that verie place some forty houses, and of the things we found therein, made freeboote and pillage" (8). It was in the context of these events and probably other like experiences that could not but have deeply demoralized her that Pocahontas was baptized a Christian, given the name Rebecca, and married to Rolfe. And like the captive white women of whom she was the Native counterpart, her body and her sexuality—indeed, her life itself—were thus placed in the service of English colonialism and, subsequently, of the American nation. Thus was the captive thoroughly captivated.

The next spring (1615) her son was born; the next (1616) Pocahontas, with her husband and child and an entourage of Indian attendants, sailed to England, once again on a ship commanded by Argall. The trip was no doubt planned so that Pocahontas/Rebecca might serve as a living advertisement for the Virginia Company's enterprise; she was put, as Frances Mossiker expresses it, "on the payroll and on parade" (209). And the next spring, 1617, after having been received and entertained by both Queen Anne and the bishop of London and meeting for the last time with Smith, the group started their journey home, ironically enough once again in ships commanded by now-Admiral Samuel Argall (Mossiker 254–79). By the time they reached the mouth of the Thames at Gravesend, Pocahontas, whose health had declined throughout her year in England, was too ill to continue the homeward voyage; she was brought ashore, where she died and was buried. She was no more than twenty-two when she died.

Her son Thomas, a child only two years old and also ill, was left behind in England to be cared for first by Sir Lewis Stukely and later by Thomas's uncle, John's brother Henry Rolfe (Mossiker 289). Thomas never saw his father again; Rolfe died in 1622, the same year as the "massacre" led by Opechancanough, perhaps even in the attack at the hands of his Indian wife's people. Thomas did not return to Virginia to take up the management of his vast holdings of land in the vicinity of Jamestown until he was a young adult, sometime between 1635 and 1640 (Mossiker 311). His English upbringing left its permanent imprint: In 1646, Thomas was commissioned as an officer in the Virginia colonial militia and assigned to guard Fort James against attack by Indians (Mossiker 313).

The English colonists in the seventeenth century were engaged in a brutal ongoing process of self-definition at the Indians' expense, of preserving their precarious racial and cultural identities against the hapless

Indians who were unfortunate enough to be in their way. Taking note of the way the borders between the two cultures in Virginia were policed by the English in terms of allowing no colonists out and allowing—or forcing—only exceptional Indians in is a reminder once again, as Peter Hulme writes, that "Boundaries, whether physical or social, are places of danger" (148). That was certainly true in the English colonies in the seventeenth century, as evidenced by the response to the captivity experiences of white women like Rowlandson and the treatment of Native women captives like Pocahontas. And the process of defining a white America in opposition to its "dark others" has continued in the ideological use that was made of both figures in subsequent centuries as a mythic national history and identity were created.

Pocahontas, then, like her white woman captive counterpart, has been held captive within our literature as well; in fact, Pocahontas seems to have become inextricable from epic visions of America.[30] Her usefulness in symbolizing the continent as a female America who is virginal, seductive, open and receptive to English settlement has persisted, and many poets and writers have continued to find in her a fruitful figure for epic assertions of American history and identity. For the poet Joel Barlow in his 1807 nationalist epic, *The Columbiad*, she was the American Medea whose protective service to the "queen of colonies" (Virginia) transformed the continental landscape: "Receding forests yield the laborers room, / And opening wilds with fields and gardens bloom" (540).

In the twentieth century, writers as different as Hart Crane and John Barth have enlisted the Pocahontas legend for their own very different epic purposes. Crane began to plan his most ambitious work, an epic poem of America to be called *The Bridge*, in the decade following World War I, another postwar period of national introspection and redefinition. In a 1927 letter about his plans for the poem, he unproblematically adopts the ages-old symbolic function of Pocahontas-as-continent, exploiting the history and the legend without questioning it: "Pocahontas is the mythological nature-symbol chosen to represent the physical body of the continent, or the soil" (248) and "Pocahontas (the continent) is the common basis of our meeting" (of the two races, white and Indian; 251). Of Part II of *The Bridge*, titled "Powhatan's Daughter," Crane wrote in the same letter, "The five sub-sections . . . are mainly concerned with a gradual exploration of this 'body' whose first possessor was the Indian" (Crane 248).

Crane's Pocahontas is, because of her gender, apparently neither an Indian (that status is reserved for the Native male who "possessed" her) nor even a real historical human being, but is instead pure symbol, the "soil" of the continent that first the Indian male and then the Euro-American male must possess in order to claim his status as American. And Crane also fuses the virgin and mother roles that Pocahontas narratives have conventionally highlighted. She is the American Madonna, both eternal virgin and our founding mother:

> There was a bed of leaves, and broken play;
> There was a veil upon you, Pocahontas, bride—
> O Princess whose brown lap was virgin May;
> And bridal flanks and eyes hid tawny pride.
>
> (70)

> She is the torrent and the singing tree;
> And she is virgin to the last of men.
>
> (74)

Like the Christian Madonna's, her virginity, though perpetual, does not compromise her maternal role:

> . . . and [you shall] read
> her in a
> mother's
> farewell gaze.
>
> (77)

This Pocahontas gives birth to the nation and nurtures it into "adulthood" (independence from England and the closing of the western "frontier"), whereupon her role, like that of so many romanticized Indians in nineteenth-century literature, is to bid her offspring farewell and then fade into mythic history. Pocahontas's function in *The Bridge*, then, as in so many earlier figurations of her legend, is to secure the establishment of an American nation in a landscape that is her "body" and to provide a site where white Euro-Americans can replace Indians in a refigured identity as "Americans." Crane thus literalizes her symbolic function, and in the poem Pocahontas is the enabling subtext that underlies not only the poem but the nation itself:

> *Who is the*
> *woman with*
> *us in the*
> *dawn? . . .*
> *whose is the*
> *flesh our feet*
> *have moved*
> *upon?*
>
> (57)

John Barth's 1960 novel, *The Sot-Weed Factor* (revised in 1967), is a brilliant and darkly comic parody of English colonialism in America, published in its revised edition against the backdrop of the neocolonialist U.S. immersion in the war in Vietnam. The novel traces—and fictionalizes—the progress of one Ebenezer Cooke from England to America in the late seventeenth century, as he and his tutor, Henry Burlingame, travel to the Maryland colony where Eben is to take up the management of a family estate and Henry, who as an infant was discovered floating in a Maryland river by an English sea captain and raised as his adopted son, searches for the truth of his origins.

Barth uses Cooke, an actual historical figure and author of an "anti-epic" poem, "The Sot-Weed Factor" (1708), as the agent of his broad attack on romantic conceptions of the founding of America. The poem records Cooke's disillusionment upon finding Maryland not, as he had imagined, a glorious place filled with noble Englishmen, but instead "a sewer" filled with "naught but scoundrels and perverts, hovels and brothels, corruption and poltroonery!" (Barth 457).

Barth appears to have taken Crane's line "And she is virgin to the last of men" and run with it to its imaginative limits. In the novel, Eben and Henry search for and eventually find the lost *Ur-text* of the founding of

America, which contains the secret "true" story of Pocahontas, in which the survival and success of the English colonial effort depend upon John Smith's accomplishing a very literal penetration and conquest of Pocahontas as the symbol of the continent. Smith, as in his *Generall Historie* a captive of Powhatan, learns that he will be killed unless he is able to penetrate the heretofore-impenetrable Pocahontas and relieve the maiden of her maidenhead, a task to which innumerable young Powhatan warriors have proved unequal. Barth thus reverses the legendary rescue story by making Smith the one who must rescue the all-unwillingly-virginal Pocahontas from an intolerable virginity and re-writes the symbolism of Pocahontas as the virginal body of the continent and the accompanying romantic Smith-Pocahontas legend as a dirty joke of epic proportions: to accomplish his Herculean task, Smith, "but passing well equipt for Venereal exercise" (732), resorts to a phallus-fortifying poultice involving secret herbs and spices and a dried eggplant. He succeeds, to Pocahontas's eternal pleasure and gratitude, and *voila!* America.[31]

DECOLONIZING POCAHONTAS

Rayna Green has said of the stories of Native women, "Whether it comes directly from the storyteller's mouth and she writes it down or someone writes it for her, the story has to be told" (introduction, *That's What She Said*, 2). Pocahontas has been the dominant mythic and iconic figure of Native American womanhood since the early seventeenth century, as Green herself and other scholars have demonstrated.[32] This threshold figure, this woman who, in body and legend, was the meeting place of cultures and races, has moved a number of Native women writers to offer other readings of Pocahontas's role in the drama of English colonialism, to "write her story for her," intervening in the traditional Anglocentric versions of the Pocahontas legend and refusing the silence of Pocahontas herself on which the legend depends. That silence is an important reason why Pocahontas has been, as Rayna Green has written, both "an intolerable metaphor for the Indian-White experience" and an "unendurable metaphor for the lives of Indian women" ("Pocahontas Perplex" 714).

Pocahontas's dilemma, caught as she was in the web of contention between two cultures, prefigured that of contemporary Native people and the choices they must continually negotiate around issues of identity and culture. The prototype of the silent Indian woman who welcomes, accepts, and loves white men and their culture, losing herself in the process, has been an especially inhibiting image for Native women writers striving to overcome subjection and speechlessness; it also has inspired them to revise the Pocahontas figure in various guises, the stories told about her, and the role she has played in American cultural history.

Paula Gunn Allen's poem "Pocahontas to Her English Husband, John Rolfe" revisits the Pocahontas story and revises it by supplying the voice that is missing in colonialist versions. Allen's Pocahontas is a woman wise beyond her years, possessing a wisdom that is the fruit of her experience but that eludes the notice of Rolfe—and, by implication, of all of Anglo-American culture. She speaks to Rolfe from the grave, reminding him that his very survival, and implicitly that of all his cohort, was due to her superior knowledge and her generous guidance, protection, and instruction:

> Had I not cradled you in my arms
> oh beloved perfidious one,
> you would have died.
> And how many times did I pluck you
> from certain death in the wilderness—
> my world through which you stumbled
> as though blind?

(8)

That Allen's Pocahontas characterizes Rolfe as "blind" is especially ironic in light of Rolfe's having referred to her, in his letter to Gov. Thomas Dale petitioning for permission to marry Pocahontas, as one "blynde" who needed him to lead her "into the right waye" (in Mossiker 347)—a reference to her not being Christian. Allen's poem has a rueful, sardonic tone because the Pocahontas who speaks there recognizes that the fruit of her having shared with the English the knowledge that enabled them to survive in her country is her own death, which both prefigured and symbolized how lethal the liaison with the Old World would prove for the peoples and cultures of the New. Rolfe, however, profited immeasurably, not only from her knowledge, but from her death; she says to him,

> I saw you well. I
> understood your ploys and still
> protected you, going so far as to die
> in your keeping—a wasting,
> putrefying Christian death—and you,
> deceiver, whiteman, father of my son,
> survived, reaping wealth greater
> than any you had ever dreamed
> from what I taught you and
> from the wasting of my bones.
>
> (9)

The tradition is that Pocahontas taught Rolfe how to grow tobacco successfully—as Leslie Fiedler put it, "tobacco [sprouted] where her divine ass had touched the earth" (86)—and it was the success of that crop that made possible the economic survival of the Virginia colony. The drama of Pocahontas, then, as Allen inscribes it here, is the drama of colonialism itself—writ small in the ancient, private, domestic tragedy of one woman's life, but writ large in the subsequent history of the nation that made her its founding heroine.

Allen uses as an epigraph to her poem a passage from Charles Larson's *American Indian Fiction* in which he characterizes Pocahontas as "a kind of traitor to her people" but also says, "The crucial point, it seems to me, is to remember that Pocahontas was a hostage. Would she have converted freely to Christianity if she had not been in captivity?" (Larson 27; epigraph in Allen 8). That "crucial point" of Pocahontas's captivity has attracted Michelle Cliff, the Jamaican writer of Amerindian-African-European ancestry who has written repeatedly and hauntingly of Pocahontas. Disturbed by her portrayal as traitor, Cliff instead sees Pocahontas as a victim. In her essay "Caliban's Daughter," Cliff writes:

Pocahontas' name has been synonymous with collaborator and traitor, consort of the enemy, a woman who let herself be used, intellectually, sexually, against her own people. . . . But the truth is not so: Pocahontas was kidnapped by colonists and held against her will, forced to abandon the belief system of her people and to memorize the Apostle's Creed, the Lord's Prayer, the Ten Commandments, outwardly appearing submissive to her captors. She was taken to England and there displayed, a tame Indian, the forest behind her, supposedly cleansed of any aboriginal longings. She became known as the "friend of the earliest colonists, whom she nobly rescued, protected, and helped," as is written on her memorial tablet in St. George's Church. She is memorialized there as Rebecca Wrolfe, her true name, which translates as "getting joy from spirits," erased. (49)

Cliff's reading here revises the characterization of Pocahontas as a "traitor to her people," or "our first [Uncle] Tom." Cliff's Pocahontas does do all that the legend says, but does it under duress. She is thus an emblematic casualty of colonialism, one who, as an emblem, might move others to resist her fate.

In her novel *No Telephone to Heaven*, Cliff's protagonist is Clare Savage, a Jamaican girl who has been raised within British colonial Caribbean culture and who has gone to England to take a doctorate in literature. In a chance visit to Gravesend, Clare comes upon the statue of Pocahontas in the memorial garden at St. George's Church:

She stood and walked toward it—from a distance her training suspected allegory. Bronze. Female. Single figure. Single feather rising from the braids. Moccasined feet stepping forward, as if to walk off the pedestal on which she was kept. A personification of the New World . . . Clare walked around the statue, slowly, taking it in. The bronze-woman gave nothing else away. She went into the church and found memorials to the Indian princess. Found two stained-glass windows, one showing her baptism, full-grown, wild, kneeling at the font. Found she had been tamed, renamed Rebecca. . . . Clare stayed in the church—cold. Dim light passing through stained glass. Something was wrong. She had no sense of the woman under the weight of all these monuments. She thought of her, her youth, her color, her strangeness, her unbearable loneliness. Where was she now? (136–37)

Clare's encounter with Pocahontas at Gravesend marks a turning point in her own life, enabling a turning away from the English culture that has colonized her and a turning back to Jamaica, ultimately to the very soil of that homeland, identified in the novel with her beloved grandmother. Cliff has written of that passage, "When Clare Savage recognizes Pocahontas in that graveyard in Gravesend, she begins a series of choices, which will open her mind and memory and will take her from the mother country [England] back to the grandmother country [Jamaica], which is, in the end, her own" ("Caliban's Daughter" 49).

At the close of *No Telephone to Heaven*, Clare, in a gesture of ritual protest against the colonialist consumption of her culture and land, is killed on a movie set by what turns out to be real gunfire. The closing scene of the novel is not only painfully violent, but also lyrical; as Cliff herself describes it in another essay, Clare is "burned into the landscape . . . but she is also enveloped in the deep green of the hills and the delicate intricacy of birdsong" ("Clare Savage as a Crossroads Character" 266). Insisting on her understanding of the landscape of Jamaica as female, Cliff returns Clare to that colonizing trope of the feminized New World landscape that Pocahontas has so often represented, but it is a return with a difference because of Native perceptions of the earth as mother, as grandmother. That is to say, Clare's reunion and merger with the grandmother/soil of Jamaica signifies her death as a colonized subject and leaves open the possibility of a resurrection or rebirth from the womb of the maternal earth. Just as her encounter with Pocahontas moves Clare to undertake the journey of return that culminates in her fusion with the mother landscape, so Clare's death might move others to undertake similar journeys, revolutionary decolonizing forays into the discourses of colonization that figure the feminized landscape as a willing partner in her own subjugation.

Pocahontas, as the body in which the two races, conqueror and conquered, met, was both literally a foremother to successive generations of Americans[33] and figuratively a mother to all those of mixed Indian-white heritage. For Native people, though, and particularly for Native women writers, the metaphoric significances of Pocahontas as "the mother of us all" (Young) differ dramatically from those that Anglo-American culture has assigned. In her role as mother of the first recorded Indian-white child in North America, Pocahontas hovers as a backdrop for treatments of the experience of divided self, divided heritage, in the writing of many Native women.

Paula Gunn Allen, for instance, in her poem "Dear World," watches her mother dying of lupus and sees the destructiveness of that disease as a metaphor for the struggle between Indian and white that, for her mixed-blood mother, is fought on the most intimate frontier:

> A halfbreed woman
> can hardly do anything else
> but attack herself,
> her blood attacks itself.
> There are historical reasons
> for this.
> I know you can't make peace
> being Indian and white.
> They cancel each other out.
> . . . .
> in such circumstances,
> when volatile substances are intertwined,
> when irreconcilable opposites meet,
> the crucible and its contents vaporize.
>
> (56–57)

Linda Hogan too, another of Pocahontas's daughters,[34] struggles with her mixed identity in the poem "The Truth Is." The speaker in the poem is quite literally split, the hand in her left pocket "a Chickasaw hand," the hand in her right pocket, and the foot in her right shoe, white. She plays with the metaphors that could help resolve the tensions she feels with her plural identities against the painful history she knows so well:

> . . . I'd like to say
> I am a tree, grafted branches

bearing two kinds of fruit,
apricots maybe and pit cherries.
It's not that way. The truth is
we are crowded together
and knock against each other at night.
We want amnesty.

(415–16)

Hogan acknowledges her mixed ancestry as problematic: "Girl, I say, / it is dangerous to be a woman of two countries." She wants to pretend that it "is nonsense / about who loved who / and who killed who," but after all knows full well "which pocket the enemy lives in" and does indeed "remember who killed who" (416). Unlike the mother in Allen's poem, though, the speaker in the Hogan poem does not self-destruct; instead she seeks accommodation, a truce between the historically warring halves of her divided self. It's as if an imagined nation begins to speak through the woman in the poem, one that arises from and can only be realized through acknowledging, realistically and with sensible caution, both heritages.

Pocahontas is a mother/grandmother figure in the writing of some contemporary Native women, one who powerfully contradicts mythic representations of her as a traitor to her people and a woman enamored of whiteness. Beth Brant, in her essay "Grandmothers of a New World," claims Pocahontas as "a Powhatan shaman" (60), a powerful grand-mother figure in the Native tradition. The glossary to Rayna Green's anthology, *That's What She Said: Comtemporary Poetry and Fiction by Native American Women*, offers this definition of the Grandmother:

Grandmother Turtle, Grandmother Spider, or just Grandma. She brought the people to earth and gave them the rules and knowledge they needed to live. Indian people have many grandmothers, real and mythic. Some are biological relatives, some adopted ones. Grand-mothers raise children; they tell stories in the winter and teach children the skills they need for survival. Grandmothers are the central char-acters in the daily and symbolic lives of Native women—indeed, of Native people. (310)

And Michelle Cliff says of this figure, "At her most powerful, the grandmother is the source of knowledge, magic, ancestors, stories, healing practices, and food. She assists at rites of passage, protects, and teaches" ("Clare Savage as a Crossroads Character" 267). One thinks too of the powerful grandmother figures in Louise Erdrich's fiction—Marie Kashpaw and Lulu Lamartine, and the elusive Fleur Pillager, so mysterious and yet so potent a figure that she seems almost to underwrite and enable the many different stories that make up Erdrich's novels—to carry them on her back, as the Iroquoian Grandmother Turtle carries the world.

To transform Pocahontas into a grandmother figure in this tradition, to give her story new and different meanings, is not only to uncouple it from its traditional forms and uses in the service of white conquest and dominance but is also to make of her a powerfully productive source of revised identity for contemporary Native women—indeed for all Native people. Marilou Awiakta writes in her essay "Amazons in Appalachia" of the diplomatic role of women in the Native tradition:

"Where are your women?"

The speaker is Attakullakulla, a Cherokee chief renowned for his shrewd and effective diplomacy. He has come to negotiate a treaty with the whites. Among his delegation are women "as famous in war as powerful in the Council." Their presence also has ceremonial significance: it is meant to show honor to the other delegation. But that delegation is composed of males only. To them the absence of their women is irrelevant, a trivial consideration.

To the Cherokee, however, reverence for women/Mother/Earth/life/spirit is interconnected. Irreverence for one is likely to mean irreverence for all. Implicit in their chief's question, "Where are your women?" the Cherokee hear, "Where is your balance? What is your intent?" They see that the balance is absent and are wary of the white men's motives. They intuit the mentality of destruction. (125)

This is the role and the identity to which Beth Brant restores Pocahontas in her "Grandmothers of a New World" essay. Brant's stated purpose is to "improve on [the traditional] tale" (48) of Pocahontas by telling another and better story of her own making, a story, however, that is grounded in resistant readings of history and in familiarity with long-standing Native belief and tradition. Brant's Pocahontas "had her own manifest destiny to fulfill. That of keeping her people alive" (51), and to that end, she became "probably the first ambassador to the English" (49):

> Powhatan and his daughter/confidant were not fools. They had a sophisticated view of the English and the other European nations who were clamoring to capture the new continent and claim it for their own. The English seemed mighty, so why not choose them to make alliances with? The continuation of the Indian people was uppermost in the daughter's and father's minds. Then, as now, survival is the most important thought on North American Indians' agendas. (49)

Observing that "Powhatan women held sway in the disposition of enemy warriors and matters pertaining to war," Brant, like other scholars I have discussed above, also rewrites Pocahontas's rescue of John Smith as a "mock execution—a traditional ritual often held after capture of enemies" and one that signified his adoption into Pocahontas's tribe and family. Her subsequent marriage to Rolfe and the birth of their son, in Brant's retelling, become not the result of Pocahontas's recognizing the superiority of white English culture and religious belief, but instead elements in her strategy to protect her own people and their way of life by forging an indissoluble alliance with the English.

If one accepts Brant's version of the Pocahontas legend, to realize what came of the dream she ascribes to Pocahontas of two cultures surviving, even thriving, side by side and intertwined, is painful indeed. Rewriting the story as she does, though, frees Pocahontas from her long captivity within the image of the submissive, love-struck, self-sacrificing woman whom the English colonists, and later white Americans, created and enshrined for their own purposes. Such rewriting also frees Native women writers from the oppressive shadow of that image and enables them to imagine other and prouder possibilities for themselves and their people.

Pocahontas's silence, which Euro-American culture has capitalized on for so long, has offered opportunities for resistance and rescripting that some Native women writers have found both inviting and productive.

By giving Pocahontas voice, by revising conventional versions of her story generated and reproduced by the dominant culture, by "talking back" to images of her that serve Euro-American interests, and by rescripting, in their own voices, cultural images of Native womanhood, contemporary Native women writers have rescued Pocahontas from her captivity within American mythology, speaking to or through or for her and other mythic figures who have cast their shadow so deeply over the history and identity of Native people and who have been made to serve and secure the white masculine identity of the American national subject.

Pocahontas died young, but her "Indian princess" legend has persisted and proliferated, especially, as Robert Tilton has demonstrated, in the nineteenth and early twentieth centuries. During that period, questions of racial dominance continued to preoccupy white America, as the "frontier" was closed and the "Indian question" and the accompanying politics and problematics of Indian removal joined with the question of slavery and, after the Civil War, of dealing with a newly emancipated slave population to trouble the scene of U.S. domestic politics. The figure of Pocahontas and the myths and legends generated around her have continued to serve as a site for asserting and reproducing racial hierarchies and the "inevitability" of the triumph of white "civilization" over America's domestic "others."

It must not be forgotten—to the contrary, it must continually be emphasized—that it was during her own years as a captive that Pocahontas was converted to Christianity and given an English name, was married to Rolfe, and gave birth to the first child of mixed Indian-English parentage recorded in North America. Her status as a hostage must, at the least, call into question her desire for conversion and marriage to an Englishman; in fact, it is not unreasonable to think of her as a victim of war and of the rape that so often accompanies it. By implication, we must question the New World's eagerness to become the christianized, anglicized bride of the Old World.

Pocahontas, an alien from a culture incomprehensible to the English, was a woman through whom the figure of the fearful New World female "monster" was subdued by christianizing, anglicizing, and domesticating her as the savior of the early colony and wife of an English colonizer. In this guise she was rendered a docile immigrant into English culture, assimilated, and subsumed. She was the counterpart to the threat of the failure of the colonial enterprise represented by the white woman captured by Indians; our Pygmalion myth, English colonialism's great success story, Pocahontas has continued to be invoked in American literature, art, and popular culture as a site for reasserting and legitimating racial and cultural dominance throughout the centuries of white efforts to claim and control the North American continent that she was made so conveniently to represent.

Voyaging to Jamestown: October 1993

From the air, the landscape is a patchwork: at the margins of the ugly suburban sprawl around the nation's capital, woods, burnished by the season, alternate with fields, cleared and squared, plowed and planted and cultivated not in the Algonkian fashion but in the style inherited from England. The fields in turn alternate with patches of lawn surrounding stately houses, mimics of the estates of an earlier era when English settlers were claiming the land and attempting to re-create it in the image of the land they'd left behind. Another more contemporary image intrudes on the pastoral scene: automobile carcasses in a vast junkyard on the edge of a lake glint and gleam in the autumn sunlight.

It's a perspective available only to those of my century. Just moments ago we sailed above a sea of autumn trees with no evidence of human habitation. The rolling eastern foothills of the Alleghenies—western Maryland and northern Virginia—look from this height much as they must have done four centuries ago, when kingdoms of another order altogether reigned here. But they couldn't have seen it as I do now. It's a humbling, even though powerful, perspective.

The Midwest I left in the darkness of early morning is further along in its progress into winter. The windstorms of the past week that turned the chairs over on the deck and blew down the ladder we'd left leaning against the house harvested the autumn leaves, or most of them, and the winter view—the trees' long, bare, gnarled and spindled branches fingering the star-speckled sky—has reasserted itself in the narrow unshaded window I look out each night as I lie in bed. My years on the prairie have accustomed me to vicissitudes of weather: its sudden turns, unpredictable violence, fierce surprises.

Here is different. And here is home. Hills and mountains and thick woods brake the buffeting winds and lashings of rain or snow, steering or stopping storms and gentling them a little, shielding the farms and towns that cling to the hillsides or huddle in the narrow valleys, sprawl in the broad ones. It would have been a pleasant and mostly easy home to the people who lived in it for centuries before the English arrived. Not paradise, perhaps, though it must have seemed like one to them, after it was wrested from them.

From high in the air on this high noon of a brilliant October day, I can see that the trees cushioning the hills of Virginia still sport their leaves. Here and there on the eastern slopes a patch of maples blazes a bright gold. Other trees, more muted, have turned also, to a dark russet-red, the color of old blood, or to a dull tawny brown. But the fields and swards are still a lush, fresh green, and ponds and rivers glisten in the midday sun.

Having grown up here, I know this land in every season: in springtime too, in April and May, so I can imagine how enchanting, how seductive it must have looked to the English when they arrived at that season: dogwood and redbud in bloom, the air fragrant with honeysuckle, the forest floor carpeted with a myriad of wildflowers, the tall and stately magnolias with their glossy leaves and, later, their creamy blossoms, fish and deer and turkeys in abundance. Little wonder they wanted to live here. But did they have to go to such murderous lengths to possess the land and make it theirs?

It's my home too, and I am struggling to learn some way to live with its history. I love this landscape that feels so maternal to me, and like those early marketing experts of the sixteenth and seventeenth centuries who wrote to advertise it to their fellow Englishmen, I want to celebrate its beauty and acknowledge my connection to it; but I want to do so without replicating the ideologies I've critiqued, without the mandate for conquest, the rapaciousness, the hunger to own and exploit that has so marred this country's past. I want to separate the gaze from the power to conquer that has for so long accompanied it; I want to refigure the gaze itself. But I don't know if that is possible. This late-twentieth-century "commanding view" that my aerial perspective gives me might allow me to see not only more, but *differently*—to see *with a difference*, if I could imagine how that would work. To see multiply, to see with "fifty pairs of eyes," as Woolf's Lily Briscoe says in *To the Lighthouse*. Maybe the best I can do is acknowledge how partial (in both senses of the word) and limited is my own way of seeing, with only one pair of eyes, these.

As we begin our descent into Dulles Airport where I'll change planes, I have a moment of regret that I did not plan to rent a car from here and drive home. It would be a four-hour drive, south through the Shenandoah Valley's spectacular early-fall displays. But there's driving enough to do tomorrow, after I dip down to collect my mother in Roanoke. "Roanoke," or "Rawanoke," in Algonkian: white shell beads, wampum or shell money. "Rawrenoke," wrote Ralph Hamor in 1615. "Row-noke," the tall, slim, golden-skinned African American woman who is our flight attendant says it. That's the familiar pronunciation; she must be a Roanoker herself. I choose to honor the Algonkian diphthong—smooth but distinct: Roanoke. Tomorrow my mother and I will leave home and drive east to the coast, to the tidewater area that was home to the Powhatan confederacy; to the site of the Jamestown settlement, where Pocahontas was imprisoned, converted, and married; to Williamsburg, colonial capital of Virginia, and to the Pamunkey Reservation, or "Pamunkey Towne" as it was called in colonial days, home of a present-day remnant of the Powhatan people. In search of Pocahontas.

I've chosen the perfect time to come. It's the "height of the foliage season," as the tourist industry has made it out to be. *Taquitock*, the Virginia Algonkians called it: the season of "harvest and fall of leafe." I remember it as my favorite season always: "Indian summer," after the first nips of cold remind us that all beauty will be extinguished, that all living things must one day die, and the year too; its time draws nigh. But for a brief, glorious stretch, we're warm again, even hot, and our limbs loosen and our spirits lift in pleasure at the respite. The air is luminous, burnished by the rich shades of ripened verdure, and fragrant of apples and woodsmoke. Virginia: now a mere fragment of the vast region Ralegh claimed and named to honor his Virgin Queen, and at her pleasure. The Algonkians called it *Attanoughkomouck*, or *Wingandacoa*, or *Tsenacommacah*, "the densely inhabited land." Gravesite of those countless inhabitants who lived here in harmony with this lovely country for so many unnumbered generations, and of their culture. Cradle of a nation that has persistently dared to describe itself as pursuing a dream of liberty and justice for all, even through the centuries of our culpable misunderstandings and grave errors, our terrible blood-stained history. *Attanoughkomouck. Wingandacoa. Tsenacommacah.* Virginia. Beautiful, and beloved. Home.

CHAPTER 3

Making a History, Shaping a Nation

TO POCAHONTAS: JUNE 1995

As soon as I heard that the world premiere of Disney's *Pocahontas* was going to take place in Pocahontas, Iowa, I knew I had to go. I called Loret and asked if she wanted to go along. She grew up on a ranch in Montana and rode a horse to school, and I knew that she was still almost always up for an adventure.

Yes, the woman at the Pocahontas Chamber of Commerce said, the premiere was going to happen on June 22, the day before the film's national release, the very first showing anywhere in the country of this long-awaited (or more precisely, long-promoted) movie. She gave me the telephone number of Ruth, the town librarian who was coordinating the event. Ruth told me the premiere was a benefit to cover the cost of the recent renovation of the Rialto Theatre on the town square; Pocahontas had been without a movie theatre for years. I asked her to reserve two tickets for me, at thirty-five dollars each, for the second show.

As it turned out, of course, it wasn't the world premiere at all, though probably no one had bothered to tell the folks in Pocahontas, Iowa, that.

On the Saturday before, the real world premiere had happened, an outdoor showing to many thousands in New York's Central Park. The news took the edge off our excitement a little, but still we were determined to go and see what even a pseudo world premiere in small-town Iowa would be like.

Loret fetched me early that morning in her new "touring car," an old and elegant silvery-grey Mercedes, and we were off, our backs to the Mississippi River and our faces toward the west, on a southeast-to-northwest diagonal to Pocahontas, in Pocahontas County, a five-hour drive from Iowa City. We wanted to get there in time to look around a little before the afternoon celebration on the courthouse lawn. The blistering heat of the Iowa summer shimmered over the pavement and above the endless fields of young corn as we sailed past; the hours rolled by as smoothly as the miles, and we were in Pocahontas in time for a late lunch.

No big surprise, of course, that Iowa has a town named Pocahontas. Many states do: "Pocahontas" was one of the banners white settlers carried with them as they marched relentlessly west. When I first did a computer keyword search on "Pocahontas" at the university library, just to see what turned up, what I found astonished me. Town names, county names, yes, lots of them; but mostly, countless geological and economic reports and studies and statistics on the Pocahontas coal vein in West Virginia, one of the biggest and richest deposits of coal in the Alleghenies. It's not hard to imagine how it got the name. *What lieth hidden in the womb of the land.*

An enormous and primitive painted statue greeted us we drove into town, of someone's 1950s idea of Pocahontas herself, with long black braids and a big ugly yellow dress. She was thick and stiff and all out of proportion, and fully two stories tall. Adjacent to the statue was a painted concrete tipi gift shop, but it was closed, the sign on the door said, because of family illness. The tacky "Indian" souvenirs inside looked very dusty. Because she's an artist herself, Loret was enthusiastic about the statue as an outsized example of American primitive folk art. Most of the townspeople, though, whenever Loret expressed her admiration, seemed embarrassed by its immense ugliness.

On our way into the center of town we passed Poky Lanes, the town bowling alley. Pocahontas (population 2,085), like most of the small towns we had passed through in the relentlessly flat landscape of northwest Iowa, collects itself for business and commercial purposes mostly in a straight line on both sides of a single wide street. An enormous grain elevator anchors the town at the bottom of Main Street, next to the railroad track. At the other end of Main Street, in the center of a square park, is the town's other anchor, an enormous classic revival courthouse. We had to wonder what sort of civic business a town and county the size of Pocahontas could have that could fill up the space in such a building. The official *Iowa Travel Guide* for this year lists "Attractions" and "Accommodations" for every town in Iowa; Pocahontas has one listing, the Big Chief Motel, under "Accommodations." And under "Attractions," nothing at all.

On this special day, though, the town had put on a festive face: Bright red "Welcome" banners flew from every lamppost, and clusters of red and white balloons hovered above the makeshift grandstand and bleachers on the courthouse lawn, presumably signifying the meeting of Indian and English that was the subject of the film. "The Rialto *IS* a Reality!" proclaimed signs posted here and there, and indeed the theatre with its handsomely restored art deco marquee was right there on Main Street, across from the courthouse.

We pulled into a parking place in front of the Ben Franklin variety store, its windows filled with Pocahontas souvenir T-shirts and miniature birch-bark canoes, and chose the Ideal Cafe as our lunch spot. We ordered—the special, homemade noodle soup and a BLT tortilla—and then looked around the place. Eight or ten people, probably the dignitaries of the town and the premiere organizers, were seated at a round table near the back, and to my surprise, there among them was Russell Means—AIM member, Indian activist, veteran of Wounded Knee, the voice of Powhatan in *Pocahontas*. His long black braids were decorated with silver conchas, and he wore a turquoise bead necklace over his black shirt. He laughed and talked amiably with the others around the table.

After lunch, Loret and I strolled up Main Street toward the courthouse lawn. The heat was withering, and we wandered into every store that was open and air-conditioned, killing time until the festivities began. We passed yet another gift shop, the Giftique, with another well-timed window display: Indian portraits, child-sized war bonnets, Pocahontas statues, refrigerator magnets in the shape of cowboy boots. This Indian motif, no matter how easily explained by the town's name or by the day's occasion, felt strangely incongruous, because Pocahontas appeared to be as thoroughly white as are most small Iowa towns.

It was still ninety-seven degrees at 4:30 when we found a spot on the lawn of the courthouse to watch the celebration. A crowd had started to arrive. Flashes of what was no doubt intended as patriotism appeared in several getups: one woman wore shorts and a shirt patterned with the stars and stripes; another wore a flag-patterned vest. A small girl was in a bright turquoise shorts-and-shirt set, fringed ("Indian style") at the sleeves, legs, and shirt hem. Another wore a fringed tan suedecloth dress that mimicked deerskin. Several pale-faced children wore beaded headbands. They were apparently the stand-ins for the real Indians, who were, Means excepted, nowhere to be seen. Booths around the edge of the lawn sold rounds of watermelon, cold Cokes, slices of homemade pie, and ice cream that melted quickly in the heat. People sat on folding chairs and fanned themselves with a slow rhythm; it was too hot for any exertion.

Then I spotted a small clutch of Indians at the fringe of the crowd. A woman in a bright cotton skirt and a T-shirt held a baby in diapers perched on her hip. Her feet, the toes and ankles swollen in the heat, were stuck into yellow rubber thongs. The baby's face was round and sweet, with full cheeks and bright black eyes and black hair that stood up in a halo all around his head. Two men in cowboy boots, jeans, T-shirts, and visored caps pulled low over their faces stood not far from the woman with her baby. They all looked around warily and stood apart, silent, from the other celebrators; they were strangers here too, I decided, maybe Mesquakie from the settlement at Tama south of here. I wondered what had brought them to town for the festivities. Maybe they were curious about this white town's celebration of Pocahontas. Or maybe they had just come to see Russell Means.

The children's chorus started things off with a listless rendition of "Zip-a-dee-do-dah" but picked up a little on "Davy Crockett." Then I caught on: a Disney theme, Disney songs resurrecting images of faithful darkies and courageous Indian fighters for the people of this white town. Yes indeed, I thought to myself, that fabled American innocence; it's a long, long story.

The Community Chorus took over after the children filed off the bleachers. They opened loudly and earnestly with a gospel song, "He's Never Failed Me Yet." Then, one by one, the organizers of the affair got up to the podium and thanked everyone who had helped them with generous outpourings of time and money and gave away endless plaques and hugged their spouses and children. There were even a few moist eyes because of the general feeling of triumph at the success of the celebration.

One of the Disney animators spoke next; he wasn't much used to public relations stuff, you could tell, and he was uncomfortable and awkward even with this small-town crowd. So he just talked about how much fun it had been to draw Pocahontas and Powhatan and the cute, funny animals. The governor was there too; he, by contrast, was perfectly at ease with PR events. He wore a suit and tie in spite of the heat, and he made a short speech about what a wonderful place Pocahontas, Iowa, was, and what a wonderful place the whole state of Iowa was. But I noticed that no one had yet said a word about the people, the Iowa people, who had given their name to this place before they were pushed west—out of the way, and out of sight.

Then Russell Means was at the podium. He stood there tall and smiling while the audience rose from their chairs to greet him and the chorus sang "The Iowa Corn Song." The crowd enthusiastically joined in on the second chorus: "I-o-way—that's where the tall corn grows!"

Means began to speak. He said how glad he was to be here in Pocahontas, Arkansas. *Arkansas?* All the traveling he was doing to promote the movie, I decided, must have gotten him mightily confused. And that wasn't the end of the confusion, either. "This is the finest movie about my people in the history of Hollywood," he said, which surprised me a lot—though admittedly that's not saying much, as my friend Stephen pointed out later when I told the story of our journey. Then "Women are our power, women are our challenge"; I was getting more and more interested. He went on, "Another reason I love this film—this is *truth*. What about twisting history? *I don't care.* I care about the children. Will they learn something good about the environment? *Yes!* Will they learn something good about Indian people? *Yes!* Will they learn about good triumphing over evil in history? *Yes!*"

By that time, my expectations of what I was going to see in that theatre would have been raised considerably, if I weren't such a cynic; from everything I'd heard and read, not to mention everything I knew about the Disney Studios, I doubted that this movie had much to teach kids about "good triumphing over evil in history." But I guess that's the Disney version of American history, sadly more familiar than the history all of us ought to know. Poor Means, I concluded, was almost as thoroughly colonized as Pocahontas herself. Or maybe he was just grinning all the way to the bank to deposit the white man's money. He closed with a kind of benediction, intoning solemnly, "Thank Pocahontas for this great land of America." I somehow couldn't bring myself to feel all that thankful just then, even if Pocahontas had slipped into the usual place of God in Means's blessing.

Then a huge haywagon hitched to a tractor pulled up to the grand-stand to fetch the governor and Means and the other movers and shakers. Big signs decorated both sides and the rear of the wagon: "Iowa LiMOOOsine"—the giant MOOO painted in a black-and-white cowhide pattern, just in case we had momentarily forgotten that Iowa is a farm state now and no longer somebody's hunting grounds. The Community Chorus kept singing energetically as the celebrities cheerfully climbed aboard, smiling and waving to the crowd, and the tractor made its slow way the short distance across the lawn and the street to the Rialto, where everybody climbed down again and the governor and Means together cut a red ribbon, officially opening the theatre after its long years of silence.

Yes, we saw the movie. We were surprised only by how completely it recapitulated the nineteenth-century romantic myth of Pocahontas welcoming and loving and rescuing the white strangers, especially John Smith, whom she falls in love with at first sight and from whom she must inevitably be tragically separated, and by how otherwise somehow empty it seemed to us. But of course it isn't so much a movie as a marketing device, something to generate desire in the hearts of America's children for Pocahontas "Barbie" dolls coloring books paper dolls lunchboxes sleeping bags stickers pillows posters figurines mugs bracelets beach towels beading kits paper plates pajamas and even Halloween costumes—no end to it, really, at least not until the next

Disney marketing device appears in our neighborhood theatres. And now that the Rialto is once again in business, the children of Pocahontas, Iowa, will no longer be left out.

We spent the night at—where else?—the Big Chief Motel, where a window air conditioner clunked and groaned all night in a feeble effort to cool the room. Next morning, we drove into a residential neighborhood nearby to find what the motel people had told us was the best thing to see in Pocahontas, and we found it: A family had hired a woodcarver from Minnesota to carve a life-size Indian chief out of the trunk of an enormous dead tree in their yard, and there he stood, literally rooted to the spot. The family had planted flowers all around the base of the statue, so that the whole thing looked a little like a memorial, or a gravesite. The woman of the house came out to enjoy what she was sure would be our admiration; while I snapped photographs, Loret made polite small talk with her, remarking on the uniqueness of such an idea— an Indian from a dead tree! The chief had a square nose and a square jaw, wore a long war bonnet, and carried a rattle in one hand and a tomahawk in the other. But of course he didn't look scary at all.

Before leaving town we stopped in at Mary's Cafe, where my breakfast of coffee and a muffin cost, so help me, thirty-eight cents. Cross-cut log rounds decoupaged with familiar images decorated the walls—a beautiful Indian princess in fringed white buckskin, the head of a bearded Jesus, Jesus knocking at the door, and *The Last Indian*, on horseback, arms extended, wearing a war bonnet but facing the setting sun, his whole face and posture an expression of resigned defeat.

We left Pocahontas behind and drove over to the next town, Rolfe (population 721), just a few miles away. Like Pocahontas, it was dominated by a huge grain elevator, but in much the same way that Pocahontas's English husband, John Rolfe, got dropped out of the myth and left out of the Disney movie, so the town named for him seemed also to have been all but forgotten. It was bleak and empty, almost a ghost town, and it depressed us just to look around. We didn't stay long—from what we saw, not many people do—and then it was back on the road again, eastbound for Iowa City, and home.

What I remember most and will remember longest about that visit is not *Pocahontas*, the eminently forgettable movie, but Means's really unforgettable speech. And the "LiMOOOsine" carrying the celebrities to the theatre. And the Community Chorus singing and singing all the while, their white faces flushed with heat and gleaming with pride and perspiration, "My Country 'Tis of Thee"—the American song to the tune of "God Save the Queen." Over and over they sang it: "God bless our native land . . . ." With apparently not a shred, not a single shred, of irony.

FACING EAST, FACING WEST

> I remain convinced that the metaphorical and metaphysical uses of race occupy definitive places in American literature, in the "national" character, and ought to be a major concern of the literary scholarship that tries to know it.
>
> —TONI MORRISON, *Playing in the Dark*

The Pocahontas familiar to the twentieth century was largely the product of the nineteenth, as both Philip Young and Robert Tilton have demonstrated. It was a time when, as Young points out, "Americans began to search intensely for their history" and so resurrected the story, shaping the history into a myth that (to echo Slotkin) allowed the nation to "remember"—but in fact allowed it to *create*—a mythohistory that was both comfortable and comforting to the dominant group, white Euro-Americans. That mythohistory offered a crucial ideological foundation for the nation's future as well; as Tilton says, "On a national level . . . it had become clear by the second decade of the nineteenth century that Pocahontas had rescued Smith, and by implication all Anglo-Americans, so that they might carry on the destined work of becoming a great nation—a task that was still in its early stages" (55).

Just as in the earlier period of colonization, stories of white women captured by Indians were also players in the post-Revolutionary dramas of constructing a new nation, partners with the Pocahontas figure in creating discursive scenes where the dramas of racial identity, both individual and national, could be played out. Looking to its past for sources to construct the identity and culture it needed, the infant nation found them in part in the related legends of the "Indian princess," lover and savior of white colonists, and of white women's captivity among "savage" Indians. In the crucible of these founding myths, the nation strove to forge both a history and an identity that helped to shape, and were in turn themselves shaped by, widely held beliefs in racial difference, the inevitability of white supremacy, the superiority of Euro-American culture, and the providential nature of the design that held Blacks in bondage and forced Native people to yield to white conquest.

Both the white woman captive and Pocahontas were such central props in the nineteenth-century effort to create and maintain a white-defined nation in America that, as we shall see, their stories continued to be pressed into service, together and separately, at moments of national and racial conflict through the twentieth century as well. Other scholars have explored the significance of the captive woman or the Pocahontas figure alone, but I see them as intimately connected, and in this chapter I want to consider the cultural work the two figures performed in concert in the nineteenth and twentieth centuries as the United States has repeatedly tried to insist on its identity as a "white" nation.

During the early years of the nineteenth century, America's process of identity formation, which had begun in the pre-Revolutionary period and which Carroll Smith-Rosenberg found at work in eighteenth-century stories of Indian captivity, was continuing. "Facing east," the process meant asserting America's recently won independence from England by forging an American identity related to but still distinct and different from that of Americans' fellow Anglophones in England. At the same time, "facing west," they asserted themselves as heirs of the English colonial project, destined to possess more and more of the continent but also distinct and different from the American Natives they would replace.

From the first decade of the nineteenth century, both the white woman captive and Pocahontas, already tried and proven figures in the enterprise of colonization, were enlisted in the effort to write a white Euro-American nation into being. The two figures together helped to create a Janus-faced national narrative that reveals the historical dynamics at work in the construction of a national identity: They engaged the discursive elements necessary to consolidate the identity of the American subject and the American nation as white and male, while at the same time their stories contained elements that perpetually thwarted the effort to achieve that consolidation in any definitive way. And because the cultural work they were assigned to do could never be satisfactorily accomplished, these figures were invoked again and again in numerous texts—verbal and visual, historical and fictional, dramatic and poetic, literary and popular—that pervaded American culture in the nineteenth century and continued to appear in the twentieth as the nation repeatedly attempted, and inevitably repeatedly failed, to construct itself as "white."

Narratives and visual images of the white woman captive and the Indian princess have been variously deployed. Sometimes the two characters operate within a single text, and at other times they are narratively fused into a single character. In still other texts one figure shadows the other, one woman's story serving as the pre-text or suppressed text on which the other woman's story is constructed. And in still other texts either the Pocahontas figure or the white captive stands alone. Even in the last instance, however, each is implicated in the other's story in some way, by virtue of the fact that they occupy the same border zone between cultures and "races," provoke the same questions and problems about the identity of the American character, and operate within the same political agenda or a closely related one.

In every instance, the persistent eroticizing of both figures demonstrates how the bodies and sexuality of white and Native women were appropriated as a terrain of racial and cultural contest in eliciting the story of the nation, always positioned at racial dividing lines and helping to police racial divisions, always raising questions about being white or dark, open or closed, secure or vulnerable, in ways that facilitated or challenged the claims of a conflicted and always unstable American identity.

Furthermore, both the figures of the Indian princess and the white woman among Indians were themselves doubled: the white-but-not-quite Pocahontas figure existed in uneasy relation to both the "savage squaw" figure[1] and the noble but not-white Native woman who cannot acculturate and so must leave or be expelled from white society. The white woman captive who, like Rowlandson, returned (apparently) "intact" to white society posed persistently unsettling questions like the ones I have suggested were raised about Rowlandson herself, of whether she had sexually crossed over, by force or by choice, the Anglo/Native divide. The returned white woman, then, coexisted with her shadowy unchaste self, representing the possible pollution of the white character of English colonial or, later, Euro-American culture. Finally, the figure of the returned white captive coexisted most uneasily with the white woman who chose to remain with her Indian captors and was thus lost to white society, leaving a gap that, despite all efforts, could not be satisfactorily closed.

These multiple figures and the stories or images they inhabit have engaged the ideology of a "white nation" in various ways. Pocahontas's transformation into the Christian Lady Rebecca Rolfe was celebrated because of the ways it symbolized the success of the project of anglicizing America; at the same time, the mimicry of Anglo identity by the anglicized Pocahontas, always almost white, yet not quite, unavoidably highlighted that such an identity was never given, but always made. Thus even in her most eastward-facing guise, the Pocahontas figure in subtle ways unsettled the white identity of the nation by reminding Americans of how contingent that identity was. As Homi Bhabha has pointed out, the "effect of mimicry on the authority of colonial discourse is profound and disturbing" ("Of Mimicry and Man" 126) because "to be Anglicized, is *emphatically* not to be English" (128).

Native women characters (as well as Native men characters) who could not or would not become acculturated as white were sometimes made to accommodate white desires by voluntarily removing themselves, or acquiescing in their removal, from the scene of civilized white society. That their disappearing was represented as their choice obscured the reality that it was Euro-Americans who were insisting on, legislating, and brutally enforcing the westward removal of Indians. These romantic Indian figures, either dying or disappearing into a misty and undefined "elsewhere" in the West, were seen as noble and heroic because their departure left the country to those supposedly destined to possess it, white Euro-Americans. Indians who refused to recognize their fate, who stood firm or fought back, provoked Euro-Americans to exercise, and so forced them to confront, their own capacity for savagery.

The white woman captive was most deeply troubling as the "woman who got away," who was captured but chose to remain with the Indians and refused to return to white society. These women—and there were a number of well-known historical ones—were literally unsettling to white America because of their ineradicable challenges to white identity itself and to assumptions about the superiority of white culture.

In its facing-west posture, then, America also faced a complex task: of making a national character that was both like and not like the Indians,[2] of adopting what were seen as admirable Indian traits that fitted them for living on this "wild" continent, while also ridding the continent of those dark others who were seen as obstructing the westward progress of white civilization. Thus it also continually confronted its own provisionality, the fragility of its claims to being "civilized" and "white" vis-à-vis the Indians.

Carroll Smith-Rosenberg has asked how the textual productions of the new nation could possibly "have affirmed the cohesion of a subject irreconcilably divided between his affinity for a white, cultured Europe and his identification with the savage newness of the American continent" (504). The twinned figures of the white woman captive and Pocahontas were enlisted in the effort to affirm a cohesive American subject, but both also repeatedly dramatized its irreconcilable divisions. The white woman captive situated the American subject's eastward-facing needs and longings yet represented also the impossibility of achieving them. The Pocahontas figure represented the westward-facing ambitions of the new nation but likewise embodied all that would make those ambitions difficult to realize. Together the two figures straddled the line between America's "affinity for a white, cultured Europe" and its "identification with the savage newness of the American continent"; moving back and forth across that line, both figures were recruited to serve the emergence of a white America, yet both also served as constant reminders that such an America never was and could never be.

THE ROMANCE OF LIGHT AND DARK

In her excellent study *Removals: Nineteenth-Century American Literature and the Politics of Indian Affairs* (1991), Lucy Maddox cites an 1833 speech by Rufus Choate, a Massachusetts politician, calling for American historical romances that would "'pour the brightness of noonday over the earth and sky'" and show not only "'the best of everything,'" but also "'a great deal more of which history shows you nothing'" (Choate 341; quoted in Maddox 89). Choate's desire to supplement history with romantic fictions of America's past arose not only from the perceived need for an indigenous American culture, but also from the desire to obscure the unpleasant facts of the nation's colonial past and so to construct a national identity founded on pride rather than shame and remorse. As Maddox says, such romantic fictions

> could perform a valuable service to the country by giving the reading public both a body of indigenous literature . . . and, at the same time, a new version of colonial history that might become a source of national pride. The sunlight of romance, Choate suggests, because it reveals only "the best of everything" and deliberately obscures all that "chills, shames, and disgusts us" . . . might help to eliminate the shadowy moral ambiguities and failures that are part of the documented record of colonial history, especially the record of Puritan conflicts with the Indians. (90)

Choate's speech sheds interesting light on the burgeoning of American Romanticism as a literary movement; it was also calling for an effort that was by 1833 already well underway. And the "light"/"dark," "sunlight"/"shadow" dichotomy he uses had, I believe, specific implications related to but exceeding those of whitewashing the often bitter realities of the nation's past. Toni Morrison has called nineteenth-century America's fascination with romance "the head-on encounter with very real, pressing historical forces and the contradictions inherent in them" (36), and goes on to say, "Romance offered writers not less but more; not a narrow a-historical canvas but a wide historical one; not escape but entanglement. For young America it had everything: nature as subject matter, a system of symbolism, a thematics of the search for self-valorization and validation . . . —and terror's most significant, overweening ingredient: darkness, with all the connotative value it awakened" (37).

The dramatic contrast of "light" and "dark," I believe, can best be understood as part of a textual and visual metaphorizing of racial identities pervasive in American popular literature and art of the nineteenth century. I read Choate's speech, then, as a call for historical fictions that would serve the political desires of white Anglo-Americans.

In Rowlandson's narrative, her descriptions of the darkness of her captors represent less a perceived racial difference than a profound cultural and spiritual one. The axes of difference between English and Indians in Rowlandson, as in seventeenth-century colonial culture generally, were Christian/heathen and civilized/savage. By the early nineteenth century, though, the critical racial questions facing the emergent nation had shifted the axis of difference, and light/dark acquired specific new meanings in popular texts and visual art representing encounters between whites and Indians.

One index of that shift is that Indians became significantly darker in visual representations during the nineteenth century than they typically had been in those of earlier eras. That visual difference reflected and reinforced white beliefs in profound and unchangeable racial difference that provided a rationale for the systematic and violent removals of Indians ever farther westward and into near-oblivion.

An example of the noticeable darkening of Indians is found in a nineteenth-century version of the "massacre" of 1622 in the Virginia colony led by Pocahontas's kinsman Opechancanough (figure 4). The drawing demonstrates the nineteenth-century proclivity for addressing the problems of the present by revisiting—and revising—the past. A dark Indian in the foreground kneels, upraised knife in hand, above a supine white man; in the background, the white woman kneeling before the door of the cabin clutches her child to her breast and extends a defending arm toward the two dark Indians who aim spear and tomahawk at the mother and child. The contrast in skin color between the colonial family and the attacking Indians is dramatic, and it both expresses and encourages white Americans' growing convictions that Indians belonged with Blacks in the category of dark racial others.[3] The imminent murder of the white family in the drawing also provides an alibi for continuing violent white "resistance" to Indian "aggression" in the nineteenth century.

By comparison, John White's drawings and watercolors of the coastal Algonkians of Virginia done in the late sixteenth century (in Hulton)—a

FIGURE 4. "A lurid nineteenth-century version of Opechancanough's warriors falling on Virginia colonists in 1622" (Josephy 205). Courtesy of the Library of Virginia.

time much closer to the historical event of the attack—depict them as much lighter, in fact, very little different in color from Englishmen, and so illustrate the beliefs common in the early colonial period that the "Americans" (unlike Africans) were of the same human family as Europeans. The nineteenth-century representations of stark racial difference— occasions when "light" met "dark" and mutually reinforced each other— not only furthered the construction of racial categories and hierarchies but also helped to anchor Anglo-American identity in its English past; at the same time they both encouraged and excused the aggressive seizure of territories occupied by Indians, now often constructed as "dark and murderous" and irreconcilably different.

Pocahontas was useful to the complex task of sustaining Anglo-America's identification with the civilized and white culture of England while at the same time separating and distinguishing itself from that culture because she could be made to serve both missions. She could be, and often was, rendered as the very type of English womanhood of the age of sensibility, but at the same time she was also portrayed as a uniquely American type, a woman of the American wilderness and an embodiment of the Indian princess who, as E. McClung Fleming demonstrates, had taken over from the earlier, more formidable Indian queen as the visual emblem of America. In highlighting the process by which an "American" woman had become English, the mythic version of her story helped to facilitate the process by which English men and women could become Americans.

But the image of the white woman captured by Indians, partner to the Pocahontas myth in the production of racial difference, shadowed the success story of the Indian Englishwoman. If Pocahontas could "become English," then the white captive could "become Indian," raising the spectre of the ease with which Englishness could be erased or abandoned and making uncomfortably visible the tenuousness of identity for English people translated to America.

While Pocahontas's adoption of some of the markers of English identity—language, name, costume, religion—could be and was celebrated in the many mythic versions of her story as an acknowledgement of the desirability of English identity, it also repeatedly insisted on that identity as constructed—an insistence that in turn heightened anxiety about the white captive's "going Native." If an American Indian woman could become English, or an Englishwoman could become Indian, then what did "being English" or "being Indian" mean? And if those opposing identities were reciprocally constructed, what became of the difference, both cultural and racial, in which territorial and racial politics were grounded?

The trajectories of identity for both Pocahontas and the white captive, therefore, in which the markers of English identity were assumed by the colonized Native or shed by her white counterpart, instated an inevitable hybridity into the history of Anglo-America.[4] That hybridity elicited the numerous nineteenth-century mythohistorical texts addressing the two figures and the questions they raised. To counter the destabilizing effects on white identity resulting from expanding global colonialism, it also elicited, in Europe as well as the United States, the essentialized "scientific" or "biological" explanation of racial difference that emerged during the nineteenth century. Choate's plea for "sunlit" American romances, and those romances themselves, can be read as engaging that discomfiting historical hybridity in America, as expressing the desire to secure an identity protecting the white colonizer and his heirs while addressing, in ways favorable to Anglo-America, the questions its hybridized history raised about the integrity of that identity. By the time of Choate's speech, texts using the figures of the Native-English or "white Indian" woman had long been engaged in that cultural work.

The first popularizer of the Pocahontas myth for American audiences was John Davis, an English traveler and adventurer who wandered through the infant nation on two separate visits in the late 1700s and early 1800s. His historical romance *Captain Smith and Pocahontas*, a fictionalized, intensely sentimental, even quasi-pornographic version of Pocahontas's history, was published in 1805.[5] It appeared the same year Lewis and Clark completed their historic expedition and less than thirty years after the Declaration of Independence and the conclusion of the Revolutionary War, when the new nation needed a history and national mythology that would allow it to identify itself both as the rightful heir of English colonialism and as a separate nation in its own right—and in its own *write*, for the process of creating the nation was as much textual as it was political. Davis's romance met those needs by engaging the questions of race, gender, and identity that the Indian "problem" as well as the institution of slavery persistently provoked for white Americans.

Boasting the compliments of no less a supporter than Pres. Thomas Jefferson on its "Testimonies" page, Davis's romance exploited both aspects of America's Janus-faced struggle for identity. It confirmed the dreams of an American nation that incorporated all it valued of English culture and tradition, while at the same time it allowed that nation to claim a place for itself on the new continent where, as Davis says, they had been "received kindly" by the Indians, who had given them "as much land as they wanted" (21). Despite that kind reception, Davis's colonists constantly fear "the barbarity of the natives" (21). When Smith is captured and taken to the Powhatan village, however, their "barbarity" is momentarily transformed into rapt attention to his "whiteness," in contrast to the "redness" of those who surround him: "[U]nspeakable was the astonishment of the women and children on beholding the prisoner, who was so unlike any human being they had ever before seen. They gazed in speechless wonder at him; some clasping their hands in dumb admiration; some contrasting the redness of their own colour with the whiteness of his" (34).

When Smith is brought before Powhatan, he cuts an impressive figure; he is the picture of "graceful manliness" and resembles "the Belvidere Apollo" (44). The classical image is not accidental; as the American Apollo, Smith is meant to be the bearer of the "light" of white Christian civilization into the "darkness" of the forest wilderness, peopled by dark-skinned Indians. The Apollonian image works powerfully on one onlooker, the young Pocahontas, "who could not conceal those soft emotions of which the female bosom is so susceptible" (44).

If Smith is the very image of the American Apollo, Pocahontas herself comes close to being an American Aphrodite. Describing her as not quite "so beautiful as Venus" (45), Davis puts Pocahontas in her familiar position of almost (but not quite) white, just as she is here almost (but not quite) Venus. She is nevertheless "of a delicate form, but admirably proportioned," with "fine, dark eyes." There is "a delicious redness to her cherub lips, a red a little riper than that which burnt on her cheek, and the nether one somewhat fully [fuller?] than the other, looked as if some bee had newly stung it. Her long black hair emulated in colour the glossy plumage of the eagle, and . . . flowed in luxuriant tresses down her comely back and neck, half concealing the polish and symmetry, the rise and fall, of a bosom just beginning to fill" (45–46).

Davis's text is obsessively preoccupied with the "female bosom," especially Pocahontas's, so much so that it threatens to become a character in its own right. Davis describes how Pocahontas's hair would sometimes "riot down her comely neck and shoulders, shading, but not hiding the protuberance of her bosom" (48; Disney's cartoon Pocahontas, with her masses of riotous hair and her exaggerated breasts, clearly owes much to Davis's version). Situating so much attention in the "female bosom" is one of the ways the novel exhibits its affinities with the emergent cult of "feeling" that gave rise to sentimental literature in America, of which Davis's novel is an early example. The focus on Pocahontas's "bosom" not only renders her an object of sexual desire, but also centers the reader's attention on the seat of her affections, highlighting the place where her love for the white men ignites and burns.

Davis's Pocahontas is, in a phrase, the Harlequin Romance heroine of the day—perhaps even the *Playboy* centerfold. His descriptions of her have proved remarkably tenacious, as Disney's Pocahontas demonstrates: Dozens of subsequent writers and artists equally devoted to trite description have continued to hold her captive within these flaccid tropes of sentimental beauty and ready if vapid sexuality. The gaze caressing Pocahontas here is the reader's, and not Smith's; he is indifferent to the beauty of the Indian maiden and loves only the country she symbolizes and the colony that, as the novel has it, he founded. The (white) reader, however, is encouraged to experience the attraction to which Smith seems immune and so to enjoy the pleasure and the power residing in the colonizing gaze.[6] Davis is explicit, though, that Pocahontas saves Smith's life out of *her* instant love for *him*, and there in the Indian longhouse, with the lovely girl's dark head bent over that of the white Apollo, "every heart melted into tenderness at the scene" (47).

Nor is it only Indian women whom Davis portrays as susceptible to fits of immediate passionate affection for the white hero. When Pocahontas's brother, Nantaquas, returns to the village and hears from her the story of her saving Smith, having first "embraced his sister for her sensibility," he "falls on [Smith's] neck with mingled rapture and admiration" (51–52). Nantaquas pleads with Powhatan to release Smith from captivity in words that vaguely echo Patrick Henry's: "Life without liberty is only a burden! . . . He wants only a little ground; you can easily spare it" (52). Foolish Nantaquas, not to realize how quickly the desire for "a little ground" would grow to a demand for all there is. But he continues to have faith in Smith, nobly resisting the evil impulses of other, unregenerate (and cannibalistic) Indians who urge an attack on the white invaders: "Let's take their scalps, drink their blood, and roast them alive," says one (59).

When Smith departs for England, he clears his reputation by declaring that he "never dropped the slightest hint about marriage" to Pocahontas, and he tells the remaining colonists to tell her he is dead, "to cure her of her passion" (87). She grieves unspeakably, "weeping along the banks of the river," her hair "deshevelled" (88). Enter Rolfe, who assuages his own acute loneliness for Smith with Pocahontas's company. Appropriately enough for the man who steps into Smith's shoes, and who is newly in love with this emblem of the continent he is hoping and helping to conquer, "the breast of Rolfe yielded to the *empire* of his passions" for Pocahontas (91; emphasis mine). When he finds her in the forest "strewing flowers over the imaginary grave of captain Smith" (92–93), she is so surprised and frightened at being detected that she faints into his arms: "He clasped the Indian maiden to his beating heart, and drank from her lips the poison of delight"; her (necessary) response is "tenderness rather than anger" (93). That response prompts an author's footnote, where Davis quotes Rochefaucault: "The female bosom is never more susceptible of a new passion, than when it is agitated by the remains of a former one" (93–94 n).

For the bereft America, apparently any old conqueror will do, and Rolfe presses his suit in this fortuitous situation: "[H]is tender embrace soon quelled her fugitive terrors" as he "encircl[ed] with his arm her unrobed, but pure form" (94). No explanation is offered for her sudden nakedness, though it signifies both her savage state and her symbolic alignment with an open and vulnerable—and pure, that is, virginal—landscape. Pocahontas, as the script demands, responds to Rolfe's embrace: "a languishing look, half concealed under the shadow of her long eye-lashes, discovered what her lips withheld, that she had been wooed by a new lover only to be won!" (95).

After their wedding, Rolfe and Pocahontas consummate the marriage, appropriately enough, in the out-of-doors, since what is being enacted is really the consummation of the "marriage" of English colonialism, in the person of Rolfe, with the countryside itself.[7] As Davis describes the scene, the features of the landscape seem to be a thinly veiled description of sexual anatomy and activity: "Sacredly private was the first intercourse of their mutual fondness. Superb forests, towering cypresses, venerable oaks, stately pines waving the long moss floating from your branches, mountains on whose summits repose the hovering clouds; rivers obstructed by cataracts, and rolling in silent majesty your streams; expanded and sublime nature! you alone were conscious of the conjugal endearments of the youthful pair" (102–3). Davis's novel established the sentimental tradition for representing Pocahontas in literature,[8] and the Pocahontas he created has been repeated, with minor variations on the theme, again and again in the succeeding two centuries, up to and including the recent Disney film.

What is particularly noteworthy about Davis's novel—and why it is worth wading through the predictable prose to identify it—is the ideological work of racialization the story performs, not despite but precisely through its eroticizing of Pocahontas, expressed in sentimental language situated in the realm of feeling, where racism often does its work. For Davis too, Pocahontas is the American continent itself—luscious and irresistible, and even better, eager to be "taken" by the white settlers who are gentlemen and heroes, taking up arms against the Indians only when provoked and demanding no more in the way of land and love than they somehow believe themselves fully entitled to.

And it is explicitly Smith's *whiteness* that both Pocahontas and Nantaquas respond to with such passionate emotion, a whiteness that, as the passage quoted above makes clear, emerges in contrast to the redness of the Indians, which in turn is produced reciprocally in contrast to Smith's whiteness. The scene calls racial difference into being and installs it in the textual universe of the novel, which then perpetrates rather than interrogates the effects of that racial difference. The emphasis on Smith's white skin (source and symbol of the "light" this American Apollo brings into the wilderness) and its power to charm susceptible Native women and men served the evolving discourses of race in America, coupled with a growing sense of a gendered and white national identity, as the racial politics of the nineteenth century were taking shape. Davis's treatment of the Pocahontas story confirmed the utility of similarly mythohistorical and sentimental literature in asserting and maintaining the supremacy of the white race at home in the new America.

Jefferson's endorsement of Davis's novel is not surprising, given that Jefferson himself in 1792 had indicated that he saw the United States as a white nation, like those of Europe. Richard Drinnon quotes from Jefferson's notes of a conversation Jefferson, as secretary of state, had with a minister from England on the legal rights of the United States "in Indian soil." Jefferson stated his conviction "'that a *white nation* settling down and declaring that such and such are their limits, makes an invasion of those limits by any other *white nation* an act of war, but gives no right of soil against the native possessors'" (quoted in Drinnon 81–82; emphasis mine). If we unravel the links between whiteness and power in the passage, it is clear that the second follows from the first—and that for Jefferson, as for so many of his compatriots before and after, white meant right(s).

Jefferson was not the only "founding father" to articulate an explicit vision of a white America. Winthrop Jordan quotes a passage from Benjamin Franklin's *Observations Concerning the Increase of Mankind* (1751) to point out that Franklin too cherished that ideal: he "was convinced that America should belong to the 'White People'" and asked, "'Why increase the Sons of Africa, by Planting them in America, where we have so fair an Opportunity, by excluding all Blacks and Tawneys, of increasing the lovely White and Red?'" (Jordan 143).[9]

The lapses and contradictions in Jefferson's attitudes on race (he was both a slaveowner and an opponent of the institution of slavery) are indicative of the shifting nature of racial discourses in the United States in the late eighteenth and early nineteenth centuries, with conflicts and contradictions that would eventually produce the abolitionist and pro-Indian movements as well as the pro-slavery Southern Confederacy and the effort to exterminate Indians and their cultures. Both Jordan and Tilton have addressed the contradictions that were evident, for example, in Jefferson's attitudes toward racial mixing of Indians and whites.[10] On the one hand, Jefferson seemed to sanction intermarriage as a means of forging a distinctive "American" population, as in 1808 when he said to a party of Indians visiting Washington, "you will mix with us by marriage, your blood will run in our veins, and will spread with us over this great island" (quoted in Tilton 24). But, as Tilton points out, "The ultimate result of such a mixture . . . would be the creation of a white, landowning race, the members of which would possess an Indian presence 'in the blood,' and perhaps even certain attractive Indian character traits, but would for all intents and purposes be Caucasian. The Enlightenment fantasy of absorption would actually be nothing less than a quiet genocide of the native population" (25).

If Pocahontas was to serve as the symbol of a white America, it was not sufficient for her simply to love whiteness; in a gesture corresponding to rendering other Indians dark, she herself had to be "whitened"— positioned at the margins of the group of dark Indians and made more closely to resemble whites in order to secure her alliance with them. This mask of whiteness, along with the redness of Indians in general, simultaneously served the discourses of racial distinctness and preserved her image as a founding heroine of the nation. In Joseph Croswell's 1802 verse drama *A New World Planted*, for example, an Indian heroine named Pocahonta, modeled on Pocahontas,[11] is described this way: "I know she's browner than European dames, / But whiter far, than other natives are" (quoted in Mossiker 178).

The "exceptional" Pocahontas was a discursive fulcrum for claims of racial difference in a number of texts throughout the century. The first of several stage dramas reworking the Pocahontas story, James Nelson Barker's *The Indian Princess; or, La Belle Sauvage* (1808), uses Pocahontas as a "good" Indian to emphasize the positive aspects of the American individual's independence from "the mass of population / That rots in stagnant Europe" (580). Celebrating America's "free atmosphere and ample range" where "man, erect, can walk a manly round" (580), the play constructs a masculinized (even "erect") and individualized American subject to contrast with Europe's "rotting masses." And a heroic Pocahontas is herself excerpted from the Indian "masses," who are "red rogues" with "coppery skins" (582), "dingy devils" with "darken'd minds" (608).

Similarly, the sentimental poet Lydia Sigourney in her poem "Pocahontas" (1841) called her "the savior of the Saxon vine" (9) that England had planted in Virginia. Saving and serving those Sigourney calls the "lily-handed youths" (3)—the ones with the *mandate* for white conquest—was for Sigourney, as for so many others, the source and sign of Pocahontas's heroic character that suited her for her role as founding mother. "Dark" Indians might have to be erased from the text of the nation, but the "Saxon vine" had to be tended and made to flourish, and Pocahontas was just the one to do it. The need to distinguish Pocahontas from other Indians and to render her near-white, firmly allied with white colonists' project of "planting" themselves in North America, was an ongoing one, however, because her hybridity meant that such an alliance could never be fully and finally accomplished—her constructed whiteness could only mask, and never eradicate, her Native identity.

Pocahontas's mythic approximations to whiteness was thus a long-lived distinction; many of the numerous nineteenth-century paintings of her (see Rasmussen and Tilton 15–47) also render her lighter in skin color than other Indians. Some, like Christian Inger's 1870 lithograph *Smith Rescued by Pocahontas* (Rasmussen and Tilton 16), make her so light-skinned as to be virtually indistinguishable from the English, in contrast to the darker Indians usually occupying the periphery—and make her thus more useful to the ideology of white dominance in America.

A representational pattern, then, emerged early in the century and persisted through and beyond it, of the heroic near-white Native woman or the vulnerable captive white woman, both visibly light against a ground of dark savagery. Joel Barlow's nationalist epic poem of America, *The Columbiad* (1807), used both figures in articulating a glorified history and prospect for the nation. That it seemed important to Barlow to include both in a "patriotic poem" whose "subject is national and historical" (preface, 375) indicates how bound into the fabric of the new nation these figures and their stories were felt to be. Despite Barlow's declaration that he wants his epic, unlike those of Homer and Virgil, to "discountenance the deleterious passion for violence and war" (preface, 382), his figure of the peace-loving (white) citizen of the republic depends for delineation and definition on a ground of undifferentiated dark Indians, savage and bloodthirsty, who must yield their place on the continent to the "race predestined" to "Plant here their arts and rear their vigorous race" (447). Barlow's "swarthy people" (454) are themselves anything but peace-loving; rather, they are aggressive and cannibalistic: "Crowds of war painted chiefs, athirst for gore / Beat their own breasts and tone their hideous roar; / . . . Their captives torture, butcher for their food / Suck the warm veins and grime their cheeks with blood" (454).

"Blest Pocahontas," though, is again an exception, and the poem promises her a reward for her courageous protection of the white "hero": "[T]hine shall be his friends, his heart, his name / His camp shall shout, his nation boast thy fame" (540). In portraying her as saving her English hero, Barlow separates Pocahontas from her natal group of "swarthy people" and makes her an honorary member of the white nation that will arise from his presence. At the same time, the rest of the Indians are banished from the human race altogether: "No power can tame them and no arts refine; / Can these be fashioned on the social plan, / Or boast a lineage with the race of man?" (454).

Barlow's poem exploits the emerging light/dark dichotomy to articulate racial differences between white Anglo-Americans and swarthy Indians with his use of both the Pocahontas legend and a fictionalized story of a white woman captured by Indians. His "Lucinda" is based on Jane McCrea, a young white woman who lived with her pro-Independence brother in northern New York during the Revolutionary War. McCrea, in love with a Tory soldier, ran away from her brother's house to meet her lover and marry him but on her way was captured and killed by Indians allied with the British troops.

In the poem, Lucinda is seized en route to her lover by two Mohawks who murder her for the bounty the British pay for patriot scalps (making the British, like the English colonials in the Hannah Dustan story, the instigator of the practice of scalping). In her posture as victim, Lucinda is a pathetic figure fusing whiteness and female sexual vulnerability: she "Spreads her *white* hands to heaven in frantic prayer, / Then runs to grasp their knees and crouches there. / Her hair, half lost along the shrubs she past, / Rolls in loose tangles round her lovely waist; / Her kerchief torn betrays the *globes of snow* / That heave responsive to her weight of woe" (635; emphasis mine). *The Columbiad* reveals the discursive differential in treatments of Pocahontas and the white captive: Pocahontas *falls in love* with her captors, but Lucinda/Jane *falls prey* to hers.

Barlow commissioned John Vanderlyn[12] to paint *The Death of Jane McCrea* (1804) as one of the illustrations to accompany *The Columbiad* (Namias 133); the painting became more popular than the poem and inspired a great number of other accounts of McCrea and her fate (Namias 119–44). Vanderlyn's painting (figure 5) resembles the scene from Davis in which Smith is brought before Powhatan to be threatened with death: in the painting, however, the genders are reversed, and it is a white woman who is about to be killed by dark savages. For McCrea, unlike Smith, no exceptional Indian savior is in sight; according to the ideology of captivity already established by the time Vanderlyn was working, Indian women can and must love Englishmen in order to consolidate the colonial project, but white women must be inviolate. In the painting, her imminent "penetration" by the Indians' phallic weapons can be read as a coded sexual violation—a reading invited by her long, tangled hair and her exposed and gleaming "globes of snow"—and therefore as an important stimulus of the outrage the painting stirred. The McCrea of the painting is a martyr to the cause of an emerging white American nation, a figure to inspire hatred among her fellow Americans toward both Indians and the British, whose allies her murderers were. Her image and story thus helped to position the identity of the new Americans between those two cultural-racial groups but distinct from both.

The painting replicates in the figure of McCrea the dazzling whiteness that in Davis's novel so astonishes the Indians when they look at Smith; triangulated with her two dark Indian assailants against the backdrop of an even darker forest wilderness, Jane's figure is the dramatic highlight of the picture as, arms extended and hair pulled back, she offers her gleaming white face and breasts to the viewer. The painting is a visual representation of how "whiteness," here as in other renditions of captivity represented by a victimized woman, emerges against a ground of "darkness"—the Indians and their untamed wilderness home—that threatens to overwhelm it. For white viewers, the painting was an emblem of the vulnerability of Anglo-American culture and therefore of the need to defend it, with violence if necessary. Richard Drinnon claims that the Vanderlyn painting "helped set the pattern for an endless series of pictorial indictments of Jefferson's 'merciless Indian Savages.' Always

FIGURE 5. John Vanderlyn, *The Death of Jane McCrea*. 1804. The Wadsworth Atheneum, Hartford, Connecticut. Purchased by the Wadsworth Atheneum.

the epic contrast was between dusky evil and fair innocence, between maddened red cruelty and helpless white virtue" (101).

June Namias points out the potentially subversive element in Jane's story: She challenges patriarchal authority when she defies her brother by running away to marry her lover and so exhibits a female independence almost as threatening to the Anglo-American social order as Indians themselves (120). Her kneeling posture in the Vanderlyn painting suggests that such independence has literally been brought low; at the same time, her Indian assailants are configured to elicit from white male viewers a racial and sexual animosity the fair female victim instigates. The painting thus offered a rich occasion for white male Anglo-American viewers to consolidate their identity against these two negative others, savage Indians and women resistant to patriarchal control.

As Vanderlyn's painting makes plain, though, whiteness was always the fundamental issue, and a sexualized femininity was the device used to bring it literally to light. In those texts that figure a white woman captive who does not return, for example, the "lost" woman's whiteness is insistently emphasized in their "Indian" names. Faith Leslie in Sedgwick's *Hope Leslie* (1827) is referred to as her husband Oneco's "white bird," and Oneco's sister Magawisca calls Faith the "lily of the Maqua's valley" (188). Ruth, the "Wept of Wish-Ton-Wish" in James Fenimore Cooper's 1829 novel of the same name, becomes Narra-mattah, or "the driven snow" (327), and Lydia Sigourney's 1846 poem about a woman captive who remains with the Indians (based on the Frances Slocum story) is entitled "The Lost Lily." These texts repeatedly insist on the desirability of whiteness by making it the source and sign of both the captive women's being cherished by their Indian husbands and white culture's grief over their loss. Above all and always, their whiteness is dramatically visible.

The insistent whiteness of the figure of the captive woman reached its apotheosis in the cold marble pallor of mid-nineteenth century sculptures like Erastus Dow Palmer's immensely popular nude, *The White Captive* (1859; in Kasson 75), and Joseph Mozier's *The Wept of Wish-Ton-Wish* (also 1859; in Kasson 95). When *The White Captive* was first exhibited, one reviewer described it as "'illustrat[ing] the power and inevitable victory of Christian civilization'" (Henry Tuckerman in 1859; quoted in Kasson 81). Such representations of beseiged white femininity seem to have offered mid-nineteenth-century white Americans a way to figure *themselves* as victims in a racialized contest—instead of the other way around—and to convince themselves that they must and would ultimately triumph, by whatever means necessary, over their racialized others.

Mozier's *Pocahontas* (1859; in Kasson 94) is also frozen in white marble, like her white captive counterparts; her whiteness here signifies her near-complete enclosure within white culture. As in so many visual representations of her, one breast is bared; she holds a cross in her hand and ponders it in a stance of arrested motion. Joy Kasson suggests that the sculpture would have carried a reassuring message to its contemporary white viewers: "Knowledge of history assures the viewer that the young girl will indeed choose to make the transition from her culture to that of the white Christian newcomers; furthermore, her choice will be motivated by love as well as religion. . . . [and] the young girl will accept, even welcome, her transformation" (93).

By the time John Esten Cooke wrote *My Lady Pokahontas* in 1885, that discursive transformation, and Pocahontas's assimilation into sentimental white culture, seem to have been fully accomplished; virtually no trace of her Indian identity remains. Cooke's story indulges in the romance, by then familiar, of thwarted love between Pocahontas and Smith, and at crucial moments in the romance the "Lady Pokahontas," to show the depth of her feeling, turns "a little white" (167), "as white as her smock" (168), or even "so white" that she appears about to faint (187). Cooke's Pocahontas is the American Miranda, heroine of the brave new world of America; he even has her attending a performance of *The Tempest* in London and brings in Will Shakespeare as a character to acknowledge that "he hath figured her [Pocahontas] in his *Miranda*, that is, *one to be wondered at*" (173). The "Lady Pokahontas" is, therefore, not only happily received in England, but, going well beyond the popular nineteenth-century plea for an indigenous American literature independent of Europe for its inspiration, Cooke makes her the American subject that inspires the English writer most revered by Americans in the nineteenth century.

Cooke's Pocahontas is a sappy girl who spends most of her time turning pale, lisping, blushing, weeping and sobbing, mostly over her "lost love," John Smith. She is a prototypical nineteenth-century sentimental heroine with impossibly tiny feet and with a Victorian modesty that keeps her constantly covered up to her chin and down to her ankles, albeit with robes lined with turkey feathers. The image is not only a dramatic change from William Strachey's description of the young Pocahontas turning cartwheels, "naked as she was, all the fort over," but also serves as a measure of the distance Pocahontas as symbol of the American continent had traveled in the eighty years since Davis's novel in 1805. For Davis, writing in the early years of the republic, Pocahontas-as-America needed to be naked and vulnerable in order to facilitate her being "taken" by English colonialism and its successor, the new Anglo-American nation. By the late nineteenth century, the "taking" was mostly accomplished, and "America" needed only the protective covering of Victorian dress to keep her white Anglo-American identity secure. The total coverage of Victorian dress in Cooke's novel also serves to conceal almost all of Pocahontas's skin, and so her racial difference; thus it is part of the white mask American writers had constructed for her through the nineteenth century.

The Pocahontas myth's usefulness in the ideological construction of a white America did not end with the nineteenth century. In 1912 her "white" identity was again addressed—and this time literalized—in Edson Kenny Odell's *The Romance of Pocahontas*. Odell not only contradicts the early Virginia historians on the subject of Pocahontas's virginity in a footnote aside declaring her marriage to Kocuom "hardly probable" (99 n); in another footnote, he raises the question of her "real" racial identity: "As to who the mother of Pocahontas was, and whether or not Pocahontas was a full-blooded Indian, there is a difference of opinion" (18 n). The "pale-face" are described as "her true brothers" (66), and Smith puzzles over her beauty, apparently inexplicable in a "full-blooded" Indian woman, as well as over her instant attraction to the whites who settle in her country:

Much [Smith] wondered at her profile,
Brow of marble curved so comely,
Nose of likeness to the white race,
Near the lines of perfect beauty.
        Could she be but Indian offspring?
Or was there a hidden secret,
Of the fountain of her being,
To account for her strange beauty
And her fondness for the white race?
(69)

The "hidden secret" is not long in revealing itself: White women from Roanoke's Lost Colony were captured and adopted and bore children to Indian men, of whom Pocahontas was one (69–70). Pocahontas's beauty, then, along with her noble character and her fondness for the English, is ascribed to the prevailing influence of her own "white blood."

Odell not only borrows the tedious metrics of Longfellow's *Hiawatha* (a relentless trochaic tetrameter) but resituates the heroic Indian antecedents of the nation celebrated in that poem to the South, as his prologue makes clear by setting the scene in "that blest of happy Southlands, / Formed by God for his dear children" (13). Odell's poem, written in the wake of the Civil War and Reconstruction when Jim Crow laws were governing race relations in the South, expresses a residual Southern nationalism and takes its part in the contention between North and South as to just which was the scene of origin for America. His insistence on Pocahontas's hitherto hidden white identity is necessitated by white supremacist views prevailing in the South at that time, which required that the guardian angel of Southern culture have a legitimate claim to "white blood." For Odell, loving whites and rescuing them were alone clearly insufficient as a foundation for Pocahontas's heroic status.

Identifying Pocahontas's mother as a white woman who was captured by Indians, but whose full story is not or cannot be told, creates a narrative pre-text or subtext of white women's captivity for the Pocahontas story Odell rewrites in his poem, as well as a "biological" explanation for the racial oscillations the Pocahontas figure had for centuries been made to perform. And once again the pairing of the two figures, Pocahontas and the white woman captive—this time made a literal kinship—comes into view in a text that captures them both to articulate and essentialize racial difference for contemporary purposes.

These visual and verbal representations of eroticized Pocahontas and white women captive figures were important players in establishing a vocabulary of racial difference in the young republic. They were repeatedly invoked to articulate a made-to-order history, one that would secure the privileged identity of a white America and further its politics around issues of race. Together they not only offered a version of America's origins that positioned whites in a "sunlit" center stage, but, by obscuring the actual past and current treatment of Native people, helped to facilitate an ongoing holocaust, the extermination of American Indians and their way of life, that such stories served so well to deny.[13] The ways these texts articulated a racial hierarchy explicitly furthered the claims of white Euro-Americans to the position of political and cultural dominance over their racial others, Black and Indian, in shaping the new nation.

THE EROTICS OF CAPTIVE BODIES

In chapters 1 and 2, I have described how both the white woman captive and Pocahontas were eroticized during the colonial era, with differing agendas and effects. From Davis and Barlow on through the nineteenth and twentieth centuries, the narrative eroticizing of both figures continued, and their sexualized bodies were deployed in ways that served the specific agendas of racialization in the young republic. These eroticized bodies make visible how deeply race and sexuality were implicated each in the other, and how the two figures, assigned the cultural work of "race-ing" the nation, converged as well as differed through the nineteenth century and beyond to help produce what Toni Morrison calls our contemporary "genderized, sexualized, wholly racialized world" (4).

As in the discourses of discovery that gendered the new world as feminine, the erotic potential of the symbolic woman provided a site for the citizen of the new American republic to consolidate an identity now more explicitly dependent on race as well as gender. The symbolic woman, however, both Native and white, also threatened to unsettle that racialized and gendered identity if her erotic potential and energies were not contained. A set of narrative and visual strategies displayed, exploited, and controlled the erotic possibilities of both the Indian princess and the white woman captive: nakedness, exposed and heaving breasts, arms extended or bound, loosened and riotous hair, kneeling or bowing postures are deployed again and again and register a crucial differential in the ways the two eroticized figures served an emerging white national identity.[14] The "heaving bosoms" of Pocahontas in the Davis romance and Lucinda in *The Columbiad* illustrate that differential: In Davis's romance, Pocahontas's signifies her ardor for a white lover, thus the validating welcome the white colonists received from the Indians; in *The Columbiad*,

Lucinda's signifies her terror and woe as she faces imminent violation by the weapons of her Mohawk attackers, thus the danger that Indians represent to white settlement of the continent. Other deployments of the eroticized bodies of Native women and white captives operate within a similar differential.

The nakedness of Native women was one of the stock tropes in both textual and visual representations in the nineteenth century, as it had been from the earliest period of New World exploration. Most paintings and sculptures of Native women in the nineteenth century feature bare breasts, as in William Powell's *Discovery of the Mississippi by de Soto* (1855), in which two bare-breasted Native women help to construct the differences between the two cultures, European and Native, that meet in the picture; they also signify once again the openness and vulnerability of the American landscape to exploration, penetration, and possession.

Powell's painting hangs in the Rotunda of the U.S. Capitol directly opposite John Gadsby Chapman's *The Baptism of Pocahontas at Jamestown, Virginia* (1840); the nearly naked Native women in the Powell painting contrast dramatically with the docile figure of the kneeling and supplicant Pocahontas, here being transformed into "Rebecca"; she of course is fully clothed in English style, in a flowing white dress, with her long dark hair bound at the nape to flow down her back. Pocahontas's dress, coiffure, clasped hands, kneeling posture, and bowed head in the Chapman painting signify her acquiescence to her abandoning of Native identity and her adoption of, and by, white Anglo-American culture, which celebrates its triumph over savagism with this image.

The vulnerability of the captive white woman's nakedness, by contrast, signifies the violence of dark savagery against her person. Her nakedness is always the result of her clothing having been torn from her by force, as in Palmer's sculpture *The White Captive* or Lucinda's "kerchief torn" revealing her snowy breasts in *The Columbiad*. Stripping the captive woman or ripping off her clothing is as much a stock trope in captivity tales, including those of the twentieth century, as is the habitual nakedness of Native women in representations of the nineteenth century and earlier. In the 1947 film *Unconquered*, set in the years just before the Revolutionary War, one scene echoes as well as caricatures the nineteenth-century figurations of the suffering white woman captive: Abby (Paulette

Goddard), the captive of an intransigently savage Indian chief (Boris Karloff), is tied to the stake, arms stretched above her head and bound at the wrists; her dress has been stripped away, and she wears only a torn white chemise that accentuates the curve of her (yes, heaving) breasts as she writhes in fear and anguish, tossing her loosened, long and tousled curls. The sexual danger figured in this scene is underscored in another, when the hero (Gary Cooper) expresses his determination to rescue her by saying darkly, "You've seen what they do to white women!"

The extended arm is another dramatic stock gesture in the nineteenth century (and beyond) in images of both the Native woman and the white woman beseiged by Indians. In the sixteenth-century de Straet engraving (figure 3), the extended arm of "America" can be read as either welcoming the European explorer or attempting to fend him off (though hindsight shows it should have been the latter). By the nineteenth century that image had split and proliferated. The extended arm of the white woman attacked by Indians in a number of representations is a clearly defensive gesture, as in Vanderlyn's *The Death of Jane McCrea* (figure 5) or in the nineteenth-century version of the 1622 Indian attack in Virginia (figure 4). The gesture, however, also opens the victimized, helpless woman to penetration by Indian weapons and so registers her perhaps unwitting, certainly unwilling, vulnerability: Her attempt to defend herself or her children renders her all the more vulnerable.

The extended arm of the Native woman, however, defends and protects not her own life, but that of the white colonists; thus it simultaneously registers her knowing acceptance of her own vulnerability and serves as a bridge connecting her to the colonizers. It is a gesture of willing self-sacrifice, as in so many of the pictorial representations of Pocahontas's rescue of Smith[15] and in Catharine Maria Sedgwick's novel *Hope Leslie* (1827), in which the noble and heroic Indian maiden Magawisca intervenes in the imminent execution of a captive white youth whom she loves by staying the blows of her father's warriors with her extended arm; the arm is severed, but the captive boy escapes.[16]

Eroticizing the bodies of these paired figures, of course, meant raising the possibility of interracial union, and a number of texts in both the nineteenth and twentieth centuries took up that vexed subject. The ambivalences and contradictions that pervaded the issue of racial mixing in the colonial and early national period are plain, for example, in Rolfe's letter asking permission to marry Pocahontas, in the antimiscegenation laws passed in the English colonies, and in the writings of Robert Beverley and Thomas Jefferson. Underscoring the equation of women with the land (and calling to mind the Pocahontas-Rolfe marriage) as well as inscribing the desirability of Englishmen, the usual proposal was for white men to marry Indian women. Robert Tilton has pointed out that the possibility of intermarriage between whites and Indians was sometimes seen as a peaceful solution to English desires to displace Indians and occupy their lands. But the issue was typically displaced historically, rendered as either an opportunity lost in the remote past or a possibility for a remote future; the usual attitude was that there "was clearly no room in the present for such a union" (Tilton 3).[17] It was also the case that the usual agenda was the racial absorption of Indians by whites (what Tilton calls a "quiet genocide"), as is plain in the following passage from William Byrd's *History of the Dividing Line* (1738): "[T]he poor Indians would have had less reason to complain that the English took away their land if they received it by way of a portion with their daughters. . . . Nor would the shade of skin have been any reproach at this day, for if a Moor may be washed white in three generations, surely an Indian might have been blanched in two" (quoted in Tilton 19). Such sentiments always coexisted with strong opposing arguments, and by the nineteenth century, those arguing against interracial marriage had for the most part gained the upper hand.

Five books appeared in the 1820s that addressed in varying ways the issue of intermarriage: James Eastburn and Robert Sands's *Yamoyden* (1820), James Seaver's transcribed narrative of the life of Mary Jemison (1824), and three novels, Lydia Maria Child's *Hobomok* (1824), Sedgwick's *Hope Leslie* (1827), and Cooper's *The Wept of Wish-Ton-Wish* (1829). All five stories reverse the prototypical paradigm of English husband and Indian wife by depicting the marriages of white women and Indian men. The gender reversal makes the racial mixing more ideologically charged; the white woman, icon of the racial purity of the nation, had to remain closed to penetration by "dark savages" if the white identity of the country was to be preserved. These texts provided sites for the highly charged erotic encounters of white and Indian to be imagined, played out, and resolved.

The taboo against sexual contact between white women and dark men has historically been one of the most rigid and powerful in American culture, deeply marking our literature, politics, psychosexuality, and social arrangements—the whole extent and fabric of American life. The prohibition was constructed by white men to keep themselves "on top"—to secure their dominance over women of their own racial group and all "other" men; it was the correlative of the assumption of white men's sexual right of access to dark women, Black and Native. The taboo has depended for its force on the assumption of a powerful heterosexual desire for white women on the part of Black and Native men; it has also required the vigorous suppression of any heterosexual desire on the part of white women for men of other racial groups, making such desire literally unspeakable. bell hooks has written of the fundamental power of this taboo:

> Under what conditions did sexuality serve as a force subverting and disrupting power relations, unsettling the oppressor/oppressed paradigm? No one seems to know how to tell this story, where to begin. As historical narrative it was long ago supplanted by the creation of another story (pornographic sexual project, fantasy, fear, the origin has yet to be traced). That story, invented by white men, is about the overwhelming desperate longing black men have to sexually violate the bodies of white women. The central character in this story is the black male rapist. . . . As the story goes, this desire is not based on longing for sexual pleasure. It is a story of revenge, rape as the weapon by which black men, the dominated, reverse their circumstance, regain power over white men. (194)

My argument that Blacks and Indians became exchangeable commodities in the discourses of American racism again requires that I read Native men as included with Black men in the category of "dark others" in whom desire was first assumed and then policed so vigorously. The construction of the Native rapist was, as we have seen, already in evidence in the seventeenth-century context of Rowlandson's narrative and responses to it like Hubbard's and Tompson's. In the 1820s, however, a number of texts addressed the possibility that white women could be attracted to noble Indian men and choose them as romantic and sexual partners.

In 1820, Eastburn and Sands's epic poem, *Yamoyden: A Tale of the Wars of King Philip*, appeared. The marriage of Nora Fitzgerald and Yamoyden is, though a happy union, emblematic of the transgressive nature of such sexual alliances for white Americans. Nora has run away into the forest with Yamoyden, disobeying her father, who refuses to accept their love for each other. That Nora's response to Yamoyden was specifically an erotic one is made plain in her father's ruminations: "In sooth his form was free and bold, / And cast in nature's noblest mold" (125). Nora, her father realizes, succumbed to Yamoyden's "glossy locks," "polished limbs," and "goodly frame" (125)—if not to the "fiendish craft" of "herb and spell" with which Fitzgerald also believes "he won her heart" (128).

The poem continually expresses such deeply conflicted perceptions of Indians as noble on the one hand and diabolical on the other. These contradictions seem less a case of narrative confusion if we read the poem as an instance of the Janus-faced narrative of American national identity, one called upon to forge the colonists' connections with Native people in order to certify their taking of the land without requiring the sacrifice of their identity as white, Christian, and civilized; in that light, the need for the coexistence of both attitudes in the poem becomes clear.

The story is not only of a woman who chooses to leave white society to marry an Indian and bear a "pledge of mixed love" (175); Nora also becomes an Indian captive when, in the Christian Yamoyden's absence from their woodland cottage, she and her infant are seized by a group of hostile Indians. Nora, who has a convenient tendency to lose her wits or her consciousness—but not her capacity to shriek—at moments of crisis, escapes with the help of a warrior who is inspired by her beauty (and who utters this accommodating, and tragically prophetic, couplet: "Beautiful Christian! I would die, / To spare thine heart one heavy sigh!" [228]). Nora is reconciled with her father, who finally forgives the "sinful one" (137), though he is at first more than reluctant to embrace her and echoes the well-known "better dead than living with an Indian" prejudice:

"Oh! I had borne to see thy bloom
Of youth, slow withering o'er its tomb—
　　Had borne to see thy hearse,
Hung with the stainless virgin wreath,
That told thy purity in death.
But thus—from heathen's couch defiled,
Polluted outcast of the wild—
I cannot brook to see my child!"

(136–37)

In a long passage that dramatically conflates Indians and witchcraft, the two forces thought to pose the greatest threat to the success of the Massachusetts colony, the Indians prepare to sacrifice Nora's child, still in their clutches, to the "Power of darkness" (172) in a devilish rite presided over by a ghastly Indian witch (176). Fitzgerald saves the child; Yamoyden in turn saves Fitzgerald from the tomahawk of an Indian warrior, losing his own life in the process. Nora lays herself down beside the mortally wounded Yamoyden and they die clasped together, the only acceptable end for such a doomed alliance, with Fitzgerald promising to raise their son—doubtless securely enclosed within Anglo culture.

The poem gathers all the major popular discourses about Indians and their relations with Anglo-Americans: Indian men desire white women; the proximity to the forest poses a threat to the integrity of whiteness and Anglo civilization; Indians, either noble and proud or savage and diabolical, are fated to die or disappear to make way for the culture of the superior race; and remnant traces of Indian life or "blood"—here, Nora and Yamoyden's son—can and must be fully absorbed into white society.

The conclusion reiterates the romanticized claim that the contest between Native and white was long over, part of a remote history in a distant past—in 1820, very clearly a convenient fiction. And it is an early instance of what would become a persistent literary as well as civic claim, that Indians belonged not in the land of the living present but in the musings of daydreams on the part of whites and in poetry *in English*:

— 182 —

'Tis good to muse on nations passed away,
For ever, from the land we call our own;
Nations, as proud and mighty in their day,
Who deemed that everlasting was their throne.

(254)

The closing lines are addressed in farewell to "Philip":

But in that land whence thy destroyers came,
A sacred bard thy champion shall be found;
He of the laureate wreath for thee shall claim
The hero's honours, to earth's farthest bound
Where Albion's tongue is heard, or Albion's songs resound.

(255)

Cooper's *The Wept of Wish-Ton-Wish* is another dramatic presentation of the devastation resulting from the mixing of races in America and clearly owes a great deal to *Yamoyden*. It too is a fictional account of events on the western Massachusetts frontier during Metacom's Rebellion. The structuring device of the novel is a captivity story, of Ruth, the young daughter of English settlers at the edge of the wilderness who is taken by Indians during an attack on their fortress home; the mother, also Ruth, believing she is rescuing her own child by seizing her and carrying her into the last stronghold of the fortress, discovers to her horror that the child she has saved is her foster daughter—the one she thought she was abandoning to the Indians—and thus that little Ruth, she of the flaxen hair, snowy skin, and blue eyes, is taken captive.

When Ruth is restored to her family years later, she has become Narra-mattah, or "the driven snow" (327), wife of Canonchet, sachem of the Narragansetts, and the mother of an infant son. Still, she seems, in that way peculiar to Cooper's other simple women, to have matured physically without a corresponding maturing of intellect. Narra-mattah's simple-mindedness is offered as both an explanation for her willingness to cohabit with an Indian and the inevitable result of such a liaison.

Confronting the reality of her daughter's mental state as well as her relation to her Indian husband and child, Ruth "muse[s] long on the desolation of a mind that had once promised to be so pure" (354). Little Ruth's sexual experience with an Indian, even with a noble chief (Canonchet is the noble savage figure in the novel whose death represents the desired disappearance of the Indians), is the evident source of her desolation, both intellectual and moral. In Cooper's sentimental universe, such a fall can be redeemed only by Narra-mattah's death. Moments before she dies, her essentialized whiteness triumphs: Her years among the savages fall away from her memory, her command of English returns, and the infant Ruth is restored intact to her mother's bosom. Her death restores the racial boundaries around the settling white family that her captivity, marriage, and motherhood have breached and secures their place on the American frontier. Ruth's half-Indian child is literally expunged from the narrative, never mentioned again after his mother's death; in refusing to accommodate the child's existence, the novel enacts white culture's stubborn refusal to acknowledge how deeply racially "crossed" its culture and its populace really are; one recurring response to the reality of mixed blood, as the novel demonstrates, is to refuse to acknowledge its existence.[18]

The Wept of Wish-Ton-Wish was Cooper's response to—and revision of—other stories of marriages between white women and Indian men, including *Yamoyden*, the Child and Sedgwick novels, and the story of Mary Jemison's captivity as a child and her subsequent long and apparently happy life among the Indians. Jemison, Eunice Williams in the early eighteenth century, and Frances Slocum (the "Lost Sister") in the late eighteenth were all well-known figures who were taken in childhood, married Indian men and bore children, and refused all efforts to persuade them to leave their Indian families and communities to return to white culture. The possibility of voluntary, successful, and loving sexual connections across racial boundaries seems to have been sufficiently threatening to the ideal of a white America to elicit dramatic contradiction from a number of writers, especially at the threshold of the westward sweep to consolidate control of the continent from sea to shining sea.[19]

The marriages of white women to Indian men in the Seaver narrative and in *Yamoyden* and the Cooper, Child, and Sedgwick novels are all represented as grounded in some degree of mutual affection and respect; however, the attitudes the poem and the novels exhibit toward such unions are, unlike Jemison's, deeply ambivalent. Leland S. Person, Jr., has claimed that in Child and Sedgwick, "the successful marriages between white women and Indian men . . . suggest terms for an alternative, female, frontier fantasy—a pact between Indians and women, an Eden from which Adam rather than Eve has been excluded" (670). I would argue, rather, that both those novels, along with *Yamoyden* and *The Wept of Wish-Ton-Wish*, open the space for interrogating women's sexual desire for "other" men only to close that space again in an unproblematized celebration of the anglicization of America.

Child, like Cooper, drew on *Yamoyden* in plotting her novel, *Hobomok*. Her heroine Mary Conant, like Nora Fitzgerald, chooses her Indian husband Hobomok in an act of defiance of her father, when she is suffering "a partial derangement of [her] faculties" (120) because she believes her English lover has been lost at sea. Mary is captive not to Indians but to a cruel father and his narrow and heartless religion, New England Puritanism.[20] The novel makes it clear that had she not been deranged by grief and mistreatment, she would never have married Hobomok. Nevertheless, his noble generosity earns her respect and eventually her love. After Mary bears a son, however, her English lover returns, and Hobomok enacts the part of the stereotypical romantic Indian when, out of love for Mary, he releases her from her marriage bonds and vanishes into the West.

When Mary and her English lover are then able to marry at last, there is little doubt that the reader is meant to celebrate the long-delayed fruition of that more appropriate passion. Mary's half-Indian boy is adopted by her white husband, grows up carrying his mother's name (which Child points out is Indian custom), and is sent first to Harvard and then to England to be educated. The Indian half of his identity is eventually erased as thoroughly as are his father's people, lost by being overwritten by white English culture—also the destined fate of the colonial landscape: "Who in those days of poverty and gloom, could have possessed a wand mighty enough to remove the veil which hid the American empire from the sight? Who would have believed that in two hundred years from that dismal period, the matured, majestic, and unrivalled beauty of England, would be nearly equalled by a daughter, blushing into life with all the impetuosity of youthful vigor?" (100).

Hobomok thus enacts the fantasy of racial "absorption" (Tilton's "quiet genocide" again) that was the nineteenth century's only imagined alternative to removal or extermination, as Carolyn Karcher points out in her introduction to the novel (xxxii–xxxiii). The bonds of friendship and marriage between a white woman and an Indian man become the ground for a narrative resolution that unequivocally favors white culture and requires the "cooperative" willing disappearance of Indians, through death, removal to the West, or absorption into the white race, a solution precipitated rather than averted by the white heroine's marriage to an Indian.

Sedgwick's *Hope Leslie* is one of the texts that, like Barlow's *Columbiad*, combine the stories of a Pocahontas-like character and a white woman captive. The combination, as in *The Columbiad*, is indicative of how deeply "American-ness" was dependent upon, and positioned between, both these founding myths. *Hope Leslie* too is set in seventeenth-century Massachusetts during the early contests between Englishmen and Indians that nineteenth-century writers and readers saw as formative of the American character.

The Pocahontas figure here is Magawisca, like her prototype the daughter of a chief and, along with her brother Oneco, a captive of the English. When their mother dies in captivity, Magawisca and Oneco are left in a state of "servile dependence in the house of [their English] enemies" (57), the Fletchers, on the western frontier of English settlement. Like the Pocahontas of legend, Magawisca develops a deep attachment during her captivity to a young Englishman, Everell, the eldest son of the Fletcher family, whom she later sacrifices her arm to save. While the father of the family and his foster child, Hope Leslie, are detained in Boston, Magawisca's father stages a raid on the Fletcher compound to free his children, and most of the family members are massacred; Everell Fletcher and Hope's sister Faith, a special favorite of Oneco's, are taken captive.

The trope of captivity continually splits, multiplies, and proliferates in this novel: Magawisca's mother is a captive of the English, as are Magawisca and Oneco; Everell and Faith Leslie are captured by Indians; Magawisca is rescued by her father and later recaptured by the English, and this time Hope, Sedgwick's protofeminist heroine, defies Puritan patriarchal authority to help her escape. Hope herself is not only captive to a restrictive Puritanism and its attempts to hold her to the patriarchal definitions of passive and submissive womanhood, but, in one of the convoluted subplots characteristic of historical romances, is also briefly captured by a debauched English Catholic villain and practiced seducer (masquerading as a devout Puritan) with designs on her virtue. The elder Fletcher's first and greatest love, Hope and Faith's mother, was captive to a cruel and domineering father in England who prevented the marriage of the young lovers. These multiple captivities as well as the many instances of masquerade and mistaken identity in the novel are indications of the radical instability of national, racial, and religious identities at the time Sedgwick was writing. They also suggest how profoundly the clarion call of the American nation, *freedom*, depended upon a radical unfreedom for its very existence—most importantly of Indians and African Americans, America's "dark and abiding presence" (Morrison 33), as well as of women within patriarchal domestic and spiritual arenas.

Hope's sister Faith is a figure in whom the white woman captive and the Native woman captive are fused: During the years of her captivity, she has become a "white Indian," the wife of Oneco, from whom she refuses to be separated.[21] Much against her will she is recaptured, or "rescued," by the English and held captive in Boston while Hope and others try in vain to persuade her to return to Anglo-American society. Oneco, masquerading as a sailor from the Mediterranean (and thus deconstructing any ineradicable difference between Indians and Europeans), rescues her to return with him to her Indian life. Faith's capture by the English and rescue by Oneco dramatically invert and rewrite the usual story of the white woman captive.

The novel repeatedly articulates a belief in Indian nobility, especially in its delineation of the character of Magawisca, but can do so because Magawisca asks little or nothing in return for the sacrifice of her arm that has liberated Everell. Her "affection for Everell Fletcher had the tenderness, the confidence, the sensitiveness of woman's love; but it had nothing of the selfishness, the expectation, or the earthliness of that passion. She had done and suffered much for him, and she felt that *his worth must be the sole requital for her sufferings*" (263; emphasis mine). Thus the novel in fact operates on the conviction that the Indians' noble suffering is justified because of the intrinsic worth of the white Anglo-American culture that supplants theirs.

Sedgwick's saga participates in the sexual deflection that Tilton has noted in the Pocahontas legend in the nineteenth century: the Indian woman and the Englishman do not come together, and so that particular possibility for an interracial union is averted. Instead, Everell ends up "properly" matched with Hope, and Magawisca (carrying a miniature of Everell that she has begged from Hope), together with her father and the rest of his entourage, conveniently disappears into a mythically mysterious faraway West: "Before dawn the next morning, this little remnant of the Pequod race, a name at which, but a few years before, all within the bounds of the New-England colonies—all, English and Indians, 'grew pale,' began their pilgrimage to the far western forests. That which remains untold of their story, is lost in the deep, voiceless obscurity of those unknown regions" (339).

Their disappearance fits the cultural assumptions of the novel because, despite its heroic Indian maiden and its recognition of the many wrongs perpetrated on Native people by the English, nowhere does the text challenge the English prerogative to settle the "vacuum domicilium" by "purchase of the natives, or by lawful conquest" (126); to the contrary, it openly celebrates the "Englishing" of America:

> We forget that the noble pilgrims lived and endured for us . . . they came not for themselves, they lived not to themselves . . . [but] to open the forests to the sun-beam, and to the light of the Sun of Righteousness—to restore man—man oppressed and trampled on by his fellow; . . . to bring down the hills, and make smooth the rough places, which the pride and cruelty of man had wrought on the fair creation of the Father of all. . . . they saw, with sublime joy, a multitude of people where the solitary savage roamed the forest—the forest vanished, and pleasant villages and busy cities appeared—the tangled foot-path expanded to the thronged high-way—the consecrated church planted on the rock of heathen sacrifice. (72–73)

One white "captive," however, Hope's sister Faith, is among that westering Pequod band; she represents one of white culture's great anxieties, the woman who is "lost" or gets away, in this case not only from English culture but from the narrative itself, in choosing to remain with the Indians, leaving the rest of her story untold. Sedgwick's novel does not so much ratify that choice as it rewrites white women's captivity in a way that acknowledges the uncloseable gap in the national "story" that women like Faith represented and whose stories hers echoes. Despite the novel's multiple "happy endings" that attempt to resolve its plot complexities, Faith's story eludes resolution, at least in any way the novel would find acceptable, and so stands in for all the ways the textual project of establishing white hegemony was also destined to remain perpetually unresolved.

Contrasting with these nineteenth-century stories of noble Native men who in one way or another win the hearts of colonial Englishwomen is the story more often perpetrated by the captivity narrative, of the sexual violence Native men were supposed to want to inflict on white women. When Rachael Plummer returned from captivity among the Comanche in Texas in 1838, she wrote a brief and sorrowful account of her experiences, filled with her suffering and grief over the loss of her children. She died a year after her return, her "constitution broke[n]" (Reese n. pag.). Plummer's narrative is replete with graphic testimony of her captors' cruelty, including her wrenching separation from the two-year-old son captured with her (who was held captive for six years before being ransomed [DeShields 26]) as well as the murder of her six-week-old infant, born five months after her capture. But on the subject of her sexual treatment during captivity, the narrative is silent.

Two popular fictional captivity stories, though, the *Narrative . . . of Mrs. Clarissa Plummer* and the *History of . . . Mrs. Caroline Harris* (published in New York in 1838, the same year as the first edition of Rachael Plummer's narrative) not only plundered the Plummer text for incidents and specific language, as William Reese has pointed out, but also, to incite racial animosity and elicit popular support for the policies of Indian removal, filled the gap left by Plummer's silence on her sexual experience. The Harris title page includes this preview of what the narrative holds: "It was the misfortune of Mrs. *Harris* and her unfortunate female companion (soon after the deaths of their husbands) to be separated by, and compelled to become the companions of, and to cohabit with, two disgusting Indian Chiefs, and from whom they received the most cruel and beastly treatment."

Fictions of captivity like those of "Clarissa Plummer" and "Caroline Harris" were embellished with lurid sexual elements not only to attract readers, but to ensure that the narratives performed their assigned work, enforcing racial differences and generating racial animosity, with the eroticized bodies of white women as the dramatic set pieces.

The eroticization of the white woman captive and of Pocahontas began in the seventeenth century with the fears about Rowlandson's sexual integrity and the rumors that she had been "forced to marry the one-eyed sachem," and with Strachey's remarking Pocahontas's girlish nakedness and Smith's claim that he "could have done what him listed" with her. Those early representations and the many that followed in their wake make clear how important it was for the project of white colonization and nation building that Native as well as Black women be seen as, and assumed or made to be, sexually open to Euro-American men, and how correspondingly important the obverse of that assumption was, that white women be closed to sexual connections with men racialized as "dark others" and "protected" from their presumed sexual aggressiveness. The guarding of those cultural and racial dividing lines, with the eroticized bodies of white women and dark women positioned at their borders, became increasingly pronounced, and increasingly visible, with the developing racial crises of slavery and Indian removal in the mid-nineteenth century.

REMOVALS

By the 1820s, on the threshold of the great push west of the Mississippi by white settlers with its accompanying politics of Indian removal, Americans' sense of their own legitimate place on the continent was growing more secure. What remained acutely unsettled was the problem of race, both in Black slavery and in the continued presence of Indians in territories desirable for white settlement. The "Indian problem" was dramatically addressed by the passage of the Indian Removal Act in 1830, resulting in all Native groups in the East having to relinquish their lands and be resettled in the territories west of the Mississippi. Almost immediately, however, whites entered and began settling lands west of the Mississippi, necessitating the continuing "removal" of Native groups farther and farther west.

As Winthrop Jordan has pointed out, "removal" had also accompanied early discussions of the emancipation of slaves in the late eighteenth and early nineteenth centuries. One of the major resistances to freeing slaves was the conviction, and the accompanying fear, that a free Black population would mean increased intermarriage and so "pollution" of white "blood." The solution was the proposed removal of newly freed slaves to "colonies" in regions not occupied by whites— including the West (Jordan 542–69). It is clear, then, that removal was a specifically racial strategy aimed at both groups figured as "dark others," one embedded in the desire to prevent racial or national hybridities, to ensure the nation's whiteness via the expulsion of the undesirable dark populations and the policing of white women's sexuality.

Removals were also being enacted on the textual front. The effort, both literary and political, of removing Indians into a romanticized, mythic "elsewhere," far to the west in the place of the setting sun, produced a pervasive image in nineteenth-century popular culture of "romantic Indians" whose "stoic acceptance of their individual fate and of the ultimate demise of their people . . . endeared these noble savages" to white audiences (Tilton 56). With their noble and self-sacrificial gestures of disappearance, death, and dismemberment, characters like Eastburn and Sands's Yamoyden, Child's Hobomok, Cooper's Canonchet, and Sedgwick's Magawisca all facilitate the survival of white English colonialism and its continuation into the future, symbolized by the "appropriate" unions of white English characters like Mary Conant and Charles Brown in *Hobomok*, Hope Leslie and Everell Fletcher in the Sedgwick novel. Indian characters who voluntarily removed themselves embodied the deep-seated desires of white Americans for Indians to disappear without whites' having to resort to violence. However, there were more than sufficient numbers of whites ready to be violent when they had to be to achieve those desires, while others read sentimental poems and novels or sat in darkened theatres, weeping over the tragic but inevitable demise of America's noble savages.

Nearly all the popular texts about Indians featured another "removal"—of the pressing issues of the nineteenth century to the remote past of the nation's beginnings. The remote *past* was a convenient stand-in for a remote *place* in these texts, all of which support in varying ways the popular idea of displacing Indians to make more room for white settlement. Historical displacement deflected the critical questions of the "Indian problem" onto the past in order to suggest that answers to the problem had already been found and needed now only to be executed; displacing contemporary problems onto the past, therefore, deftly deflected the guilt reasonable people would otherwise have had to feel over contemporary Indian policies. If the demise of the Indians and their way of life had been determined once and for all two centuries before, then nineteenth-century whites could not be held accountable simply for witnessing the final act of the predestined drama that pitted white against Indian, civilization against savagery.

The nineteenth-century texts discussed above, with the exception of Seaver's,[22] participate in that displacement of current issues into what was by the time they were written already a remote past: Davis's and Cooke's novels, Barker's play, and the Sigourney and Odell poems on Pocahontas return to the period of the earliest English settlement, in Virginia. Eastburn and Sands's epic and the Child, Sedgwick, and Cooper novels are situated in the other scene of English colonialism, the early decades of the settlement of Massachusetts. Two other nineteenth-century texts, John Augustus Stone's drama *Metamora, or The Last of the Wampanoags* (1829) and George Hollister's novel *Mount Hope; or Philip, King of the Wampanoags* (1851) return to colonial Massachusetts as well, to the time of King Philip's War, to portray Metacom as the very type of the "noble Indian"—one whose death can be figured dramatically or textually as emblematic of the passing of the Indian race.

Metamora was the most popular of all the Indian dramas of the nineteenth century; it was performed more than two hundred times over a period of sixty years after its opening in 1829 (Moody 199). Stone's Metamora utters the line that at once assures (and celebrates) the Indians' physical extinction and romanticizes their continuing symbolic presence in white America: "We are destroyed—not vanquished; we are no more, yet we are forever" (226). Interestingly enough, during the period in which the debates over the extension and preservation of slavery were becoming increasingly heated, both Stone and Hollister took advantage of the opportunity to rewrite the fate of Metacom's wife and son, who were, according to the histories of the period, captured and sold into slavery. Metamora declares to his wife that their son "shall not be the white man's slave" (211), and in the final scene of the play we learn that the boy has been slain by the white soldiers (225). Metamora has a vision of what the white man may do to his wife (and indeed did do to Metacom's wife), make a captive and then a slave of her: "He may seize thee, and bear thee off to the far country, bind these arms that have so often clasped me in the dear embrace of love, scourge thy soft flesh in the hour of his wrath, and force thee to carry burdens like the beasts of the fields" (226). To avert that fate, he takes her into a final embrace and stabs her himself, thus sparing white audiences the guilt of the actual history of her captivity as well as the trouble—and guilt—of having to kill her themselves.

Hollister's novel (which also features a young white woman captive with a brow "pale as marble" [25] and bare arms "of an unearthly whiteness" [81]) rewrites the painful history of Metacom's wife and son too, though Hollister does acknowledge their captivity. After the death of "Philip," we see his wife and son aboard "a Spanish slaver, freighted with Indian captives" (257); as the ship sails past Pokanoket, Metacom's ancestral home, both climb over the ship's rail and leap into the ocean to drown and so to join Metacom in death, "secure from the bondage to which their proud spirits could never submit" (258). Hollister describes Metacom himself, after his death, as "the uncompromising enemy of civilized society," admirably unwavering in his "untiring purpose, which, like the plumes of his own eagle, when spread to encounter the blaze of the noon-day sun, never faltered in its flight till it was quenched in the radiance of the orb of civilization, which it sought in vain to blot from the heavens" (256). The message of Hollister's novel, like that of Stone's play and so many of the century's Indian texts, is clear: Indians threaten to eradicate the "radiance" of white civilization, which, like the sun, is destined to sweep over the continent; nonwhite people, if they are heroic, accept their inevitable defeat and initiate or cooperate in their own death or disappearance.

A public image that also resurrected the past to address the empire-building ambitions of the present was Antonio Capellano's relief *The Preservation of Captain Smith by Pocahontas* (1825), one of four reliefs depicting historical white-Indian encounters that were installed in the U.S. Capitol Rotunda during the 1820s, the decade that preceded the passage of the Indian Removal Act.[23] Capellano's relief panel returns to the settlement of the Jamestown colony and, like so many other nineteenth-century renditions, echoes the romantic rescue myth, emphasizing Pocahontas's self-sacrificial gesture without addressing her interracial marriage and motherhood. Placed over the west door of the Capitol Rotunda, the relief made Pocahontas's rescue of Smith a symbolic "door to the West" for white America and thus promoted both westward expansion and the self-sacrificing Indians who would facilitate it. For white Americans of the nineteenth century, the imaginative recall of an imagined past promoted the desired resolution of the era's most troubling present problems—and its most expansive ambitions.

Pocahontas, or The Settlers of Virginia by George Washington Parke Custis (as his name indicates, a descendant of the first First Family) was produced in 1830, the same year the Indian Removal Act was passed. The play plainly inscribes both Pocahontas's popular repudiation of her "ties of blood" (207) to the Indians and, "tho' of dark complexion" (194), her necessary adoption of English culture and identity to the benefit of English colonialism. Furthermore, it engages the then-troubling questions about the appropriate solution to the "Indian problem" in ways that explicitly support the removal enacted in the 1830 legislation.

Custis's Namoutac is an Indian character who returns to his homeland with Smith and the other Jamestown settlers after a sojourn in England. He tells Pocahontas of his travels: "All which I have seen has impress'd me with the most exalted ideas of the power and grandeur of a people, who are as gods are to men. Still amid all the splendours of the courts of Europe, I have never forgot my native land, but long'd to re-visit even its poverty and nothingness" (192). His speech echoes the argument that had accompanied Anglo settlement since the earliest days of colonization: That since Indian occupation has left the land impoverished and made "nothing" of it, it is only reasonable and right that the Indians should be removed so the English can turn their hands to making it productive and profitable. Upon his return, he immediately casts off his English dress and veneer and becomes a savage Indian once more: "The sun shines for the last time upon Namoutac the English. . . . [I] will soon be Namoutac the Indian. Namoutac the English, will be no more" (192). Namoutac thus becomes an emblem of the irresistible "force of early habits" (192) and so of the inevitable failure—and thus the futility—of any effort to civilize the Indian, Pocahontas being the obvious single exception to that rule.

The warrior Matacoran is Custis's "noble Indian" who recognizes the inevitability of white conquest and who, at the end of the play, takes his necessary leave:

> The fortune of war is on thy side; thy gods are as much greater than the gods of the Indian, as thine arms are greater than his. But altho' thy gods and thine arms have prevailed, say did not Matacoran fight bravely in the last of his country's battles? . . . Now that he can no longer combat the invaders he will retire before them, even to where tradition says, there rolls a western wave. There, on the utmost verge of the land which the Manitou gave to his father . . . Matacoran will . . . die. (208)

Custis, himself a Virginian (the son of George Washington's stepson), redeems the image of Powhatan, who, as Pocahontas's father is also the ancestor of many "white" Virginians; giving Pocahontas's hand to Rolfe, Powhatan says, "Let their union be a pledge of the future union between England and Virginia" (208). Powhatan becomes himself the prophet of empire in Custis's play, foretelling the Indians' removal: He looks ceremoniously "thro' a long vista of futurity, to the time when these wild regions shall become the ancient and honour'd part of a great and glorious American Empire" and hopes that "when the tales of early days are told from the nursery, the library, or the stage, that kindly will be received the national story of POCAHONTAS, OR THE SETTLEMENT OF VIRGINIA" (208).[24]

As the frontier moved westward during the nineteenth century, so did the companion figure to Pocahontas, the white woman captive. The prospect of white women's sexual intimacy with Indians, the underlying danger in the scene of captivity, continued to pose a threat to white identity and the success of the white project to control America, while sexual intimacy between white men and Indian women was figured as accomplishing the opposite. Pocahontas's marriage to an Englishman secured her place in the catalog of heroic American figures because it helped to consolidate the identity of the colonizers and their successors as "white" and symbolized the relinquishing of her country. But the white counterpart to the legendary Pocahontas—the white woman who turned her back on her own society to embrace an Indian husband and way of life—was a profound marker for white culture of the loss of secure distinctions between Indians and whites and therefore profoundly unsettled the racial distinctions on which nineteenth-century politics were founded. The ideological counterweight to the forcible removal of Indians, therefore, was the woman captive who chose to "remove" herself from white society by marrying an Indian and entering an Indian community—women like Eunice Williams, Frances Slocum, and Mary Jemison. So unsettling was this figure that persistent and often violent means were sometimes used to retrieve such women against their will.

In 1836—the same year Texas won its independence from Mexico and became a republic—a white girl, Cynthia Ann Parker, was captured by Comanche at Fort Parker, Texas. Parker was one of several captives taken in the attack; Rachael Plummer, Parker's cousin, was another. Parker was a young girl (somewhere between nine and eleven years old) when she was taken. She spent the next twenty-four years among the Comanche; she assimilated thoroughly into the tribe, married a chief, and bore three children, one of whom was Quanah Parker, the Comanche headman who years later was to lead the remnants of his people into Fort Sill, surrendering the tribe to the U.S. Cavalry and federal governance. Quanah was still a young man in 1860 when his mother, along with her small daughter, was recaptured by whites in a raid on a Comanche hunting camp and forcibly returned to white society. In her biography of Parker, Margaret Schmidt Hacker portrays her as a tragic figure who was captive in two cultures. She lived with her white relatives after she was returned, but because she made repeated attempts to run away, she was locked up whenever she could not be watched; she was, in every sense of the word, a prisoner. When her young daughter died of fever, Parker fell into a depression from which she never recovered; she refused to eat, rejecting both literally and metaphorically the efforts of her white relatives to sustain her, and died of deliberate starvation without being reunited with her Indian family. Parker's story, like Faith Leslie's in Sedgwick's *Hope Leslie*, illustrates the frequent oscillations across racial and cultural lines of the white woman captive who is recaptured and becomes the captive of white Americans.

If captivity stories of white women were a site for consolidating beliefs in racial difference, white privilege, Native "savagery," and the legitimacy of western settlement and land claims by white Americans, it is not a coincidence that so much was made of Parker's capture at the time when Texas was asserting its identity as an independent republic of white citizens, and then again that much was made of her return on the eve of the Civil War, when Texas, then part of the Confederacy, was preparing to participate in a conflict grounded in large part in the issue of race. Parker was seen as a tragic figure by her white relatives too—not because of having been torn from the family and way of life she had known for nearly a quarter century, but because she seemed wild and untamable, a degenerate version of the woman she might otherwise have become. As with Cooper's Narra-mattah, the fact of Parker's children proved that "Indian-ness" had literally penetrated her, rendering her lost to the family that had tried so hard for so long to "redeem" her. Parker and her story became legendary, a prototype illustrating the dangers to white society and its values that intimate connection with Native people presumably presented.

One last, and yet ongoing, removal of Indians from the American scene remains to be noted: the erasure of Native presence from many arenas of contemporary American life. State or regional histories in the United States, for example, often, perhaps even usually, begin with the beginnings of white settlement. Indians "are forever," to echo Stone's *Metamora*, in the names of much in the American landscape—names of mountains, rivers, lakes, and of innumerable cities and many states. And yet they "are no more" in any clearly visible way, it seems, in Lancaster, Massachusetts, and in Pocahontas, Iowa, and countless other places between and beyond. Ghettoized in school and university curricula, natural history museums and archeological collections, American

Indians continue to be represented most often as an element of America's romantic past.

The closing of the frontier at the end of the nineteenth century brought to a "close," for the most part, the dramas of contention between Indians and whites. The stories of that contention, however, including those of white women's captivity, remained available to serve new purposes: to refigure or reassert a racially inflected national identity in the aftermaths of two world wars and as surrogates for interrogating the most dramatic racial conflict of the twentieth century, that between whites and African Americans.

RED, WHITE, AND BLACK

Annette Kolodny has pointed out that "From the first, for both their authors and their readers, Indian captivity narratives have mirrored the aspirations and anxieties of successive generations, revealing new meanings and lending themselves to startling new interpretations over time" ("Among the Indians" 26). Captivity narratives and Pocahontas stories have historically not been vehicles for anti-Indian sentiment alone; Francophobic and anti-"papist" attitudes were expressed through many captivity narratives during the colonial period, and as the American Revolution approached, Anglophobia joined forces with fear and hatred of Indians in stories of both Pocahontas and Indian captivity. In the twentieth century, those stories became part of the discursive milieu not only for postwar moments of national redefinition, but also for addressing the conflicts over racial integration that came to a crisis point at mid-century.

Michael Rogin has said, "In the popular culture of films, Westerns, and children's games, seizing America from the Indians is the central, mythical, formative experience" of the nation, traceable as metaphor in this century all the way to Vietnam (136). The twinned myths that enlisted the eroticized bodies of white and Native women to serve the project of seizing America from the Indians have been repeatedly called into service in this century as well as earlier ones, whenever the need has arisen to rearticulate or reassert the identity of the American nation.

Vachel Lindsay's poem "Our Mother Pocahontas" appeared in 1926, in the wake of the First World War and in a context of rising isolationist sentiment in the United States. Like Hart Crane, who a few years later appropriated Pocahontas's body as the literal ground of American identity in *The Bridge*, Lindsay raises the familiar issue of the two races that contend in the figure of Pocahontas, using her as a vehicle to repudiate America's European heritage and claim an American identity with and through her:

> . . . gray Europe's rags august
> She tramples in the dust;
> Because we are her fields of corn;
> Because our fires are all reborn
> From her bosom's deathless embers . . .
>   (41)

As Crane was later to do, Lindsay moves his symbolic Pocahontas in a grand sweep across the continent, all the way to "the Pacific sand" (41), as the figurehead for consolidating a reclaimed and refigured American identity separate from any European origins. And once again not only Pocahontas's "bosom" comes into play, but also the fetish of "blood" makes its crucial appearance:

> We here renounce our Saxon blood.
> . . . The newest race
> Is born of her resilient grace.
> We here renounce our Teuton pride:
> Our Norse and Slavic boasts have died:
> Italian dreams are swept away,
> And Celtic feuds are lost today . . .
>   (42)

Invoking Pocahontas's role as mother of the nation, Lindsay appropriates Native identity in a "facing west" posture, this time not to secure but to sever America's connections with Europe in the postwar period. His gesture of claiming her as the mother of the American nation, like Crane's claiming her as lover, repeats the ideological uses to which white America had put Pocahontas for well more than a century.

In the aftermath of World War II, America again paused to celebrate and renew its dedication to the principles of freedom and opportunity on which it claimed to be founded. In 1947, two years after the Allied victory in Europe and Japan, Cecil B. DeMille released *Unconquered*. Situated in the period just before the Revolution, the film reassures its postwar audience that the nation is worth the sacrifices, including the lives of the war dead, that were required to preserve it. And once again the mythic story of the white woman captive and of the conflicts between whites and Indians presents itself as an appropriate vehicle for the film's reassertions of national identity.

In one telling sequence, after Holden (Gary Cooper), an officer in the pre-Revolutionary colonial militia, manages to free the heroine, Abby, from the Indians, the pair come upon an empty settler cabin in the wilderness. It is a romantic, bucolic setting, and they take shelter in the cabin for the night, assuming that the owners have fled to the fort for safety from the marauding Indians, and fantasize that they too are settlers.

The next morning, the magic of the setting is broken when Holden finds the whole family not far from the cabin, massacred and apparently mutilated (the bodies are never shown, but a savage horror impossible to represent is hinted at). Abby wakes to find Holden digging a grave. Seeing the bodies, she shudders with revulsion and exclaims, "No one has a chance in this wilderness! Nobody can fight it; it'll always be wilderness. Savages will burn, torture, and kill, until they get it back." Holden replies reflectively yet grandly, "People like the Salters can never be stopped, Abby. The Indians can kill them and run them off, but more will keep coming. The Salters are the new world, unconquered, uncon-querable. Because they're strong and free. Because they have faith in themselves—and in God."

Holden's message celebrates the fact that, despite the loss of American lives, the recent war has not mutilated the nation itself; he affirms the rightness of America's victory as well as the traits—strength, desire for freedom, faith in the Christian God—which have historically brought the nation its supposedly deserved victory over all its enemies, including

Indians, and which will enable Holden and Abby and other Euro-American people to take possession of and *hold* the continent.

After Holden has liberated the British outpost from the Indian siege that threatened to overrun it (he loads wagons with the bodies of dead but propped-up English soldiers to deceive the Indians into thinking reinforcements have arrived), he and Abby are poised at its gate, and so at the threshold of the "frontier," and must decide: east to Boston or west to what Holden has earlier described as "the edge of the end of the world"? They choose, of course, west—the course of empire.

The film demonstrates that the strategy of addressing national issues of the moment by revisiting the mythicized past has been a recurrent one in American cultural history; it celebrates the nation's 1945 victory by returning, like so many nineteenth-century texts, to the conquest of the continent as the defining myth of the nation, and the Indians serve as the surrogates for any and all of America's enemies, actual or perceived.

Unconquered relies on the captivity trope to emphasize differences and distinctions between Euro-Americans and their enemy "others." During the same period, a grade-school play by an unknown author, *Kidnapped by the Indians*, was performed in 1948 in Roanoke, Virginia, which also made Indians the surrogates for the nation's enemies in that war.[25] The play deals with the capture of Jemima Boone, Daniel Boone's daughter, and two other young girls by "Chief Hanging Maw." The Indians are referred to in the play as "Yellow Boys"—almost certainly an expression of the prejudice of the time against the Japanese, a displacement onto a familiar American target of residual race animosity toward the recent Asian enemy. In the play, the Indians are clumsy, stupid, and inept; the white girls who are their captives are plucky and defiant; Boone and company have no trouble tracking and defeating the Indians with a minimum of bloodshed, and good humor prevails throughout. The play invites children to identify with the enterprising and clearly superior whites and to enjoy and congratulate themselves for being on the winning side against America's "yellow" enemies. In both *Unconquered* and *Kidnapped by the Indians*, race and racial identity are plainly visible in constructing the victorious America, indicating how deeply questions of race have been implicated in efforts to define the American nation.

By the middle of the twentieth century, of course, Indians presented virtually no threat whatever to the hegemony and power of white culture. And yet, beginning in the mid-1950s, the figure of the captive woman and stories of Indian captivity were used once again to address contemporary racial issues in a number of popular Westerns. This was, I believe, a response to the renewed panic over racial mixing that swept the nation in the wake of the 1954 Supreme Court decision, *Brown v. the Board of Education*, which overthrew the "separate but equal" doctrine and mandated racial integration of the schools "with all deliberate speed." The *Brown* decision was universally viewed as the most significant challenge to the supremacy of whites in the United States since emancipation in 1863; popular fears were situated specifically in the possibility of racial mixing that would likely result from Black and white children attending school together. Cultural anxieties over the spectre of Black-white miscegenation in the wake of the *Brown* decision were often displaced in popular literature and film onto the historical race conflict between Indians and whites, where convictions of white supremacy could be reasserted and reenacted in that safely removed and remote scene in which whites had already "won" a racial contest. Because the Pocahontas legend and stories of white women's captivity had historically been an important discursive terrain for articulating racial difference and policing racial mixing, they were once again at mid-century recruited to perform their familiar cultural work of racialization.

The representational overlapping of Indians and Blacks in racial discourses has had a long history in the United States. One very early instance, during the colonial era, is found in Cotton Mather's story of Mercy Short's satanic possession in *A Brand Pluck'd out of the Burning* (1693), in which the "devil" tormenting the seventeen-year-old Mercy is figured as an Indian, but in a way that links him explicitly with Blacks and places both Blacks and Indians among the company of devils:

There exhibited himself unto her a Divel having the Figure of A Short and a Black Man; and it was remarkable that altho' shee had no sort of Acquaintance with Histories of what has happened elsewhere, to make any Impressions upon her Imagination, yett the Divel that visited her was just of the same Stature, Feature, and complexion with what the Histories of the Witchcrafts beyond-sea ascribe unto him; he was a wretch no taller than an ordinary Walking-Staff; hee was not of a Negro, but of a Tawney, or an Indian colour; hee wore an high-crowned Hat, with strait Hair; and had one Cloven-Foot. (261)

That process of overlapping persisted in the twentieth century, when the successful resolution of the "Indian problem" was recalled as a surrogate for addressing Black-white race relations, now in the forefront as the major race crisis for the nation. In D. W. Griffith's *The Birth of a Nation* (1915), the white heroine, Elsie Stoneman (Lillian Gish), is held captive by the power-hungry and lustful "mulatto," the ominously named Silas Lynch, who plans a quick forced marriage to Elsie. He says to her, "See! My people fill the streets. With them I will build a Black Empire and you as Queen shall sit by my side." Elsie's reply is to threaten him with "a horsewhipping" for his "insolence." With a diabolical leer, Lynch forces his embraces on her and, when she refuses to respond, he binds her and locks the door to prevent her escape. Elsie in this scene is strongly reminiscent of the white woman held captive by Indians; her lacy white garment is torn, her hair disheveled, she is held against her will and threatened with forced sexual intimacy (and so with being an agent of racial mixing), and she faints away repeatedly. Before Silas's "affront" in the form of a marriage proposal, Elsie has been a staunch proponent of racial equality and opponent of the Klan riders whose beginnings the film traces; she has broken off her engagement when she learns that her lover is a founder of the Klan. It takes only the leering Silas and the looming threat of rape by this dark villain to turn Elsie into a cheering fan of the Klan when they ride into town and rescue her, whereupon she falls joyfully into her white Klansman's arms. In the film the tropes of Indian captivity, especially the threat of sexual violation of a white woman by a dark man, are engaged to elicit and encourage race prejudice, and the captivity tradition merges vividly with anti-Black sentiment.

Henry Louis Gates, Jr., has cited an especially grotesque instance of how the accomplished conquest of one race, Indians, was used to terrorize another, African Americans. In his essay "The Face and Voice of Blackness," Gates reproduces a postcard labeled "Pub. by Harkrider

Drug Co., Center, Tex." from 1908, during the era of Jim Crow segregation in the South. The postcard features a photograph of five Black men, lynched and hanging from the branches of a tree. The photograph is captioned on the postcard "Scene in Sabine County, Texas, June 15, 1908," and below the photograph is printed this verse:

THE DOGWOOD TREE

This is only the branch of the Dogwood tree;
    An emblem of WHITE SUPREMACY.
A lesson once taught in the Pioneer's school,
    That this is the land of WHITE MAN'S RULE.
The Red Man once in an early day,
    Was told by the Whites to mend his way.

The negro, now, by eternal grace,
    Must learn to stay in the negro's place.
In the Sunny South, the Land of the Free,
    Let the WHITE SUPREME forever be.
Let this a warning to all negroes be,
    Or they'll suffer the fate of the DOGWOOD TREE.

(xxxii, figure 6)

The layered ironies of the postcard's use of the dogwood tree for purposes of promoting such literally murderous racism are remarkable: the tree has long been associated in popular folklore with the crucifixion of Jesus.

Such virulence in white efforts to police race mixing, of course, is generated by the fact that of all the myths that pervade American culture, the myth of racial purity is the most fragile. America has never been, and indeed could never be, a "white nation." Whenever people of different racial identities live and work together, their intermingling is inevitable, regardless of the force of prohibitions against it. The very existence of legal strictures against racial mixing of whites with Indians and Blacks in the English colonies indicates that such mixing was already occurring in those early years of colonization; only a practice that presents itself as a problem elicits the effort to regulate it.

Robert Tilton, for example, in discussing early Anglo-American attitudes toward racial mixing, quotes from a 1757 letter by Peter Fontaine, a Virginia clergyman:

> But here methinks I can hear you observe, What! Englishmen inter-marry with Indians? But I can convince you that they are guilty of much more heinous practices, more unjustifiable in the sight of God and man . . . for many base wretches amongst us take up with negro women, by which means the country swarms with mulatto bastards, and these mulattoes, if but three generations removed from the black father or mother, may, by the indulgence of the laws of the country, intermarry with the white people, and actually do every day so marry. Now, if instead of this abominable practice which hath polluted the blood of many amongst us, we had taken Indian wives in the first place, it would have made them some compensation for their lands. They are a free people, and the offspring would not be born in a state of slavery. We should become rightful heirs to their lands, and should not have smutted our blood, for the Indian children when born are as white as Spanish or Portuguese. (quoted in Tilton 22)

The passage demonstrates the force of color prejudice against those of African descent and the pre-nineteenth-century positioning of Indians as closer to whites than Blacks; it also indicates that mixed-race people in Virginia had been around for at least three generations by the mid-eighteenth century and were freely intermarrying at that time with people of white identity. The phenomenon of mixed blood, therefore, lies at the very foundations of America and "colors" in the most literal way its population as a whole. As Albert Murray has written, "[T]he United States is in actuality not a nation of black people and white people. It is a nation of multicolored people. There are white Americans so to speak and black Americans. But any fool can see that the white people are not really white, and that black people are not black. They are all interrelated one way or another" (3).

That the historical mixing of white men and Black women, by rape as well as consent, has produced a racially mixed Black population in America is widely acknowledged; the phenomenon of "passing," combined with the historical proximities of differing racial groups, would necessarily also produce a racially mixed "white" population. "Racial purity," then, is a discursive construct, no more and no less, arising within discourses of racial difference and policed within those discourses.

American obsessions with policing racial identities and guarding against racial mixing have persisted throughout the four centuries since Europeans arrived on the continent. Ruth Frankenberg's study of contemporary white women in interracial relationships is situated within "a cultural and legislative history that constructs whiteness as a biologically pure category. The desire for racial purity and the power to enforce it by defining out people of diverse ancestry have in fact largely been preserves of white Americans," she claims (98). One of Frankenberg's subjects, a white woman who came of age in the South in the 1970s, had this to say about the prohibitions she learned very early against interracial sex: "[I]n high school you're taught really strictly what to do and not do around sex. I mean, it's bad to be a slut, anyway. But . . . to have sex with a Black man is like being the worst slut in the world" (quoted in Frankenberg 71).

The myths of Black men lusting after and raping white women, and of "sluttish" white women who have consensual sexual relations with Black men, have long-standing analogs in the stories from the seventeenth century onward, of Indians' savage sexuality inflicted on helpless white women, and of women who "went Native," choosing to remain with Indian partners and refusing to let themselves be reclaimed by white culture.

A 1964 television documentary by Douglas Leiterman and Beryl Fox, *One More River: The Mood of the American South in 1964*, illustrates the rhetorical connections between the historical racist hostility toward Indians and that which many whites harbored toward African Americans during the years of struggle for civil rights.[26] In the film, a professional broadcaster who identifies himself as Wally Butterworth of the Defensive League of Georgia delivers a virulently racist diatribe; among his remarks are a series of characterizations of Black Americans that echo directly and exactly the ways early colonizers of North America characterized the Indians: Blacks have no language, Butterworth claims; they have no culture; they have built no cities, and no houses "save of sticks and mud";

they don't settle in one place, but "roam like animals"; and they are unshod, their "black bare feet" treading over the riches of the African continent, riches they do not recognize as such until "the white man" points them out. Butterworth also makes very explicit that it is the spectre of racial mixing—he terms it "mongrelization"—that he most fears and hates.

In the same film, Black students who at the time were integrating white southern universities express their clear understanding that the sexual taboo is at the heart of the controversy over integration. Butterworth's anxiety over the sexual "violation" of white girls and women by Black men establishes a clear connection between mid-century racism directed at Black Americans and the long history of racist violence practiced against not only African Americans but also Native people, generated in part by tales of the threatened "violation" of white women captives.

In the wake of the *Brown* decision, a number of captivity stories appeared in popular media that addressed the issue of race and racial mixing, including two John Ford Western films, *The Searchers* in 1956 and *Two Rode Together* in 1961, a paperback Western novel by Gordon D. Shirreffs, *Bugles on the Prairie*, in 1957, and a John Huston Western film, *The Unforgiven*, in 1960. All revisit the stock features of earlier captivity tales, focusing specifically on the issue of sexual connections between races, confronting the sexual threat that dark men pose to white women (and thus implicitly to the power of white men) and reaffirming the sexual prerogative of white men to "their" women. The coincidence of these racializing echoes suggests that such texts too, like those of the nineteenth century, are revisiting the mythic past, recalling it to do the work of racial policing of white women's sexuality that the contemporary prospect of racial integration elicited.

Ford's *Two Rode Together* pairs a small-town Texas marshal (James Stewart) and his friend (Richard Widmark) in a quest pressed on them by the residents of the town, to "redeem" a group of captive whites from the Comanche by trading guns for captives. The marshal is opposed to the mission because he believes that once "Indianized," captives cannot readapt to civilized society; his opposition is overcome by his partner's enthusiasm for the project, however, and the two visit the encampment of the Comanche chief, Quanah Parker. No mention is made in the film of the historic Quanah's "captive" white mother, or of his being himself of mixed race.

Among the town's residents is a couple whose young daughter was captured when she was a child. The marshal discourages them from holding out hope of her return by saying, "Comanche mate their women early. If she's still alive, she's probably got a couple half-breed kids by now." The two men do indeed find the girl, and all their worst fears are realized: she is one of two white women who have been forced to become the "squaws" of Comanche men. Both women are dirty, haggard, grey-faced, and hunched over; they creep around the camp in a subservient posture, keeping their eyes on the ground, and finally refuse to be returned to their families because of the "shame" of their experience. They beg instead that their families be told they are dead—and the 1950s slogan "Better dead than Red" here takes on a new significance.

Another young woman (Shirley Jones) whose brother was taken captive as a small boy longs desperately for his return. He is among those brought back, but the savagery he has absorbed during the years of captivity cannot be erased. He no longer understands English, he must be kept bound because he attacks his white rescuers and family members whenever he is free, and he tries to run away at every opportunity. His sister is dissuaded from expecting her brother's full restoration when the Widmark character tells her, "He's forgot his English—he just grunts now, grunts Comanche. And given the chance, he'd rape you, then trade you off to one of the other bucks for a good knife, or a gun." The film explicitly warns against interracial contact—a clear message for its contemporary audience—by depicting the power of "savagery" to erode the "civilized" character of whites unfortunate enough to be forced to become intimate with the racial other.

Both *The Searchers* and *Bugles on the Prairie* have a Civil War background, hinting at the real race issue that both film and novel mean to address. And in both, a white woman captive is the ground on which the race struggle is fought. *The Searchers* replicates the racial and sexual ideologies I have traced in earlier captivity stories. Ethan Edwards (John Wayne) is a Confederate soldier who returns to his brother's homestead in Texas at the end of the Civil War. His loyalty to the Confederacy has not been extinguished by defeat and predicts the racial hatred that motivates his behavior in the narrative. Shortly after his return, most of his brother's family are massacred by Comanche; only the two daughters, Lucy and Debbie, are taken alive, and Ethan's search for the girls constitutes the action of the film. He soon finds Lucy, the older girl, in an isolated canyon, dead—and naked. Sexual atrocities are hinted at but remain unspeakable; Lucy's sweetheart, Brad, when told she is dead, asks with horror, "Was she . . . did they . . .?" Ethan replies with passion, "What do I have to do, draw you a picture? Don't ask me! For as long as you live, never ask me!"

Ethan's monomaniacal search for Debbie (Melville's Ahab comes to mind) continues for years, until she is a young woman, and when Ethan finds her (played now by Natalie Wood), his worst fears are realized: she is living in the tipi of a Comanche chief named Scar. Ethan has expressed this (again unspeakable) fear earlier to Martin (Jeffrey Hunter), Debbie's eighth-Cherokee foster brother (whom Ethan harasses by calling him a "half-breed"): "If they don't kill her, they'll keep her and raise her as one of their own until she's old enough to . . . ." Just as in *Yamoyden* and *The Wept of Wish-Ton-Wish*, death and sexual consort with an Indian are equally disastrous, even equivalent, and when Ethan and Martin find Debbie alive and living in Scar's tipi, Ethan's first impulse is to shoot her; Martin stops him by shielding Debbie's body with his own. Ethan rages that Debbie is no longer his "blood kin" because "she's been living with a buck," and in Ethan's final pursuit of Debbie, it is not certain he will not shoot her until the last moment, when instead he picks her up and says, "Let's go home."

Whether or not she chose it, Debbie's suggested intimacy with a Comanche "buck" (not coincidentally, also a pejorative term applied to Black men), has rendered her own racial identity questionable, just like that of three young women, former captives, who are shown to Ethan and Martin during their search. Their blank stares, babbling tongues, and lunatic smiles demonstrate that their minds have been destroyed by the experience of captivity (presumably including rape). "It's hard to believe they're white," says one of the cavalrymen who rescued them. "They're not, any more," replies Ethan.

Shirreffs's paperback Western novel *Bugles on the Prairie* also replays all the cliches of captivity tales: it features a handsome white hero whose quest is to free a beautiful captive maiden in sexual danger from her captors, the brutal Apache. The hero, Fletcher, says to his brother, "She was young . . . and beautiful. She might be an Apache squaw even now. Unless— . . . They might have had their way with her. . . . I've seen what some of those bloody bastards can do to a white woman. They're chaste as all hell with their own woman. But a white woman is part of their loot; no more, no less" (14).

When Fletcher finds Isabel at last, she is alive and sexually "intact," having saved herself from violation by feigning the simple-mindedness that Cooper's fair victim in *The Wept of Wish-Ton-Wish* actually suffers. Isabel's passivity, even for the 1950s, is remarkable; her strategy of pretending to be weak-minded is the one action she is capable of, and it is required to keep her sexually "untainted" and thus a suitable love interest for Fletcher.

The novel uses depraved mixed-race characters to warn its mid-century audience against the dangers of the mixing of blood; both Fletcher's betrayer, Luz Campos (whose sexual availability to all comers proves the aptness of her name), and Yaqui, a violent and rapacious outcast from both Indian and white cultures, are the "half-breed" enemies of the white hero. Yaqui is drunken, bestial, deceitful, and above all ugly; he desires all white women, especially the captive maiden Isabel, and vents his lust on them whenever he can, as well as on the hapless Luz. In a hand-to-hand knife battle with Yaqui, Fletcher, though wounded and exhausted, proves his racial superiority by killing the half-breed. Yaqui embodies all the worst fears of racial mixing that the prospect of racial integration raised in white America at mid-century.

The mixed-blood character of Martin in *The Searchers* is more complex and depicts the intimate, interior struggle for racial dominance. It is his task in the course of the film to prove his "whiteness," to repudiate his Indian blood and exorcize the ghost of his own mixed racial heritage, by accompanying Ethan faithfully in his search for Debbie; by rejecting the Indian "wife" Look, whom he inadvertently acquires in a clumsy bargain (Look is the mirror in which Martin must confront his own Indianness); and finally by being the one who shoots and kills Scar. In that act, he kills the Indian in himself and earns the right to return with Ethan and Debbie to the white community and to contribute to the white conquest of the frontier, a project his rejection, indeed literal slaughter, of his Indian identity both protects and furthers. His cooperating in the effort to find, rescue, and restore Debbie to white society is proof of his allegiance to white culture and its racial and political values. Martin's identity quest can be read as representing that of the country as a whole, contending with its history of racial encounters, both intimate and inimical, and engaged in an ideological struggle to define itself as "white" or "not."

John Huston's *The Unforgiven* is the most complex of the mid-twentieth-century interrogations of race by way of a captivity story. In the character of Rachel Zachary, both the captive white woman and the Pocahontas figure are fused, and both figures oscillate in the racial contest that rages around, within, and through her. Rachel (Audrey Hepburn) is the foster daughter of the Zachary family, ranchers on the nineteenth-century western "frontier." The father of the family has been murdered by Kiowa, generating a virulent hatred of Indians among the family; the eldest brother Ben (Burt Lancaster) has taken over the role of family patriarch.

The family story is that the father found the infant Rachel in a pioneer wagon; both parents, he said, had been killed by Kiowa, and Zachary brought the baby home to his wife to raise as their own. Now Rachel is grown, and the Kiowa make several visits to the Zachary cabin in peaceful but insistent attempts to "buy" Rachel from her family; the assumption is that they want her as a wife for their chief, and so the presumed desire of dark men for white women comes into view. But when a mysterious and half-demented stranger appears in the community, claiming that Rachel is in fact an Indian—"a red heart injun. . . . Red heart whelp as ever was"—the film's racial drama begins, in all its complexity.

When Rachel's suitor, Charley, is killed by Kiowa, Rachel, who has heard nothing about the stranger's allegations of her history, goes to comfort the family and offer her condolences. Charley's mother flies into a rage when she recognizes Rachel and screams at her: "Don't touch me! Don't touch me! Get out of this house! Dirty injun with your injun ways! Ain't you done enough—wound yourself around my son Charley to get yourself a litter of half-breeds to run around my Charley's cabin! Squaw! Kiowa squaw! RED NIGGER AS EVER WAS!"

The townspeople propose to "strip her naked," to examine her body and determine her "identity," but Ben threatens to shoot anyone who touches her, and the Zacharys leave for home. There they find that Kiowa have been at the cabin in the family's absence (the middle brother, Cash, says, "I smell injuns!"). The mysterious stranger has apparently reported Rachel's identity to the Indians as well, and they have left a pictographic scroll that tells of a Kiowa girl baby who was stolen years before by white men with guns. Suddenly it becomes clear that the Kiowa attempt to "buy" Rachel with ponies has been an effort not to acquire a bride, but to retrieve the young woman who is the daughter of their old chief and sister of the young one.

Thus Rachel's identities as both white and Indian begin to oscillate, as does her "captive" status. Stolen from the Kiowa, she has been without knowing it the captive of her white family; now the Kiowa are attempting to recapture her against her will. Culturally identified with whites, she is rejected by the white community and even by one of her brothers: when her Indian identity is revealed, Cash says, "My sister's an injun?!" and urges Ben to "send her away." When Ben says, "She's stayin'; we're all stayin'," Cash replies passionately, "I'm not stayin'! Not with a red-heart nigger!"

Rachel finally "knows" herself as Indian when, looking the very image of Pocahontas in the Chapman painting of the baptism—dressed in a long and flowing white gown, her dark hair bound at the nape and flowing down her back—she goes into her bedroom, unbuttons her bodice, and examines her skin. She then looks at her image in a mirror and, tears filling her eyes, marks her forehead with a streak of black lampsoot. The mark signs her as both Indian and "dark," cancelled out of white culture by the revealed secret of her identity.

Rachel's role as a Pocahontas figure is most clear when her Kiowa brother returns once more to the Zachary cabin in an effort to reclaim her. Though the Indians have come in peace, Ben responds with weapons, and a full-fledged firefight ensues. When her Kiowa brother breaks into the cabin and reaches out his hand to her, calling her "sister," Rachel must choose: Indian or white? Like the Pocahontas of legend, Rachel chooses white identity over Indian: she fires a gun point-blank, killing her Indian brother. Like Martin's figural fratricide in *The Searchers*, Rachel's literal one signifies a rejection of her Indian blood and confirms her allegiance to white culture; furthermore, in an odd development, her white "brother" Ben, who has served as her "father" since Will Zachary's death, becomes suddenly her lover too: he proposes that they leave the area (presumably to keep the secret of her Indian ancestry) and head for Kansas City to get married.

If the claim that Westerns of the mid-1950s and early 1960s were addressing the contemporary racial struggle between whites and Blacks seems tenuous, the recurring phrase "red niggers" in *The Unforgiven* is powerful evidence of what their concern actually was. Just as the "space invasion" films of the 1950s were coded expressions of Cold War nationalism and constructed a Soviet enemy as extraterrestrial aliens, so, I believe, these Westerns of the period were addressing the domestic racial crisis that threatened the status of America as "white." The security of the nation was threatened from without by the military might of an opponent, and its identity as a "white nation" was threatened from within by the prospect of racial integration. America responded to the first with futuristic fantasies of military triumph and to the second by replaying the mythic histories of the past that had so often been used to celebrate white conquest of the continent.

The discourses of race, or attitudes toward race, have of course not been monolithic at any point in American history; like all other social discourses, those around race have always been deeply conflicted and often contradictory. My interest here has been largely in the ways the figures of Pocahontas and the white woman captive have cooperated within those particular discourses of race that work to promote and consolidate, rather than challenge or destabilize, the ideal of white superiority and thus supremacy in America. That history of the cultural work done by most renditions of the captivity or Pocahontas stories, though, has also been countered by other texts that have taken up both stories in order specifically to challenge and to refigure the ways they have inscribed race, racial dominance, and desire: In the twentieth century, Louise Erdrich has revised the Rowlandson narrative; Peter Hulme has reinterpreted Pocahontas's "rescue" of Smith; and Native women writers have returned to the Pocahontas legend to rescript it.

The nineteenth century also had its revisions of these culturally powerful stories. Tilton cites two abolitionist texts from the antebellum period that the authors signed with the pseudonym "Pocahontas": William Hillhouse's *Pocahontas; A Proclamation: With Plates* in 1820 and Emily Clemens Pearson's *Cousin Franck's Household, or Scenes in the Old Dominion* in 1852 (Tilton 149–62). Both authors were apparently inspired to adopt the pseudonym precisely because of the preponderance of Pocahontas stories that perpetuated rather than challenged racial arrangements and hierarchies in the United States.

One nineteenth-century narrative of Indian captivity, that of Sarah Wakefield published in Minnesota in 1863, was written to protest the U.S. government's treatment of Indians (Namias 204–61), using Wakefield's familiarity with Indians as a result of her captivity as the source of her authority. Wakefield was taken captive with her children during the Dakota uprising in Minnesota in 1862; one of the Indians, Chaska, became her protector during her six-week captivity, defending Wakefield and her children on several occasions against other Indians who wanted and attempted to kill them. When the Dakota were subdued, Chaska was taken prisoner along with nearly four hundred others. Despite Wakefield's public testimony on Chaska's behalf that he had more than once saved her life, he was hanged along with thirty-seven other Dakota men. June Namias calls Wakefield's story, published a few months after the hangings, not "an anti-Indian tract" but a "pro-Indian story" (240).

Because Wakefield dared to take an Indian's side against the power of the white state, she was subjected to the familiar and time-worn accusation leveled at returned captive women: of changed loyalty because of sexual intimacy with her protector. An officer involved in the trials and executions wrote in a letter to his wife, "[O]ne rather handsome woman . . . had become so infatuated with the red skin who had taken her for his wife, that, although her white husband was still living at some point below, and had been in search of her, she declared that were it not for her children, she would not leave her dusky paramour" (quoted in Namias 226).

In recent years, sympathy for Indians has become less risky than it was for Wakefield, as America has witnessed a resurgence of popular interest in Native American cultures and a renewed romanticization of Indian life. Michael Blake's 1988 paperback Western novel *Dances with Wolves*, from which the enormously successful 1990 film was adapted, engages the racial tropes of the 1950s captivity Westerns in order to rewrite their racial values, and while the usefulness of his simple reversal of the usual figuration of "bad Indians and good settlers" must be questioned—in Blake's novel, as in the film, almost all whites are cruel and bestial, and all Indians, except the Pawnee, well intentioned, dignified, and noble— it is interesting to note some of the ways *Dances with Wolves* responds to the tradition of the captivity story.

The heroine of the novel is a white woman who, like Cynthia Ann Parker, was taken by Comanche when she was a young girl (the film relocates the story among the Lakota) and has spent most of her life with "the People," assimilating thoroughly, as did Parker, into the tribe. The novel makes clear, as the film does not, that Stands-with-a-Fist fears the white cavalryman Dunbar when she first sees him precisely because she is afraid he will recapture her and return her by force to white society— another echo of Cynthia Ann Parker's story. The cavalry unit that later captures Dunbar (now a "white Indian," Dances-with-Wolves) has been sent into the territory explicitly to retrieve captive women and children (a revealing gender distinction), by force if necessary. Blake also rescripts the captivity prototype in making Stands-with-a-Fist not at all "tainted" by sexual intimacy with the Indian husband who has just died when she enters the story; her prior sexual relationship with an Indian is no obstacle whatever to her suitability as a love object and sexual partner for Dunbar, the white hero who, like other "white Indians" in American cultural history, chooses to assimilate into Indian life, a life that both the novel and film represent as infinitely superior to that in white society. *Dances with Wolves* engages the earlier representations of captivity to respond to and rewrite the ideologies of race, gender, and sexuality that earlier captivity stories, including those of the 1950s, had promoted.

Not all recent returns to the captivity tradition, however, have aimed to unsettle the ways it served romanticized histories of the colonizing of the continent. An edition of Rowlandson's narrative was published in 1988 in Arizona by a Christian fundamentalist, Mark Ludwig, who makes plain in his introduction that he hopes Rowlandson's story will inspire a return to the religious values that he claims founded the nation.

Ludwig dedicates his edition of Rowlandson to "the men and women who built this nation with their tears and with their prayers"; he is silent about the tears and prayers of those from whom the country was taken. Claiming that "Mary Rowlandson has a special message for our generation" (vi), Ludwig, like the seventeenth-century Puritan divines before him, usurps and dehistoricizes Rowlandson's experience as a metaphor for contemporary Christians' struggle against what he sees as ungodly forces:

> The Christians of this age find themselves embattled with those who would redirect the course of our nation, and attempt to reestablish it on principles which are entirely at odds with the Bible and with God. While we may not have come to the point of bloodshed yet, the battle is very real and vicious. The stakes are nothing less than our freedom to worship and serve God, as well as all of the prosperity and blessing which has resulted from doing His will. (vi)

Like the preface writer of the first edition of Rowlandson's narrative, Ludwig makes her text and her experience a political as well as religious story, relevant to the spiritual and civic "crises" that he perceives in contemporary America:

> Centuries later we are faced with the task of rebuilding a nation which has been ruined by sin. I say "ruined" because it is hard to find another word for a nation where thousands of babies are sacrificed every day to the idols of license and convenience, and where homosexuals have more political clout than Christians. . . . In the days to come, we are going to need a faith no less tenacious, and a perseverence [sic] no less enduring than Mary Rowlandson's. (vii)

Ludwig's interpretation of Rowlandson's text connects with those of her Puritan community in the seventeenth century; it is a vivid reminder of the longevity of the ideologies that pressed Rowlandson's text into the service of white supremacist views, along with those that followed it through the centuries.

The issue of white supremacy in America is far from settled. A 1996 article by Leonard Zeskind in *The Nation*, "White-Shoed Supremacy," reports on a movement that calls itself an "American Renaissance":

> Over Memorial Day weekend, Samuel Jared Taylor's "American Renaissance" newsletter will convene 150 university professors, journalists and clergymen in Louisville, Kentucky's Seelbach Hotel for gentlemanly discussion—coats and ties required. They will catalogue a growing list of indecencies, including theft of the national shrines by bands of multicultural brigands and an imminent demographic tsunami that will swamp European-Americans altogether. They will lament the genetic link between the black race, crime and I.Q. as a sobering but scientific fact.
>
> At the end, a solution will present itself: resurgent white racial consciousness as a precursor to old-fashioned white supremacy. Nothing hateful, mind you, just the stuff that once made America great. They call it "white separatism" now. (21)

Zeskind's report on the "American Renaissance" movement is only one among many reports of a resurgent white nationalism in America of the 1990s. In such a climate, perhaps it isn't surprising to find Ludwig placing Rowlandson's narrative into the theopolitics of the religious right or Disney Studios making a film like *Pocahontas*. The very vigor of these repeated articulations of white supremacist convictions, however, as Dana Frank has recently remarked, is evidence that "white rule must always be in danger of slipping, or they wouldn't have to work so hard to shore it up" (29).

That white supremacist ideologies in this country have been repeatedly challenged is evident in the existence of alternative histories that writers like Erdrich, Hulme, Allen, Brant, Blake, and others have drawn from the stories of Pocahontas and captive white women as they have in various ways returned to and rewritten those stories. In other words, there are counter-narratives to the white-supremacist stories of what has "lain hidden in the wombs" of this land from the beginnings of English colonization.

In John Barth's *The Sot-Weed Factor*, Eben Cooke's English tutor, Henry Burlingame, discovers in his quest for his own identity that he is, in fact, part Indian. And, having discovered John Smith's secret eggplant recipe for overcoming his phallic inadequacies (the legacy of his English forebear, the first Henry Burlingame, who passed the affliction down to all his male progeny), Henry manages to impregnate Eben's twin sister, Anna, before disappearing into the Maryland wilds to take up residence with the Indians, presumably having found Indian life more seductive than English.

Eben's wife, Joan, and his sister, Anna, are brought to bed simultaneously, but Joan perishes in childbirth, together with their newborn daughter; to spare his unwed sister the shame of public knowledge of her illegitimate child, Eben claims her son to be his and Joan's child, whom his sister will help him raise. He installs the boy as heir to Malden, his Maryland estate, and gives him the Cooke family name. But "Andrew Cooke," scion of English gentry in colonial Maryland, is actually the son of a man who is part Indian, and so is himself likewise of mixed race. Thus Barth irreverently deconstructs the pretensions of white identity and privilege on which myths of national origins, class, social status, and property have so often rested in America.

A more recent novel, Bharati Mukherjee's *The Holder of the World* (1993), turns to the story of white women's captivity to explore and finally explode their usual arbitrary constructions of identity, individual and national, around race and women's sexual desire. The novel is the story of the "Salem Bibi—meaning 'the white wife from Salem'—Precious-as-Pearl" (13), who is also Hannah Easton, born in the Massachusetts colony in 1670. Mukherjee engages the historical record of the settlement of the Massachusetts colony in her novel: Hannah's father comes to Massachusetts from England, and on his way to the westward edge of white settlement, pauses in Lancaster, where he has dinner "at the home of John White" (Mary Rowlandson's father) and is "offered a modest bookkeeping job by White's son-in-law, the Reverend Joseph Rowlandson, Lancaster's first minister" (24). He moves on, buys land, marries Rebecca, a neighbor's young daughter, and fathers Hannah; on her first birthday, he dies of a bee sting (26). The young widow Rebecca secretly takes an Indian lover, a defiance of Puritan sexual codes that her position on the very edge of the wilderness makes possible.

When Hannah is five, King Philip's War erupts; that historical conflict serves as the backdrop for the first of Mukherjee's revisions of the captivity prototype. Because the war makes it impossible to continue their liaison as usual, Rebecca runs away with her Nipmuc lover, who smears her old clothes with blood, strews them about the house, and sets the house afire to make it appear that Rebecca has been the victim of an Indian attack. They leave the child Hannah behind to be raised by another Puritan family, and Rebecca, "peel[ing] her white, radiant body out of the Puritan widow's somber bodice and skirt as a viper sheds skin before wriggling into the bush" and putting on "something new and Indian and clean to wear" (29), "vanishes into the wilderness, [escaping] her prison, against prevailing odds that would have branded her" (30–31).

This scene of a fictionalized Indian captivity, refigured as Rebecca's escape, allies her with the other "lost" women who chose Indian life over English. Since reference has been made earlier to Rebecca's "fertile womb" (26), it is no surprise to learn at the end of the novel that she bore five more children with her Nipmuc lover. Rebecca's escape, coinciding as it does in the novel with the time of Rowlandson's captivity, serves as a dramatic counter to the narrative that initiated the captivity tradition.

The child Hannah grows up a quiet and dutiful Puritan. When she is still a young woman, her best friend, Hester, gives her Rowlandson's narrative to read (51); Hester, whose aunt was among those who died in the Lancaster attack, is a "compliant" woman who "entrusted herself to marriage for deliverance" (51) but who also has enough erotic imagination to "fancy herself abducted by heathens" (52). Hester's fantasies help Hannah to "remember" her own mother's disappearance, rewriting its character from loss into opportunity. Accordingly, after Hester drowns, Hannah, now prepared for adventures of her own, impulsively marries the Irish adventurer to whom Hester had been engaged; Gabriel eventually takes her with him to India in pursuit of his fortune. Gabriel disappears some years later, and Hannah becomes the captive—"prisoner" or "guest" (218)—and finally the passionate and sexually fulfilled lover of Raja Jadav Singh. When Singh is killed in battle, Hannah makes her way back to Massachusetts with her infant daughter, "the proof of *her* 'Indian' lover, the quick, black-haired and black-eyed girl called Pearl

Singh" (284).[27] There she finds her mother with her "five half-Nipmuc children" (284), and all live together in Salem until Rebecca dies in 1720 and Hannah in 1750.

Hannah's daughter Pearl, the narrative reports, "born in 1701 somewhere in the South Atlantic on the long voyage home, saw in her old age the birth of this country, an event she had spent a lifetime advocating, and suffering for" (284). In having Pearl working for and witnessing the "birth" of America, Mukherjee inscribes a multiracial and multicultural element into the very foundations of the country, much as Barth does in *The Sot-Weed Factor*.

The web of Mukherjee's novel connects two scenes of English colonialism: New England and India, with the problematic and ambivalent term "Indian" as their connecting node. The "white" wombs of Anna Cooke in *The Sot-Weed Factor* and of Rebecca and Hannah Easton in *The Holder of the World* bring forth a powerful counter-narrative to the dominant history of Indian captivity in white America: In Mukerjee's novel in particular, Indian captivity is a scene for enacting a woman's powerful sexual desire, a desire that transgresses the racial and cultural divisions that stories of captive women have so often been used to evoke and guard. That desire also produces the blending of races as well as cultures in the children born of these passionate unions.

Crucial as the usual versions of these stories have been as instruments for articulating and policing race in America, then, they have never been about race alone. Dependent upon gender for constructing race, legendary accounts of Pocahontas and the white woman captured by Indians have also depended upon race for a reciprocal construction of gender. The legends spoke a familiar femininity: that the bodies and sexuality of women belong to men; that women are properly the *objects*, but never the *subjects*, of desire; and that women belong *at home*, a home dependent for its definition upon masculine control and the presence and exploitation of women's sexual and reproductive bodies. Mediating the relations between disempowered "dark other" men and dominant white men who drew their power from the enforced powerlessness of women and racially "other" men, the white woman captive and Pocahontas have been instruments for legitimating the conquest of the land and establishing it as "home" to white Euro-Americans.

These paired figures have throughout U.S. history wielded enormous cultural power; narratives and mythic retellings of their experiences have been an ideological linchpin in the long history of white conquest and white supremacy in the New World. Sufficiently resilient to be adapted to shifting and even contradictory scenarios and purposes, both the white woman captive and her Native counterpart have been invoked at critical moments when questions of racial and national identity have been in the forefront of the consciousness of white America. Whenever their stories have offered a challenge to ideologies of conquest, they have most often been manipulated, suppressed, or rewritten to support those ideologies; for that reason they have also attracted writers like Erdrich, Allen, Hulme, Barth, and Mukherjee whose work rewrites the essentialist notions of gender and identity on which the concept of a "white nation" rests.

Against such a "map" of America, therefore, stands another: one inscribed by the refusal of some, including women, to cooperate in constructing such a nation and by "transgressive" liaisons—social, sexual, political—across racial dividing lines that have produced a richly multiracial, multilingual, multicultural United States. One such revisionary cartography of the nation in miniature is offered in Mukherjee's novel in the house in Salem, Massachusetts, where Hannah and Rebecca Easton and their assortment of half-Indian children make their home. It is one among many possible alternative cartographies of America and readings of American history and culture that render imaginable the project of reconstructing and reshaping the American nation.

THE PRAIRIE: AUGUST 1992

> What I am after is . . . a more organic panorama, showing the continuous and living evidence of the past in the inmost vital substance of the present.
>
> —HART CRANE

It's a beautiful midwestern late-summer day. At midday the sky is high and bright blue overhead, with a few floaty white clouds for contrast.

Sunlight dapples the leaves in the woods around the edge of the yard and warms the flowers in the pots on the porch, making them raise their blossom heads and extend their leaves. They had looked decidedly droopy and contracted in the chill of early morning.

The whole world, including me, is glad for a little warmth. I woke up early this morning, 5:30, when the sky above the trees in the tall bedroom window was just faintly washing with light. The house was cold for an August morning; the outside thermometer at the kitchen window had dipped below 50, probably a record low. But then it's been an altogether uncharacteristic Iowa summer, with only occasional touches of the drenching heat we're used to. The corn is growing well, though—it's tall, much taller than I, and thick and green, with a crown of bright gold where the tassels cascade up and over the top. This unexpected bright coolness, combined with the usual lush vegetable green of late summer, makes the day seem jewel-like and rare, a day not to be squandered.

By noon a pleasant warmth has established itself. Five hundred years ago today, Columbus had already left Spain and his first voyage to Asia was underway. That is, to what he thought would be Asia. I could, no doubt should, stay at home and indoors, reading and writing more about that voyage and all that happened on this continent in its wake. Today, though, in the heartland of the continent Columbus "discovered," I'm more inclined to head out on an expedition of my own. Bill and I decide to bike over to the Rochester Prairie, one of my favorite Iowa spots, where I haven't been for several years.

We put the bikes in the back of the truck and drive from Iowa City to West Branch, leave the truck there, and head out into the countryside. As usual, I've underestimated the distance and overestimated my stamina on a bicycle. It turns out to be a long way, probably ten or twelve miles, much of it uphill. But I enjoy the ride. On either side of the road, the corn is high, the landscape in its subtle Iowa way quite beautiful, the red barns and silos a picture against the deep green waves of corn. Several of the farms carry a proud certificate on a gatepost: Century Farm, indicating that it has been in the same family for a hundred years. Some of the signs are pretty weathered; maybe it's been more than a hundred years since some of these families staked their claim, plunked themselves down, and started to till and plant. Never mind that other people had been living there before them, and for centuries, too. To people looking to "civilize" the country by planting, the rich black soil of Iowa must have looked like black gold, like money in the bank.

We reach the Cedar River, cross the bridge, and pass the first road, the one that leads to the town dump, then turn right onto the second road, the one to the cemetery. The road is a shock after the smooth pavement; my bike bucks at the gravel and slows to a slide in the patches of sand. Soon we're almost at the entrance; Bill decides to ride on ahead, but I drop my bike in the weeds beside the road and walk up to the cemetery.

The entrance is a wide metal gate with an arch at the top. Metal letters spell out the name across the arch: Rochester Cemetery. Somewhere along the way, someone decided it should be a prairie—maybe as a commemorative gesture to what this part of the world looked like when some of the people buried here arrived and saw it for the first time. Or maybe as a celebration of the beauty and fecundity of what they'd claimed and kept as theirs. Now it's grown up and wild with prairie flowers and other native plants, not at all groomed and tended in the usual way of cemeteries—except for the section up the hill far to the left, where the new graves are.

The place is familiar but every time new, every time of year different. Now it's thick with the profligacy of late summer. The flowers are profuse and tangled and tall, mostly white and yellow-gold, accented with the lavender-pink of sweet red clover. Most numerous are the black-eyed Susans. There are sunflowers, too, here and there—as Adrienne Rich says in "An Atlas of the Difficult World," "something that binds the map of this country together . . . from Vermont to California." From her poem I learned that the sunflower or girasol root is the Jerusalem artichoke, the tuber "that has fed the Indians, fed the hobos, could feed us all," as Rich puts it. A lot of food is going to waste beside the roadways of America, hidden at the root of these sturdy, lovely flowers. When Mary Rowlandson wrote of her time among the Indians, one of the things she mentioned is gathering and eating "Harty-choakes." I remember wondering, when I first read her narrative, what she meant—in seventeenth-century Massachusetts, certainly not my favorite pizza topping. Now, having read Rich's poem, I think I know. She must have learned from the Indians to eat the roots of sunflowers. I've never eaten a Jerusalem artichoke, but I've seen them in the stores, knobby and covered with a papery brown skin. I make a mental note to try one.

Queen Anne's lace is here too, in profusion, and the gold coreopsis are higher than my head. I spot some tiny and delicate white flowers blooming in tall sprays; I don't know their name, but I think how they would make a lovely bridal bouquet. I step over the leaves and stems of other flowers no longer in their blooming season: wild columbine, larkspur, phlox, yarrow, rambling rose. The pods of wild peas hang heavy on the vines, their green shading to yellow as the peas ripen. Bees and butterflies swarm around the fragrant, columned blossoms of creamy vetch; I'm careful of my step when I walk by a patch of it, fearful of a bee sting or of crushing a butterfly.

The mammoth and majestic oaks stretch their immense branches to shade much of the cemetery. Their leaves are saturated with the deep, deep green of late summer, the most intense green they'll achieve this year. They are poised to shift their palette in a few weeks, sooner if the chilly nights persist. The tangle of flowers at my feet—and now, at this peak time of year, even at my waist and shoulders—fills me with a sensuous delight, draws me down to the earth and to the contemplation of its fragile and miraculous productivity, its only apparently infinite capacity for renewing itself. But the trees lift me up again, away from the earth and its minute, amazing processes, lift my eyes toward the sky and to the contemplation of larger matters. They must be wondrously old, these oaks. Maybe they were already here, a scattering of young saplings, when the first white settlers moved into this territory. Now, along with the baroquely twisted cedars that give the river its name, they shelter the graves of many of those they greeted here so long ago.

I make my way through the tangle of prairie grasses and flowers to the rise at the far end of the cemetery, watching for snakes as I go. Beggar lice, the parent plants eager to extend the range of their offspring, cling to my socks, shorts, and shoes. Some prairie grass I don't know the name of has sent up delicate seed stalks from its round green tufts; the seeds, a dull but definite red, suspend from the gracefully curved stalks and tremble there like drops of faded blood.

From the top of the rise I look out over a broad expanse of descending fields and forests toward the river. This is my favorite place in the prairie, my reason for coming back again and again. Here are clustered the oldest of the gravestones, dating from the earliest time of white settlement in Iowa. Those graves are at my back now, as I look out and away from the prairie to drink in the view.

As always, it takes my breath away. The earth slopes downward in gentle, voluptuous curves to the cleft of the valley where the river runs. It looks for all the world as warm and welcoming as a mother's lap. The light of the late afternoon is a hazy gold and lovingly caresses the tops of the hills. I try to imagine what those first white settlers must have thought when they stood here and looked out for miles over this fertile valley, how seductive the scene must have been. I can imagine how easily they must have fallen in love with what they'd found, a place profoundly inviting, looking as if it could let itself be called "home." No wonder this seemed the right spot to stop and stay and stake a claim, to live and then to die, and when it came to that, to consign the bodies of their dead to this particular earth.

The verdant growth of the prairie makes it more difficult than at other times of year to locate the gravestones and read their faint inscriptions, but I soon find the family graves of the Kesters, Samuel and his several wives. Little markers remind me that some little Kesters, of various maternal origins, didn't make it very far into the biblical three score years and ten allotted to a human lifespan. Other families' plots confirm the familiar social history: women died young, many very likely in child-birth, though some lived to a surprising old age. Children succumbed in great numbers. Men frequently outlived two or even three wives. Women's graves so outnumber those of men in this part of the cemetery that the soil in this spot strikes me as quite literally engendered by the number of female bodies laid to rest here. The image of "Mother Earth" suddenly takes on new meaning. I think again of how this burying ground marks the individual failures but collective success of whites in taking over all the land here.

But I know very well that it's stories that tell us how to see, stories that tell me now as I stand here how to look at the land before me, how to read this landscape, that tell me in fact what I see, what I can see. This part of Iowa is just west of the Mississippi, that mighty river which was the threshold for white expansion into the West in the nineteenth century.

The Mississippi was the border between the "white" East and the Indian West in the Indian Removal Act of 1830; according to its terms, those Century Farms shouldn't be here. As usual, though, white ambitions fast outstripped white promises, and the Iowa Territory was opened to white settlement in the 1830s. All those tales and movies of my childhood told me it was heroes that "claimed the West"; my seeing this land now as feminized, inviting, with the capacity to nurture me, is the residue of the colonizing gaze that gendered the continent as female and ripe for the taking. More recently, a rediscovery of traditional Indian respect for the earth has been popularized as part of the environmental movement, and bumper stickers featuring a blue and green planet and enjoining us to "Love Our Mother" are everywhere. When I look out on this beautiful vista, the metaphors that spring at once to mind are of a female body, an inviting and nurturing maternal presence. And no wonder; those metaphors have been given to me, urged upon me.

I recall Mary Lou telling me recently about Lily Briscoe, a character in Virginia Woolf's *To the Lighthouse:* Lily, who is a painter, knows that one pair of eyes are never enough to see a thing in all its complexity. "One wanted fifty pairs of eyes to see with," Lily thinks to herself; and even then, "Fifty pairs of eyes were not enough." Well, I have only one pair of eyes. But I can confront the partiality of what I see, acknowledge all I don't see, and remind myself that it is powerful and privileged *stories* that shape my seeing of this place. Displace the way of looking that has been privileged by the dominant stories—that's what I have to try to do. Maybe fall silent and listen instead of look—attend to the silences, leave spaces to signify all that this cemetery and restored prairie have covered up, spaces for other stories to be heard, room for voices other than my own. What would those stories sound like? How would I look at this valley, at these gravestones, if those stories too were familiar to me?

Because I was just at the Mesquakie Powwow in Tama last week, I'm more aware than usual of the cultural palimpsest of this countryside, of how the most recent accretions bury what lies beneath. Another kind of removal. The Mesquakie lived and hunted on many thousands of acres of the hills just west of the Mississippi as late as the early nineteenth century. Their hunting grounds could have encompassed the hill on which I stand. They had been relocated here from the east, from what is now Wisconsin, and were subsequently again relocated west, to Kansas, to land where trees are more scarce even than in Iowa—no doubt not a happy situation for a people who had once been at home in the eastern woodlands. The Mesquakie didn't like Kansas one bit, were homesick for trees, so they sold their ponies and petitioned the governor of Iowa to use the money to purchase in their name a large tract of land, eventually more than three thousand acres, along the Iowa River. The governor had to make the purchase because it was against the law at that time for an Indian to buy land in the United States and its territories. They stayed; five hundred or so Mesquakie live there still. I wonder if any of the folks I stand among here ever met up with a Mesquakie, and if so, what happened.

And I wonder now, I think for the first time in all the many visits I've made to this place, about the people who might have stood on this spot before there were any graves with markers bearing English names and German names. History is a funny thing—so many things get left out. I wonder what the land that spreads itself out before me now looked like to the people who once lived here. And what must the white settlers have looked like to those first people when the whites arrived with their cows and Conestogas?

After a final glance around, I leave the cemetery and call to Bill, and we head back to Iowa City, and home. The uphill climbs of the trip out have their payoff now, and I coast on long stretches that cool me off and rest my tired legs. My bottom is numb from the pressure of the seat, and my hands start to tingle from gripping the handlebars. When I coast, I can put a little more of my weight on the pedals and lift my bottom slightly off the seat for relief, and I can loosen my grip on the handlebars and let the blood flow back into my palms and fingers. I find myself wondering what your bottom would feel like if you sat on a hard board wagon seat for a thousand or more miles, crossing prairies that had no roads, just wagon tracks to show where other wagons had gone before, if any had. How can I admit the courage and endurance of those people who came west, leaving bodies of children and women and men by the way, facing and fearing, but not understanding, the wrath of the people they displaced? How can I feel pity for their struggles, suffering, and losses, while remembering, refusing to forget, their blind ignorance and the devastation they wrought for people who were already here? Where can I place my own history and identity against the backdrop of that drama?

The day and the excursion are almost over. A cooling breeze blows over my face and arms as I head home, winding west, toward the setting sun, through the waving fields of corn. The oceans of Iowa. In a few weeks the corn will start to dry in the fields; the stalks will turn the dull of gold not spent but stashed, and the silos will be full. The oaks in the cemetery will turn a dull gold too, and bronze and copper and crimson, and pigs will live in fear for their lives. It's not glamorous, but it's gold nonetheless, the gold the Europeans came here for and found, though in forms they hadn't imagined. I read somewhere a few years ago that Iowa has more millionaires per capita than any other state. That surprised me, because there's so little show of wealth here. I decided it must be because the land people own is worth so much. Even if you haven't got a hundred dollars in the bank, if you own a big farm, you're a millionaire in Iowa. I guess the Mesquakie and the Sauk used to be the millionaires around here. Now the Mesquakie have the lowest per capita income and the highest unemployment rate of any people in the state.

In a few days I'll load the car and turn my face east once again, reverse the westward trek of the white settlers and the track of the sun, drive back to New England, once the land of the Massachusetts, Pequod, Wampanoag, Narragansett, Mohegan; back to the Connecticut River valley that I now call, for the time being at least, home. This particular Iowa summer is over.

Massachusetts is different from Iowa, no doubt about it. But some things they have in common. Their names, for instance—Indian words, names of Indian people. Histories, some of them privileged and oft-told, some of them silenced, bind the map of this country together too, I think, even more firmly than sunflowers.

Yes, really to see this place, this land, requires more than one pair of eyes, more than fifty even. And to tell the story of this prairie—of this whole *country*—would take a chorus: many voices, many stories, not always harmonious, in fact probably dissonant more often than not. That we can make room for the stories, all of them, is our last and best hope. And then we'll each of us have to learn to listen in a new way—with new ears, maybe with fifty pairs of ears, or even more—to the complex song that chorus would sing.

⟨Notes⟩

1. MARY ROWLANDSON MAPS NEW WORLDS

1. In the Old Style calendar, the year's date changed following the vernal equinox instead of on January 1. Dates between January 1 and March 24 in years prior to the calendar shift are frequently designated with both years, though I have used New Style dating throughout. The calendar shift explains the discrepancy between the Old Style date of the attack on Lancaster that Rowlandson gives in her narrative—February 10, 1675—and the date based on the modern calendar, which would be 1676. See also the chronology of the war in Richard Slotkin and James Folsom's *So Dreadfull a Judgment* (46–52).

2. For a survey of the extent and prominence of captivity materials in North America, see Kathryn Derounian-Stodola and James Levernier, *The Indian Captivity Narrative 1550–1900,* and June Namias, *White Captives.* The sheer volume of the material both books cover vividly demonstrates how important the figure of the white woman captive has been in American cultural history.

3. My primary sources for Rowlandson's biography and family history are Kathryn Derounian, Kathryn Derounian-Stodola and David Greene, Robert Diebold, David Greene, and Douglas Leach.

4. According to the anthropologist and writer Michael Dorris, "most Native American peoples considered land to be an abstract commodity similar in kind to air or water or fire—something necessary for human survival but above personal ownership. While the notion of a group['s] or a person's rights to use a certain piece of property was widespread, there was almost no corresponding idea of 'title,' or land owned exclusively and permanently by those who didn't

directly work it" ("Discoveries" 158). It is likely, then, that, as with other exchanges, the indigenous people and the Europeans understood very differently what was happening when they "sold" and "bought" land.

5. I use terms like "Indian," "savage," "America," "New World," and "discovery" acutely aware of how imbued they are with Eurocentric (mis)perceptions. They would be most appropriately qualified throughout with quotation marks, but in the interests of the reader's ease I have not done that. Nevertheless, I want to acknowledge that the vocabulary is problematic, and I employ the familiar language of conquest with full awareness of those problems.

6. Abbot, 161. The actual kinship relation between Massasoit and the two brothers is not clear. Charles Burke says, "While Wamsutta and his brother have always been considered the sons of Massasoit, it is possible that this relationship was assumed on the basis of English law. All we know of the practices of the tribes in the northeast indicates that succession followed the female line, which would have Massasoit followed by his brother or his sister's son. Thus Wamsutta and his brother who followed him were possibly the nephews of Massasoit" (52).

7. Also sometimes spelled Weetamo or, in Rowlandson's narrative, Wattimore or Wettimore (150). English spelling was not regularized until the eighteenth century, so variant spellings are common in English writing prior to that time.

8. Rowlandson's description of Weetamoo's treatment of her during her captivity offers evidence of that enmity; Weetamoo is the only member of the group with whom Rowlandson has consistently strained relations. Rowlandson repays her mistress's harsh treatment when Weetamoo's baby dies. A company of other Indians come to support and share Weetamoo's mourning (to "howle with her," Rowlandson says [145]), but Rowlandson "[can] not much condole with them" (145). Even taking into account Rowlandson's recent loss of her own child and the resentment she is sure to have felt toward the Indians because of Sarah's death, her response to the death of Weetamoo's child seems remarkably heartless: "there was one benefit in it, that there was more room" (144).

9. Quotations from Rowlandson's narrative, including those from the preface, are taken from the Lincoln edition and will be cited parenthetically in the text.

10. David Minter cites Rowlandson as the prime example of such typological interpretation of the captivity experience: "[W]hat we see in her, at least as she comes to us in her narrative, is a nearly perfect internalization of a social code which possessed, despite its distinct social bias, a capacity for giving heroic proportion and definite meaning to individual adventure" (346–47).

11. Christopher Castiglia also sees white women's captivity as having posed a "radical challenge to systems of male domination" (45). He writes, "the captivity narrative allowed women authors to create a symbolic economy through which to express dissatisfaction with the roles traditionally offered white women

in America, and to reimagine those roles and the narratives that normalize them" (4). Castiglia's analysis seems to me to be a somewhat ahistorical one, or at least one that collapses historical differences in the possibilities for interpretation in different periods, in his ascribing of a recognizably more contemporary feminist consciousness to the captives and women readers of captivity accounts in earlier periods. Certainly such an analysis as the one he offers is possible from our late-twentieth-century reading positions—indeed Castiglia's interest in the captivity narratives' potentially destabilizing effects and challenges to white male hegemony is close to my own—but I would argue that there is no evidence that such a "liberationist" reading of captivity by either the captives themselves or readers of the accounts was likely or even possible before at least the nineteenth century. Thus I find his reading of nineteenth-century narratives more persuasive than his reading of Rowlandson, which I find flawed as well by his unhistoricized reading of Rowlandson's attitudes on race.

12. Hawthorne's account appeared in the *American Magazine of Useful and Entertaining Knowledge* 2 (May 1836); Thoreau's in *A Week on the Concord and Merrimack Rivers* (1849), 238–40; Whittier's legend of the Dustan story, "A Mother's Revenge," is included in *Legends of New England* (1831), 125–31. Kathryn Whitford discusses these and other versions of the story in "Hannah Duston: The Judgement of History."

13. June Namias too writes that "there is evidence that the earliest Englishmen did not see Indians as 'red'—this racialist epithet was a late eighteenth- and nineteenth-century usage" (87).

14. For an elaboration of the kinship connections between Blacks and Indians in America, see William Loren Katz, *Black Indians: A Hidden Heritage*. Katz claims that "Today just about every African-American family tree has an Indian branch" (2). See also Bennett, *Before the Mayflower*, 321–22.

15. Edmund S. Morgan specifies the years between 1670 and 1682 (the year of the first publication of Rowlandson's narrative in Boston and London) as the period when the process of legally conflating Indians with Blacks occurred in the Virginia colony: "In 1670 the question had been raised whether Indians sold in Virginia by other Indians (who had captured them in tribal wars) should be slaves for life or for a term of years. At that time it was decided that servants who were not Christians and who were brought into the colony by land (Indians from other regions) should serve for twelve years or (if children) until thirty years of age. The same act stated that non-Christian servants brought 'by shipping' (Negroes) were to be slaves for life. Thus Africans purchased from traders were assumed to be slaves but Indians were not. In 1682 the assembly eliminated the difference, making slaves of all imported non-Christian servants. Since only Indians and Africans fitted this description and since the assembly had already

decided in 1667 that conversion to Christianity after arrival did not alter the status of a slave, the act of 1682 set the further development of slavery on a squarely racial foundation. Indians and Negroes were henceforth lumped together in Virginia legislation, and white Virginians treated black, red, and intermediate shades of brown as interchangeable. Even the offspring of a mixed Indian and white couple were defined as mulattoes" (329).

16. That a woman captive would choose to remain with her captors rather than being "redeemed" and returned to her home culture was a threat, and sometimes a reality, that produced enormous anxiety among the colonizing population because of all it symbolically signified. For the story of one such woman who made that choice, Eunice Williams (captured in Deerfield, Massachusetts, in 1704, when she was seven), see John Demos, *The Unredeemed Captive: A Family Story from Early America.* Williams's father, John Williams, was the minister at Deerfield when it was attacked; he was also taken prisoner but was later released. His narrative of his own captivity, *The Redeemed Captive, Returning to Zion* (1707) was, along with Rowlandson's, one of the best known of the early Puritan captivity narratives.

17. For evidence that Mather was the author of the preface, see Minter, 336 n, and Derounian, "Publication, Promotion, and Distribution," 240–42.

18. I have used one of the first published versions of Rowlandson's narrative, the London edition of 1682, in the collection of the British Library. That edition appeared simultaneously with the 1682 Cambridge first edition, no copy of which is now extant. See Derounian, "Publication, Promotion, and Distribution," for details about the narrative's early publishing history. Quotations from Joseph Rowlandson's sermon are from the 1682 London edition; its pagination is erratic, but I have cited the page numbers as they are printed. The preface has sometimes been included with Rowlandson's text in later editions, but the sermon has not been. For a discussion of the full publication history of Rowlandson's narrative, see Diebold's critical edition.

19. This is how the preface is signed in the London edition (Diebold c). Early American editions printed "Per Amicam" ("For a Friend") or "Ter Amicam," roughly "Thy three-fold friend" (Slotkin and Folsom, 367 n). The Lincoln edition uses "Ter Amicam," as does the version printed in Slotkin and Folsom. I have chosen to follow Diebold's preference. For a discussion of the differing preface signatures, see Derounian, "Publication, Promotion, and Distribution," 240.

20. Michael Rogin notes that in the Puritan lexicon, "to justify" meant "to save for God" (137).

21. See Diebold, x. June Namias suggests that the sexual reticence most Indians exhibited toward their captives might have been due in part to their anticipation that the captives might be adopted into the tribe; the captors were

cautious about infringing incest taboos by sexual intimacy with someone who might become a sister or brother, daughter or son (Namias 89).

22. According to the narrative, of Rowlandson's two sisters who were with her in the garrison when the Indians attacked Lancaster, one was shot and killed during the attack and the other was taken captive but ransomed about the same time as Rowlandson (120, 154–55). N.S.'s story bears some resemblance, however, to Rowlandson's account of the fate of Goodwife Joslin (128–29), which she does not witness herself but hears from other captives. The similarity may indicate that N.S. read the narrative before its publication and misremembered it or that he had heard the story secondhand, embellished it, and applied it, knowingly or not, to the wrong woman.

23. The "one eyed Sachem" was known to the English as John Monoco (his English-given name includes as a surname the Latin version of "one eye"). He was a Nashaway leader who took part in the attack on Lancaster in which Rowlandson was captured (Diebold x).

24. The "wine to drink out of their Captains throats" is, of course, English blood. In representing Metacom and his men as bloodthirsty vampires, Tompson deploys the well–worn trope of New World cannibalism found in so many of the discovery tracts. For a discussion of how the trope of cannibalism served the colonization of the Americas, see Peter Hulme's *Colonial Encounters*.

25. See, for example, my discussion in chapter 3 of James Fenimore Cooper's characterization of Narra-mattah, or "The Driven Snow," in *The Wept of Wish-Ton-Wish* (1829).

26. See also my discussion of Ludwig's introduction in chapter 3. I am indebted to Gary Ebersole's *Captured by Texts* for bringing the Ludwig edition to my attention.

27. The differences in the language of the title pages of Rowlandson's narrative in different editions support this suggestion. The 1682 Cambridge edition is titled "The Soveraignty & Goodness of God, together, with the faithfulness of his promises displayed: being a narrative of the captivity and restauration of Mrs. Mary Rowlandson"; there is no mention whatever of her captors. The title of the London edition of the same year does mention "the heathens": "A true history of the captivity & Restoration of Mrs. Mary Rowlandson, a minister's wife in New-England: wherein is set forth the cruel and inhumane usage she underwent amongst the heathens for eleven weeks time, and her deliverance from them." The 1720 Boston edition, however, once again makes no mention of the Indians but emphasizes the spiritual trials of captivity with this addition to the 1682 Cambridge title: "Commended by her, to all that desire to know the Lords doings to, & dealings with her." By the time the narrative was reprinted in Boston in 1770, the title had been amended to include strong anti-Indian

sentiment: "A narrative of the captivity, sufferings and removes, of Mrs. Mary Rowlandson, who was taken prisoner by the Indians, with several others, and treated in the most barbarous and cruel manner by those vile savages." Both 1770 editions as well as the 1771 edition carried that title.

28. Willard's treatment of Rowlandson's text also illustrates how representations and interpretations of Indian captivity produce and police gender along with racial ideologies. Referring to the passage from the narrative (quoted below, on 65) where Rowlandson reports that from the time she was first taken captive, she refused the use of tobacco, Willard says, "Her captivity seems to have thoroughly cured her of one habit, which however excusable it may be in men, is certainly rather disgusting in the fair sex, we mean the use of tobacco. *Pauvre tabac!* Mrs. R. gives it as violent a counterblast as did ever James of royal memory" (113). Willard here articulates a nineteenth-century gender/class division in the use of tobacco, even though pipe smoking seems to have been a common and socially accepted practice among seventeenth-century colonial Englishwomen.

29. While I agree with the theoretical implications Anderson draws from captivity narratives, including Rowlandson's, his reading of Rowlandson's history and even of her text is filled with errors. He asserts, for example, that "she had been born and spent all her young life in the no less un-European Massachusetts. . . . she [had] never been within three thousand miles of England" (314). He also inexplicably refers to her as "the nineteen-year old, newly married Mary Rowlandson"; in fact she was around forty when she was captured and had been married twenty years. In another error, he says that when she was finally ransomed, she returned home to Lancaster (315). Rowlandson does report passing through the ruins of Lancaster en route to Boston after her ransom (161–62) and says "a solemn sight it was to me" (161), but, as I have indicated, she was after her captivity never again "at home" in Lancaster.

30. Rowlandson obviously is referring here not to skin color, but to the Indians' use of body paint. Their being "always before Black" indicates her captors' usual color of body paint during her captivity, while here it is red, the shift no doubt part of the ritual she observes.

31. Directly contradicting a Puritan stereotype, Rowlandson makes a point of saying, "He was the first Indian I saw drunk all the while that I was amongst them" (157).

32. Jill Lepore makes the very poignant argument that "Rowlandson's release from captivity was predicated on . . . Indians' own bondage" (145). Lepore's excellent history, *The Name of War: King Philip's War and The Origins of American Identity*, was published just as this book was going to press, so I was unable to incorporate her insights as fully as I would have liked. See especially her impor-

tant chapter on the enslavement of Indians during and immediately after the war, "A Dangerous Merchandise," 150–70.

2. CLOSE ENCOUNTERS OF THE FIRST KIND

1. In her poem "Pocahontas from Her New World" (its title suggesting a neat reversal on the notion of discovery), Pamela Hadas does indeed show Pocahontas writing. The three sections of the poem are letters Pocahontas writes while she is in England, addressed to the three significant men in the story as we know it—Powhatan, John Smith, John Rolfe. Most interestingly, each "letter" (she claims she is actually writing for herself, "so I may say / what else I might not say of what I see" [3]) is interrupted by Rolfe, who chides her for writing and fears the power that possessing written language can give her: "I fear / you may have learned the use of words too well" (3); and "if I hear you cough once more, / I'll take your quill and ink away for good" (7). Pocahontas complains to herself, "Can I not sit down with quill and ink / but John must come and read my stiff beginning?" (11). The implication of Hadas's poem is that there could very well have been some written record by Pocahontas herself of her experiences with the English, but it was lost or destroyed by someone—perhaps her husband— who thought it either unimportant or subversive.

2. A number of critics, including Louis Montrose, Peter Hulme, and Annette Kolodny, have written about the ways European ideologies of gender and sexuality cooperated with those of race in the production of the rhetorics of "discovery" and "settlement" of the New World or were imposed upon it in the process of exploration. I have drawn from their work as well as extended it in several ways in what follows.

3. Kolodny has focused on the ways the American landscape was gendered as feminine in *The Lay of the Land: Metaphor as Experience and History in American Life and Letters*. Chapters 1 and 2, where she cites extensively instances from the documents of discovery in which the "land-as-woman symbolization" (ix) is established, are especially relevant to my work here. Kolodny's purpose in examining that metaphor, though, differs from mine; her original impetus, as she says, was her awareness of "our current ecological and environmental ills" and "growing distress at what we have done to our continent" (ix). While I share her concerns, my intention here is to examine another, though related, function of the metaphor of the land-as-woman: the role such engendering played in the political history of a racialized Euro-American nation and national identity.

4. The poem is undated in the anthologies I consulted, but presumably it, along with Donne's other secular love poems, was written before 1600, during

the years when Donne was living as a Renaissance "gentleman" in London, before his marriage and some years before his ordination to the Anglican priesthood in 1615. For the full text of the poem, see *The Complete Poetry of John Donne*, 57–58.

5. Cabot had touched on the North American continent in England's name in 1497, five years after Columbus's landfall in the Bahamas, but it was to be nearly a century before English exploration with an eye to colonial settlement was to begin. In the 1580s two English colonies were attempted in "Virginia": the colonists abandoned the first, and the second, the famous "Lost Colony of Roanoke Island," mysteriously disappeared altogether. Jamestown, founded in 1607, was the first English settlement to survive, though in that case too, as in Plymouth later, the colonists' survival was due entirely to the assistance of the local Native population.

6. For a thorough discussion of the social and sexual politics of Ralegh's rhetoric in the *Discovery*, see Louis Montrose, "The Work of Gender in the Discourse of Discovery."

7. For other discussions of the politics of representation in this engraving, see both Montrose, "Work of Gender," and Hulme.

8. Vespucci's explorations in 1499 followed closely on Columbus's. The German mapmaker Martin Waldseemueller was the first to use the name "America" for the New World, in a map drawn in 1507.

9. "The Fourme of Solempnizacion of Matrimonye," in *The Boke of Common Praier* (London, 1559; rpt. London: 1890), 123.

10. From the perspective of the history of European settlement of the New World, England's defeat of the Spanish Armada in 1588 not only established England as a world naval power—the significance usually assigned in world history classes in American schools—but also gave England the incentive to contest Spain's colonial enterprises in the New World and thus opened the door to English exploration and colonization of North America.

11. The representations of "hermaphrodites" or "sodomites" found in the New World, while not central to my inquiry here, are nonetheless worthy of brief notice. The explorers found among the Native people a fluidity of gender identities that challenged the rigid gender binarism of Judeo-Christian Europe. The berdache, or "man-woman," tradition common among indigenous American culture groups (see Walter L. Williams) elicited responses ranging from curiosity to murderous outrage. LeMoyne, a participant in French attempts to colonize Florida in the mid-sixteenth century, made a drawing of hermaphrodites that was later engraved by De Bry and included in the *Historia Americae* (34). The text accompanying the drawing describes them as "a mixture of both sexes" who are

"considered odious by the Indians, but as they are robust and strong they are used to carry loads instead of beasts of burden" (De Bry 34). Alvar Nuñez Cabeza de Vaca reported his own observations: "I saw a most brutish and beastly custome, to wit, a man who was married to another, and these be certaine effeminate and impotent men, who go cloathed and attired like women, and perform the office of a woman: they carry no bowes, but bear very great and waightie burdens: and among them we saw many such effeminate persons" (quoted in Hulton 205 n.34). The colonists' and explorers' anxiety of gender at least occasionally provoked a grotesquely violent response, as can be seen in another De Bry engraving from Benzoni's *La Historia del Mondo Nuovo*, captioned "Sodomites savaged by mastiffs"; the accompanying text reports that "when Balboa was crossing the isthmus of Panama he had forty hermaphrodites killed by dogs" (De Bry 132).

12. See Peter Hulme's discussions of cannibalism as the spectral "other" from whom Robinson Crusoe distinguishes himself and against whom he thus consolidates his identity when he "finally knows who he is"; he knows he "is not a cannibal" (198).

13. The "Indian queen" figure, which in early world cartography was used to symbolize "America" as one of the world's four continents, also "was depicted, . . . in size, as being Amazonian" (Fleming 67).

14. Sigmund Freud in "The Taboo of Virginity": "Decapitation is to us a well-known symbolic substitute for castration" (239). I am indebted for this reference to Michael Paul Rogin in *Ronald Reagan, the Movie*, 343 n.31.

15. That Native people of the Americas were figured as cannibals, and that their cannibalism was used to justify their brutal treatment, are especially ironic in light of the fact that cannibalism erupted among the English colonists at Jamestown during "the Starving Time," the winter of 1609–10: Some of them ate the flesh of other colonists who had died of disease or starvation, some roasted and ate an Indian killed during an attack on the settlement, and another colonist killed, butchered, salted, and ate his wife, a crime for which he was executed (Morgan 73; Woodward 117).

16. Montrose ("Work of Gender" 6) cites de Certeau's use of the phrase in *The Writing of History*, xxv–xxvi.

17. The term "wanton" in the seventeenth century, according to the *Oxford English Dictionary*, included the meanings "Lascivious, unchaste, lewd, . . . given to amorous dalliance"; other meanings, though, especially applied to children, were "unruly," "naughty," "unmanageable," "playful," "sportive," "unrestrained in merriment." Strachey's choice of attributive here is revealing of the position of the observer as well as the behavior of the observed; Pocahontas clearly

exhibited spirited behavior that would not have been tolerated in an English girl, so that the colonists would have seen it as indicating her being "unmanageable." Unself-consciously exposing her genitals (apparently, as Strachey indicates, not unusual among Algonkian girls who had not yet reached puberty) made her vulnerable to the sexualized (invasive) gaze of the English colonists. Only after puberty, Strachey reports, did Algonkian girls develop a sense of sexual privacy: "being once twelve yeares, [the younger women] put on a kind of semecinctum lethern apron (as doe our artificers or handycrafts men) before their bellies, and are very shamefac't to be seene bare" (*Historie* 65).

18. This image of Pocahontas as available to the lustful gaze of the colonists recalls another, later instance where Native women's genital "geography" is conflated with the continent's being "discovered" and mapped by the "penetrating" gaze of the European explorer. Leslie Fiedler quotes a passage from Meriwether Lewis's journal, a comment about the grass girdles worn by the Assiniboine women: "[They are] of a sufficient thickness when the female stands erect to conceal those parts usually covered from familiar view, but when she stoops or places herself in many other attitudes this battery of Venus is not altogether impervious to the inquisitive and penetrating eye of the amorite" (quoted in Fiedler 73).

19. "Pocones" was the root of the pokeberry bush, dried and powdered; when mixed with animal fat, it made a red–tinted body paint, used by the Indians both for body decoration and to protect the skin against the sun and insect bites. See Strachey's *Historie*, 63–64, and Vaughan, 8.

20. Lemay points out that Adams wrote the essay in 1862, though it did not appear in print until 1867.

21. A unit of the Virginia Cavalry during the Civil War was the "Guard of the Daughters of Powhatan," which carried Pocahontas's image (wearing a red cross around her neck) on their company ensign (Rasmussen and Tilton 40).

22. Lemay devotes a footnote to this possibility (108–9 n). See also Barbour (24–25) and Mossiker (81), as well as the discussion by Helen Rountree, a historical anthropologist who has studied Powhatan culture, in *Pocahontas's People*, 38–39.

23. Quotations from Rolfe's letter to Gov. Thomas Dale are from appendix C in Mossiker's *Pocahontas: The Life and the Legend*, 344–48. This passage is found on 346; subsequent quotations will be from this source and will be cited parenthetically in the text.

24. In John Davis's 1805 novel, *Captain Smith and Pocahontas*, Rolfe joins Pocahontas in pining for Virginia when both are in England, though his reasons for "homesickness" are rather different from hers: "Not only Pocahontas, but Rolfe sighed in secret for the romantic scenery, the deep retirement of the still

virgin soil of the western continent. In Virginia he was entitled by the right of his bride to lands of immeasurable extent" (110–11).

25. The complexities of antimiscegenation legislation in Virginia were intricate and almost comic, as the state tried to pass racist laws that would prohibit interracial marriage but provide loopholes for the whites who claimed descent from Pocahontas (see Feest 80). It was a long-standing obsession, as the state persevered in defining and protecting racial identities; an "Act to Preserve Racial Integrity" was passed as late as 1924, complete with the usual loophole for white Virginia aristocrats who claimed descent from Pocahontas (Tilton 29). Legal prohibitions against interracial marriage were not repealed in Virginia until 1968 (Tilton 30). An analagous dilemma arose for the Melungeons in North Carolina and Tennessee. Having harbored and intermarried with escaped slaves, they were very mixed racially. Tennessee declared them "free persons of color," permitting their continued intermarriage with people of African descent. The North Carolina legislature in 1855, however, acting on the belief that the Melungeons were really Croatans, and so were the "white" descendants of the Lost Colony of Roanoke Island, declared them white and, under the provisions of antimiscegenation laws, forbade their marrying Blacks (Katz 129).

26. For Tilton's full discussion of how attitudes on racial mixing influenced the Pocahontas narrative, see his chapters "Miscegenation and the Pocahontas Narrative in Colonial and Federalist America" (9–33) and "The Pocahontas Narrative in the Era of the Romantic Indian" (58–92).

27. Lydia Maria Child, in "An Appeal for the Indians" (1868), tells of the "beautiful wife" of Osceola, the nineteenth-century Seminole leader, being "torn from him and sold into slavery," provoking Osceola to fight "like a tiger" against the whites (223). There is no reason to believe that her fate was unique or even unusual; Yehudi Webster claims that during the period before slavery was abolished, of the Native population of North America "approximately 10 percent . . . was enslaved" (107).

28. Both *The Log of Christopher Columbus* and his 1493 letter to Ferdinand and Isabella are filled with numerous instances of Native people being forcibly taken by the explorers; capture of Native women as well as men, therefore, was routine from the earliest period of contact. Nor were the captivities confined to the early periods of colonization alone; the practice of removing Indian children from their families and communities and transporting them long distances to Indian schools continued through the first decades of the twentieth century. These schools were designed to separate Native children from their language, traditions, and culture and so very deliberately to deconstruct their Native identities. These experiences were, then, very real captivities, analogous to Pocahontas's. See James Welch's description of his parents attending Indian boarding schools

in the 1930s in *Killing Custer*, 227–29. See also *Indian School Days* by Basil H. Johnston and *They Called It Prairie Light: The Story of Chilocco Indian School* by K. Tsianina Lomawaima.

29. The longevity of the assumption of white men's sexual access to Native women is illustrated by a novel by Larry Watson, *Montana 1948*, a story of the habitual but long-hidden sexual abuse of Native women by a white physician in a small Montana town in the mid-twentieth century.

30. Tilton discusses the similarities of the Pocahontas story to elements of classical epics and the part her story played in the perceived need for an American epic in the post-Revolutionary period (49–52).

31. A cultural icon as solemnly sacred as the nineteenth century's Pocahontas inevitably invites parody, and Barth's was not the first irreverent rendering of her story. John Brougham's 1855 New York burlesque *Po-ca-hon-tas, or the Gentle Savage* ("An Original Aboriginal Erratic Operatic Semi-Civilized and Demi-Savage Extravaganza, being a Per-Version of Ye Trewe and Wonderrefulle Hystorie of Ye Rennownned Princesse" [403]) was a broadly comic attack on the romanticized story as well as on other popular renditions of the "romantic Indian" of his day. In the twentieth century, Philip Moeller's play *Pokey, or The Beautiful Legend of the Amorous Indian* (1918) makes her a sexually overeager monomaniac in her determined pursuit of a white husband; her lines consist mostly of repeated "Um, Um, Um!" (130–31), signifiying kisses, and a reluctant Rolfe can barely extricate himself from her "mad embrace" (130). Moeller also re-writes the rescue story; in his play, a captive Smith is threatened not with execution but with marriage to Pocahontas; he escapes by persuading Rolfe to save him by taking his place as her husband. A song from from the turn-of-the-century New York musical stage is also suggestive of the bawdy possibilities of the romanticized legend: "Who Played Poker with Pocahontas When John Smith Was Away?" (*Music from the New York Stage 1890–1920*, Pearl Records, vol. 1, 1890–1908).

32. See Rayna Green, "The Pocahontas Perplex: The Image of Indian Women in American Culture," and Leslie Fiedler, *The Return of the Vanishing American*.

33. Many thousands of white Americans, among them a number of the so-called First Families of Virginia, claim descent from Pocahontas, a claim Vine Deloria has attacked as a false and futile gesture on the part of whites of support and concern for Indians (*Custer Died for Your Sins* 27). See also Robertson, *Pocahontas's Descendants*.

34. For a discussion of the role of miscegenation or intermarriage between white men and Native or other ethnic women in American literary history, see Mary Dearborn, *Pocahontas' Daughters: Gender and Ethnicity in American Culture*.

3. MAKING A HISTORY, SHAPING A NATION

1. See David Smits's article "The Squaw Drudge: A Prime Index of Savagism" for a thorough discussion of how that figure was employed in the service of Euro–American imperialism.

2. See Philip J. Deloria's *Playing Indian*, a historical study of white Americans' appropriations of Indian dress and identity from the Boston Tea Party to the counterculture movements of the twentieth century—and of how that recurring masquerade has functioned in the formation of an always-insecure American identity.

3. For other examples from the period of Indians rendered dramatically darker than whites, see the frontispiece illustrations of the *Narrative of . . . Mrs. Clarissa Plummer* (1838) and the *History of . . . Mrs. Caroline Harris* (1838), both reprinted in the *Garland Library of Narratives of North American Indian Captivities*, vol. 54. In Alonzo Chappel's engraving *Pocahontas Saving the Life of Capt. John Smith* (1861; in Rasmussen and Tilton 16), the Indian warrior who attempts to thwart Pocahontas's rescue of Smith is not only very dark-skinned but also has stereotypically Black facial features, an indication of the discursive and representational merger of Blacks and Indians in the nineteenth century and beyond.

4. See Homi Bhabha, "Signs Taken for Wonders," for the argument that mimicries of the colonizing power by the colonized are "signs of spectacular resistance" that produce a hybridization of history (181).

5. According to Hubbell, "the earliest of [Davis's] four versions of the Pocahontas story was . . . introduced into his novelette *The Farmer of New Jersey* (1800). An improved version appeared in his *Travels* (1803). In 1805 Davis . . . published . . . *Captain Smith and Pocahontas*, and . . . later in the same year he brought out . . . *The First Settlers of Virginia*" (187), in which the Smith-Pocahontas story was embedded.

6. There is some ironic tension in the way Davis's novel constructs the reader's "gaze" as masculine and the fact that, as Tilton claims, Davis was hoping to capture "the growing, largely female, audience for fiction in America" (35). An investigation into the complexities of how the reader is constructed as gendered in Davis or other captivity or Pocahontas texts is beyond the scope of my inquiry here, though the issue has surfaced in minor ways in other discussions, specifically of captivity romances. Commenting on the titillating aspects of nineteenth-century representations of Indian-white sex in popular captivity tales, Gary Ebersole figures the reader as white and male (and a masturbator?) when he observes that versions of the "male fantasy" of "forbidden sexuality" have "been in print continually from at least the time of Capt. John Smith's account of Pocahontas," and that "Through the consumption of captivity

narratives . . . the male reader could maintain his moral propriety, while tasting forbidden pleasures in the privacy of his own room" (206). Peter Beidler, to the contrary, in his review of contemporary Indian romance novels, assumes it is true that "white women constitute the dominant audience for the Indian romance" (99) among contemporary readers. Perhaps the gendering of readers as both male and female is another indication of the appeal of these genres to white readers of both sexes; at least, to my knowledge, no one has suggested that the reader is ever anything but white.

7. Lydia Sigourney in her poem "Pocahontas" (1841) makes the Pocahontas-Rolfe marriage explicitly a marriage of two worlds, here quite literally old and new: "Peace waves her garland o'er the favour'd place / Where weds the new-born West with Europe's lordly race" (15).

8. Tilton describes Davis's novel as "a precocious expression of what would come to be known as American Romanticism" (35), and certainly it is part of the romantic impulse Morrison describes and Choate's speech encourages; I see it as perhaps more clearly an important progenitor of the sentimental genre of "women's fiction" of the nineteenth century.

9. It is unclear whether, in his use of the term "Tawneys," Franklin is referring to Indians or to a lighter-skinned group of the "Sons of Africa." By "White and Red," of course, Franklin means not whites and Indians, but whites alone; he is drawing on the commonplace poetic tropes of "ivory skin" and "ruby cheeks and lips" in the English love poetry of the Renaissance and after.

10. See Winthrop Jordan, 429–81, for a thorough discussion of Jefferson's often contradictory attitudes on race and racial mixing. See also Tilton, 24–25.

11. Tilton stresses the ways Croswell's drama differs from rather than draws upon Pocahontas's history and calls his echo of her name a "hook" (48) to attract the attention of an audience. Certainly the story departs from that of the historical Pocahontas (for example, in its New England rather than Virginia setting), but the close connection to her name persuades me that the Pocahontas figure, especially her racial profile, is indeed being invoked here.

12. Vanderlyn was later to paint the *Landing of Columbus at the Island of Guanahani, West Indies, October 12, 1492* (1847), one of four murals that hang in the Rotunda of the U.S. Capitol (Fryd 55).

13. David Stannard argues for the term "holocaust" as an appropriate one to describe the European treatment of America's indigenous peoples in *American Holocaust: Columbus and the Conquest of the New World*.

14. These figurations of the dissected bodies of both Pocahontas and the white captive suggest that the eroticized encounters of white and Indian challenged and disrupted what Homi Bhabha calls "the phobic myth of the undifferentiated whole white body" ("Of Mimicry and Man" 133).

15. See, for example, in Fryd, the 1825 Antonio Capellano relief in the U.S. Capitol Rotunda, *Preservation of Captain Smith by Pocahontas* (22), and an 1817 engraving, *Pocahontas Ran with Mournful Distraction to the Block* (25); in Rasmussen and Tilton, John Gadsby Chapman's 1836 *Pocahontas Saving the Life of Captain John Smith* (15); Alonzo Chappel's 1861 *Pocahontas Saving the Life of Capt. John Smith* (16); Victor Nehlig's 1874 *Pocahontas Saving John Smith* (17); and Paul Cadmus's 1938–39 mural *Pocahontas Saving the Life of John Smith* (17), formerly in the Parcel Post Building in Richmond, Virginia.

16. The dramatic inclusion of the outstretched arm in Pocahontas paintings done after the publication of Sedgwick's novel suggests that perhaps the Pocahontas/Magawisca influence was reciprocal and Sedgwick's noble Indian princess shaped later representations of Pocahontas, much as earlier ones of Pocahontas influenced Sedgwick's construction of her story and character.

17. By the late nineteenth century, when the project of consolidating white control of the continent was more or less complete, contemporary attitudes toward men who married or cohabited with Indian women had lost their idealism; such men were often referred to as "squaw men" and disparaged as "morally depraved fugitives from the law, offscourings of civilization, and a blend of the worst of civilized and savage societies" (Smits, "'Squaw Men,'" 48).

18. Cooper's preface to the novel, however, acknowledges his debt to "The Rev. J. R. C., of *****, Pennsylvania" for "The kind and disinterested manner in which you have furnished the materials of the following tale" and with his mention of the "descent" of this man, whom Cooper calls "truly an American," hints that his story not only has its basis in the ancestral lore of his benefactor, but that the man is descended from the child of Canonchet and Narra-mattah (iii). Tilton also notes the contradictions in Cooper's praise of the mixed ancestry of "Rev. J. R. C." and the novel's evident opposition to interracial union (70–72). For other discussions of nineteenth-century attitudes toward those of mixed race, see Smits, "'Squaw Men,'" and Tilton 60 ff.

19. *The Last of the Mohicans* (1826), probably Cooper's most well known and widely read novel, also flirts with but finally evades the love between a white woman and an Indian man. Cooper makes the attraction permissible because Cora Munro has "tainted" blood; she is the daughter of a West Indian woman, one of whose ancestors was an African slave. Thus Cora is made available to the affections of the noble Indian Uncas as a woman of "pure" white blood could never be. However much sympathy the attraction of this strong woman and heroic man might generate, the anxiety it produced was greater and its anticipated consummation had to be averted to preserve the ideal of white primacy in the wilderness. Cooper accomplishes this task by having Cora and Uncas die together at the novel's end. The demise of both the Indian and the woman of

"mixed blood" leaves the scene to whites "with no cross," as Cooper's Natty Bumppo says to describe the purity of his own white "blood."

20. Child was not alone in her use of the captivity trope to represent a state of enslavement other than to Indians, as in Mary's case to a tyrannical father. Other scholars have noted that the Indian captivity narrative has served as a textual model for other writing—that Indian captivity itself has been a metaphor for other kinds of oppressive bondage, including slavery and domestic abuse. The slave narratives of the nineteenth century owed much to the captivity narratives' precedent; see, for example, Jean Fagan Yellin's introduction to Harriet Jacobs's slave narrative. Yellin argues (xxxiv) that Jacobs refuses rather than adopts the passivity which Yellin believes characterizes women in captivity—a perception of the captivity narratives I do not share. One late-eighteenth-century woman, Abigail Abbot Bailey, apparently used the narrative structures familiar to her from captivity narratives (including Rowlandson's) in telling her own story of being trapped in a marriage to a violent and abusive husband who tricks her into leaving her home and traveling with him into the wilderness, where he holds her hostage until she engineers an escape. See Ann Taves's edition of Bailey's memoirs, *Religion and Domestic Violence in Early New England*, especially Taves's introduction, 15–19.

21. Ethnohistorian James Axtell has explored the phenomenon of whites who became "Indian" in his essay "The White Indians of Colonial America."

22. Seaver's story of Mary Jemison is not as historically remote as the other texts, but Jemison was a very old woman (in her eighties) when she recounted her life story to Seaver; thus her captivity and two marriages to Indian men had taken place more than half a century before the book was published in 1824.

23. See Fryd's discussion of the reliefs and how they enacted the racial postures of a burgeoning white empire (9–41). She characterizes the themes of the four reliefs as "Assimilation" (19), "Segregation" (25), "Land for Peace" (28), and "Subjugation" (32) and claims that together, "these stereotypical images of the Indians provide[d] an excuse for their subjugation by what white Americans believed to be a superior and civilized culture" (41).

24. Custis's Powhatan was prophetic in another way: Tales of both Pocahontas and Indian captivity have at least since the mid-nineteenth century continued to be "told from the nursery" as a means of constructing young Americans as white and instructing them in their destined prerogative. *Little Ferns for Fanny's Little Friends* (1854) a collection of didactic children's stories by the sentimental writer "Fanny Fern," includes "'Bald Eagle'; or, The Little Captives," the story of two white children who are captured and adopted by a powerful chief. The story opens with the coy question "Do you like Indians?" and instructs its young readers that a negative response is the proper one: "Our forefathers did n't

admire them much. They had seen too many scalps hanging at their belts, and had heard their war whoops rather too often, to fancy such troublesome neighbors" (162). It too, like other texts of the period, deftly but inaccurately places Indian-white conflicts outside the "troublesome" present and into a comfortingly distant past: "You would n't have relished living in those days, would you? . . . I'm very glad you are not obliged to live in such days" (163). The children outwardly adapt to Indian ways but never abandon their "true" identity; eventually they escape, reaching the safety of an army camp in Charleston just in time to avoid recapture, and are "so glad to get among white people again" (169–70). The story's southern setting reveals that it is engaging not the distant past but indeed the very recent efforts to rid the South of its Native inhabitants; the forced displacement of the southern tribes lasted well into the 1830s (Josephy 320–33). The story teaches young white Americans that Indians are "troublesome neighbors" who belong not in their present time and space but to the past; in that way it supports forced removal and resettlement and helps to write the American landscape as the appropriate home of whites alone. Fern's story is an early example of the didactic children's stories about early encounters of whites and Indians that continued to appear well into our own century.

25. I am indebted to the poet and novelist R. H. W. Dillard (named for the nineteenth-century southern poet Richard Henry Wilde, himself the author of a famous nineteenth-century poem on Indian captivity, "The Lament of the Captive") for this reference and for providing me with a typescript of the play. Dillard was a member of the cast, playing the part of Sam Henderson, sweetheart of one of the captive girls.

26. I am indebted to Gerald O'Grady, visiting scholar in Afro-American Studies at Harvard, for bringing this film to my attention and making it available to me.

27. Mukherjee's use of the names Hester and Pearl indicates that she means also to rewrite another American story—Hawthorne's *The Scarlet Letter*—in her novel which, in telling the story of the Salem Bibi's passionate "adultery," does not punish but instead allows the full flowering of female sexual desire: in Rebecca with her Indian lover, Hannah with *her* Indian lover, and Beigh Masters, the narrator of the story, a contemporary New Englander who is searching out Hannah's story, with *her* Indian lover, a man whose family has immigrated from India to America.

Works Cited

Abbot, Jacob. *King Philip*. New York: Harper, 1900.

Accorsi, William. *My Name Is Pocahontas*. New York: Holiday House, 1992.

[Adams, Henry.] "Captain John Smith." *North American Review* 104.214 (January 1867): 1–30.

Allen, Paula Gunn. *Skins and Bones: Poems 1979–87*. Albuquerque: West End, 1988.

Allen, Theodore W. *The Invention of the White Race*. Volume Two: *The Origin of Racial Oppression in Anglo-America*. London: Verso, 1997.

Anderson, Benedict. "Exodus." *Critical Inquiry* 20 (Winter 1994): 314–27.

Armstrong, Nancy, and Leonard Tennenhouse. "The American Origins of the English Novel." *American Literary History* 4.3 (Fall 1992): 386–410.

Athey, Stephanie, and Daniel Cooper Alarcon. "*Oroonoko's* Gendered Economies of Honor/Horror: Reframing Colonial Discourse Studies in the Americas." *Subjects and Citizens: Nation, Race, and Gender from Oroonoko to Anita Hill*. Ed. Michael Moon and Cathy N. Davidson. Durham, NC: Duke UP, 1995. 27–55.

Austin, Mary. "An Indian Captivity." Rev. of *Narrative of the Captivity and Restoration of Mrs. Mary Rowlandson*. *The Saturday Review of Literature* 21 June 1930: 1150–51.

Awiakta, Marilou. "Amazons in Appalachia." *A Gathering of Spirit: Writing and Art by North American Indian Women*. Ed. Beth Brant. Rockland, ME: Sinister Wisdom, 1984. 125–30.

Axtell, James. "The White Indians of Colonial America." *The European and the Indian: Essays in the Ethnohistory of Colonial North America*. New York: Oxford UP, 1981. 168–206.

Baker, Houston A., Jr. "Archeology, Ideology and African American Discourse." *Redefining American Literary History*. Ed. A. LaVonne Brown Ruoff and Jerry W. Ward, Jr. New York: Modern Language Association, 1990. 157–95.

Baldwin, James. "Here Be Dragons." *The Price of the Ticket: Collected Nonfiction 1948–1985*. New York: St. Martin's, 1985. 677–90.

———. "Stranger in the Village." *The Price of the Ticket: Collected Nonfiction 1948–1985*. New York: St. Martin's, 1985. 79–90.

Barbour, Philip L. *Pocahontas and Her World*. Boston: Houghton Mifflin, 1970.

Barker, James Nelson. *The Indian Princess; or, La Belle Sauvage*. 1808. Rpt. in *Representative Plays by American Dramatists 1765–1819*. Ed. Montrose J. Moses. New York: Dutton, 1918. 565–628.

Barlow, Joel. *The Columbiad*. 1807. Rpt. in *The Works of Joel Barlow*. Vol. 2. Gainesville, FL: Scholars' Facsimiles and Reprints, 1970. 371–866.

Barth, John. *The Sot-Weed Factor*, 2d ed. 1967. Rpt. New York: Anchor Doubleday, 1987.

Beidler, Peter G. "The Contemporary Indian Romance: A Review Essay." *American Indian Culture and Research Journal* 15.4 (1991): 97–126.

Bennett, Lerone, Jr. *Before the Mayflower: A History of Black America*. 5th ed. Chicago: Johnson, 1982.

Bhabha, Homi K. "Of Mimicry and Man." *October* 28 (Spring 1984): 125–33.

———. "Signs Taken for Wonders: Questions of Ambivalence and Authority under a Tree outside Delhi, May 1817." *"Race," Writing, and Difference*. Ed. Henry Louis Gates, Jr. Chicago: U of Chicago P, 1985. 163–84.

The Birth of a Nation. Dir. D. W. Griffith. Griffith Feature Films, 1915.

Bizzell, Patricia. "Opportunities for Feminist Research in the History of Rhetoric." *Rhetoric Review* 11.1 (Fall 1992): 50–58.

Blake, Michael. *Dances with Wolves*. New York: Fawcett Gold Medal, 1988.

Bodge, George Madison. *Soldiers in King Philip's War*. Boston: For the Author, 1906.

Bradford, William. *Of Plymouth Plantation 1620–1647*. Rpt. New York: Random House, 1981.

Brant, Beth. "Grandmothers of a New World." *Ikon* 8 (1988): 48–60.

Breitwieser, Mitchell Robert. *American Puritanism and the Defense of Mourning: Religion, Grief, and Ethnology in Mary White Rowlandson's Captivity Narrative*. Madison: U of Wisconsin P, 1990.

Brooks, Cleanth, R. W. B. Lewis, and Robert Penn Warren, eds. *American Literature: The Makers and the Making*. 2 vols. New York: St. Martin's, 1973.

Brougham, John. *Po-ca-hon-tas, or The Gentle Savage*. 1855. Rpt. in *Dramas from the American Theatre 1762–1909*. Ed. Richard Moody. Cleveland: World, 1966. 397–421.

Burke, Charles T. *Puritans at Bay: The War against King Philip and the Squaw Sachems.* New York: Exposition, 1967.

Busia, Abena P. A. "Silencing Sycorax: On African Colonial Discourse and the Unvoiced Female." *Cultural Critique* 14 (Winter 1989–90): 81–104.

Cabell, James Branch. "The Fourteenth Letter: To the Lady Rebecca Rolfe, Called Pocahontas." *Ladies and Gentlemen: A Parcel of Reconsiderations.* New York: McBride, 1934. 197–209.

Calloway, Colin G., ed. *Dawnland Encounters: Indians and Europeans in Northern New England.* Hanover, NH: UP of New England, 1991.

Castiglia, Christopher. *Bound and Determined: Captivity, Culture-Crossing, and White Womanhood from Mary Rowlandson to Patty Hearst.* Chicago: U of Chicago P, 1996.

Certeau, Michel de. *The Writing of History.* Trans. Tom Conley. New York: 1988.

Chapman, George, Ben Jonson, and John Marston. *Eastward Hoe.* London: 1605.

Child, Lydia Maria. "An Appeal for the Indians." 1868. Rpt. in *Hobomok and Other Writings on Indians.* Ed. Carolyn L. Karcher. American Women Writers Series. New Brunswick, NJ: Rutgers UP, 1986. 216–32.

———. *Hobomok.* 1824. Rpt. in *Hobomok and Other Writings on Indians.* Ed. Carolyn L. Karcher. American Women Writers Series. New Brunswick, NJ: Rutgers UP, 1986. 1–150.

Choate, Rufus. *The Works of Rufus Choate.* Ed. Samuel Gilman Brown. Boston: Little, Brown, 1862.

Cliff, Michelle. "Caliban's Daughter: The Tempest and the Teapot." *Frontiers* 12.2 (Fall 1991): 36–51.

———. "Clare Savage as a Crossroads Character." *Caribbean Women Writers: Essays from the First International Conference.* Ed. Selwyn R. Cudjoe. Wellesley, MA: Calaloux, 1990. 263–68.

———. *No Telephone to Heaven.* New York: Dutton, 1987.

Columbus, Christopher. *The Columbus Letter of March 14, 1493.* Trans. Richard Henry Major. Chicago: Newberry Library, 1953.

———. *The Log of Christopher Columbus.* Trans. Robert H. Fuson. Camden, ME: International Marine, 1987.

Cooke, Ebenezer. "The Sot-Weed Factor." 1708. Rpt. in *Colonial American Poetry.* Ed. Kenneth Silverman. New York: Hafner, 1968. 282–301.

Cooke, John Esten. *My Lady Pokahontas, A True Relation of Virginia. Writ by Anas Todkill, Puritan and Pilgrim.* Boston: Houghton Mifflin, 1885.

Cooper, James Fenimore. *The Last of the Mohicans.* 1826. New York: New American Library, 1962.

———. *The Wept of Wish-Ton-Wish.* New York: 1829. Rpt. *The Complete Works of J. Fenimore Cooper*, vol. 30. New York: Putnams, n.d.

Crane, Hart. *The Complete Poems and Selected Letters and Prose of Hart Crane.* Ed. Brom Weber. New York: Anchor, 1966.

Croswell, Joseph. *A New World Planted.* Boston: 1802.

Custis, George Washington Parke. *Pocahontas, or the Settlers of Virginia.* 1830. Rpt. in *Representative American Plays 1767–1923,* 3d ed. Ed. Arthur Hobson Quinn. New York: Century, 1925. 181–208.

Dances with Wolves. Dir. Kevin Costner. Orion Pictures, 1990.

d'Aulaire, Ingri, and Edgar Parin d'Aulaire. *Pocahontas.* New York: Doubleday, 1946.

Davis, John. *Captain Smith and Pocahontas. An Indian Tale.* Philadelphia: For the Author, 1805.

Dearborn, Mary. *Pocahontas' Daughters: Gender and Ethnicity in American Culture.* New York: Oxford UP, 1986.

De Bry, Theodore. *Discovering the New World.* Ed. Michael Alexander. New York: Harper & Row, 1976.

Deloria, Philip J. *Playing Indian.* New Haven: Yale UP, 1998.

Deloria, Vine. *Custer Died for Your Sins: An Indian Manifesto.* 1970. Norman: U of Oklahoma P, 1988.

Demos, John. *The Unredeemed Captive: A Family Story from Early America.* New York: Knopf, 1994.

Derounian, Kathryn Zabelle. "A Note on Mary (White) Rowlandson's English Origins." *Early American Literature* 24 (1989): 70–72.

———. "The Publication, Promotion, and Distribution of Mary Rowlandson's Indian Captivity Narrative in the Seventeenth Century." *Early American Literature* 23 (1988): 239–61.

Derounian-Stodola, Kathryn Zabelle, and David L. Greene. "Additions and Corrections to 'A Note on Mary (White) Rowlandson's English Origins.'" *Early American Literature* 25 (1990): 305–6.

Derounian-Stodola, Kathryn Zabelle, and James Arthur Levernier. *The Indian Captivity Narrative 1550–1900.* Twayne's United States Authors Series. New York: Twayne, 1993.

DeShields, James T. *Cynthia Ann Parker: The Story of Her Capture.* St. Louis: For the Author, 1886. Rpt. in *Garland Library of North American Indian Captivities,* vol. 95. New York: Garland, 1976.

Diebold, Robert Kent. "A Critical Edition of Mrs. Mary Rowlandson's Captivity Narrative." Diss. Yale U, 1972.

Donne, John. "Elegie: Going to Bed." *The Complete Poetry of John Donne.* Ed. John T. Shawcross. New York: Anchor Doubleday, 1967. 57–58.

Dorris, Michael. "Discoveries." *Paper Trail: Essays.* New York: HarperCollins, 1994. 145–62.

———. "Indians on the Shelf." *Paper Trail: Essays*. New York: HarperCollins, 1994. 122–32.

Drinnon, Richard. *Facing West: The Metaphysics of Indian-Hating and Empire-Building*. New York: New American Library, 1980.

Eastburn, James Wallis [and Robert C. Sands]. *Yamoyden: A Tale of the Wars of King Philip*. New York: Published by James Eastburn, 1820.

Ebersole, Gary L. *Captured by Texts: Puritan to Postmodern Images of Indian Captivity*. Charlottesville: UP of Virginia, 1995.

Erdrich, Louise. *The Beet Queen*. New York: Holt, 1986.

———. *The Bingo Palace*. New York: HarperCollins, 1994.

———. "Captivity." *Jacklight*. New York: Holt, Rinehart, and Winston, 1984. 26–27.

———. *Love Medicine*. New York: Holt, Rinehart, and Winston, 1984.

Feest, Christian. *The Powhatan Tribes*. New York: Chelsea House, 1990.

"Fern, Fanny" [Willis, Sarah Payson Parton]. *Little Ferns for Fanny's Little Friends*. Auburn: Derby & Miller, 1854.

Fiedler, Leslie. *The Return of the Vanishing American*. New York: Stein and Day, 1968.

Fitzpatrick, Tara. "The Figure of Captivity: The Cultural Work of the Puritan Captivity Narrative." *American Literary History* 3.1 (Spring 1991): 1–26.

Fleming, E. McClung. "The American Image as Indian Princess, 1765–1783." *Winterthur Portfolio* 2 (1965): 65–81.

"The Fourme of Solempnization of Matrimonye." *The Boke of Common Praier*. London: 1559. London: 1890.

Frank, Dana. "Southern History Inside Out." Rev. of *Gender and Jim Crow: Women and the Politics of White Supremacy in North Carolina, 1896–1920*, by Glenda Elizabeth Gilmore. *The Nation* 263.14 (November 4, 1996): 29–31.

Frankenberg, Ruth. *White Women, Race Matters: The Social Construction of Whiteness*. Minneapolis: U of Minnesota P, 1993.

Freud, Sigmund. "The Taboo of Virginity." *Freud: On War, Sex, and Neurosis*. Ed. Sander Katz. New York: Arts and Sciences, 1947. 219–41.

Fritz, Jean. *The Double Life of Pocahontas*. New York: Putnam, 1983.

Fryd, Vivien Green. *Art and Empire: The Politics of Ethnicity in the U.S. Capitol, 1815–1860*. New Haven: Yale UP, 1992.

Gates, Henry Louis, Jr. "The Face and Voice of Blackness." *Facing History: The Black Image in American Art 1710–1940*. By Guy C. McElroy. San Francisco: Bedford Arts, 1990. xxix–xliv.

———. *Loose Canons: Notes on the Culture Wars*. New York: Oxford UP, 1992.

Geddes, Virgil. *Pocahontas and the Elders*. Chapel Hill: Abernethy, 1933.

Glaser, Lynn. *America on Paper: The First Hundred Years*. Philadelphia: Associated Antiquaries, 1989.

Green, Rayna. "The Pocahontas Perplex: The Image of Indian Women in American Culture." *Massachusetts Review* 16.4 (Autumn 1975): 698–714.

———, ed. *That's What She Said: Contemporary Poetry and Fiction by Native American Women*. Bloomington: Indiana UP, 1984.

Greene, Carol. *Pocahontas: Daughter of a Chief*. Chicago: Children's Press, 1988.

Greene, David L. "New Light on Mary Rowlandson." *Early American Literature* 20 (1985): 24–38.

Hacker, Margaret Schmidt. *Cynthia Ann Parker: The Life and the Legend*. Southwestern Studies No. 92. El Paso: Texas Western, 1990.

Hadas, Pamela. "Pocahontas from Her New World." *Beside Herself: Pocahontas to Patty Hearst: Poems*. New York: Knopf, 1983. 3–16.

Hamor, Ralph. *A True Discourse of the present estate of Virginia. London: 1615*. Richmond: Virginia State Library, 1957.

"Harris, Caroline." *History of the Captivity and Providential Release Therefrom of Mrs. Caroline Harris*. New York: Perry and Cooke, 1838. Rpt. in *Garland Library of North American Captivity Narratives*, vol. 54. New York: Garland, 1977.

Hawthorne, Nathaniel. "The Duston Family." *The American Magazine of Useful and Entertaining Knowledge* 2 (May 1836): 395–97.

———. "Young Goodman Brown." *Mosses from an Old Manse*. 1846. *The Centenary Edition of the Works of Nathaniel Hawthorne*, Vol. 10. Columbus: Ohio State UP, 1974. 74–90.

Hogan, Linda. "The Truth Is." *No More Masks!: An Anthology of Twentieth-Century American Women Poets*, rev. ed. Ed. Florence Howe. New York: HarperCollins, 1993. 415–16.

Hollister, G. H. *Mount Hope; or, Philip, King of the Wampanoags: An Historical Romance*. New York: Harper, 1851.

hooks, bell. "Reflections on Race and Sex." 1990. Rpt. in *Daughters of the Revolution: Classic Essays by Women*. Ed. James D. Lester. Lincolnwood, IL: NTC, 1995. 193–201.

Howe, Susan. "The Captivity and Restoration of Mrs. Mary Rowlandson." *The Birth-mark: Unsettling the Wilderness in American Literary History*. Middletown, CT: Wesleyan UP, 1993: 89–130.

Hubbard, William. *The Present State of New-England*. London: 1677.

Hubbell, Jay B. "The Smith-Pocahontas Literary Legend." *South and Southwest: Literary Essays and Reminiscences*. Durham, NC: Duke UP, 1965. 175–204.

Hulme, Peter. *Colonial Encounters: Europe and the Native Caribbean 1492–1797*. 1986. London: Routledge, 1992.

Hulton, Paul. *America in 1585: The Complete Drawings of John White*. Chapel Hill: U of North Carolina P, 1984.

Johnston, Basil H. *Indian School Days*. Norman: U of Oklahoma P, 1988.

Jordan, Winthrop. *White over Black: American Attitudes toward the Negro, 1550–1812.* Chapel Hill: U of North Carolina P, for the Institute of Early American History and Culture, Williamsburg, Virginia, 1968.

Josephy, Alvin M., Jr. *500 Nations: An Illustrated History of North American Indians.* New York: Knopf, 1994.

Karcher, Carolyn L. Introduction. *Hobomok and Other Writings on Indians.* By Lydia Maria Child. New Brunswick, NJ: Rutgers UP, 1986. ix–xxxviii.

Kasson, Joy S. *Marble Queens and Captives: Women in Nineteenth-Century American Sculpture.* New Haven: Yale UP, 1990.

Katz, William Loren. *Black Indians: A Hidden Heritage.* New York: Atheneum, 1986.

Kolodny, Annette. "Among the Indians: The Uses of Captivity." *New York Times Book Review* 31 Jan. 1993: 1+.

———. *The Land before Her: Fantasy and Experience of the American Frontiers, 1630–1860.* Chapel Hill: U of North Carolina P, 1984.

———. *The Lay of the Land: Metaphor as Experience and History in American Life and Letters.* Chapel Hill: U of North Carolina P, 1975.

———. "Letting Go Our Grand Obsessions: Notes toward a New Literary History of the American Frontiers." *Subjects and Citizens: Nation, Race, and Gender from* Oroonoko *to* Anita Hill. Ed. Michael Moon and Cathy N. Davidson. Durham, NC: Duke UP, 1995. 9–26.

Larson, Charles. "The Children of Pocahontas." *American Indian Fiction.* Albuquerque: U of New Mexico P, 1978. 17–33.

Leach, Douglas Edward. "Mary White Rowlandson." *Notable American Women, 1607–1950.* Cambridge: Harvard UP, 1971. Vol. 3: 200–2.

Lemay, J. A. Leo. *Did Pocahontas Save Captain John Smith?* Athens: U of Georgia P, 1992.

Lepore, Jill. *The Name of War: King Philip's War and The Origins of American Identity.* New York: Knopf, 1998.

Lindsay, Vachel. "Our Mother Pocahontas." *The Chinese Nightingale and Other Poems.* New York: Macmillan, 1926. 39–42.

Lomawaima, K. Tsianina. *They Called It Prairie Light: The Story of Chilocco Indian School.* Lincoln: U of Nebraska P, 1993.

Longfellow, Henry Wadsworth. "The Song of Hiawatha." *The Poetical Works of Henry W. Longfellow.* London: Moxon, 1870. 169–276.

Ludwig, Mark. Introduction. *The Captive: Mary Rowlandson.* Tucson, AZ: American Eagle, 1988. v–vii.

Maddox, Lucy. *Removals: Nineteenth-Century American Literature and the Politics of Indian Affairs.* New York: Oxford UP, 1991.

"Mary Rowlandson." *Oxford Companion to American Literature.* 4th ed. 1965.

Mather, Cotton. *A Brand Pluck'd out of the Burning*. 1693. *Narratives of the Witchcraft Cases 1648–1706*. Ed. George Lincoln Burr. New York: Scribner's, 1914. 253–87.

Mather, Increase. *A Brief History of the War with the Indians in New England*. 1676. *So Dreadfull a Judgment: Puritan Responses to King Philip's War*. Ed. Richard Slotkin and James Folsom. Middletown, CT: Wesleyan UP, 1978. 79–163.

Melville, Herman. *The Confidence Man: His Masquerade*. 1857. New York: Oxford UP, 1991.

Mills, Charles W. *The Racial Contract*. Ithaca: Cornell UP, 1997.

Minter, David. "By Dens of Lions: Notes on Stylization in Early Puritan Captivity Narratives." *American Literature* 45 (1973): 335–47.

Moeller, Philip. *Pokey, or The Beautiful Legend of the Amorous Indian. Five Somewhat Historical Plays*. New York: Knopf, 1918. 127–57.

Montrose, Louis A. "Professing the Renaissance: The Poetics and Politics of Culture." *The New Historicism*. Ed. H. Aram Veeser. New York: Routledge, 1989. 15–36.

———. "The Work of Gender in the Discourse of Discovery." *Representations* 33 (Winter 1991): 1–41.

Moody, Richard. Introduction. *Metamora, or The Last of the Wampanoags*. By John Augustus Stone. *Dramas of the American Theatre 1762–1909*. Cleveland: World, 1966. 199–204.

Moon, Michael, and Cathy N. Davidson. Introduction. *Subjects and Citizens: Nation, Race, and Gender from Oroonoko to Anita Hill*. Durham, NC: Duke UP, 1995. 1–6.

Morgan, Edmund S. *American Slavery, American Freedom: The Ordeal of Colonial Virginia*. New York: Norton, 1975.

Morrison, Toni. *Playing in the Dark: Whiteness and the Literary Imagination*. Cambridge: Harvard UP, 1992.

Morton, Thomas. *New English Canaan, or New Canaan*. 1632. Rpt. Amsterdam: 1637.

Mossiker, Frances. *Pocahontas: The Life and the Legend*. 1976. New York: Da Capo, 1996.

Mukherjee, Bharati. *The Holder of the World*. New York: Knopf, 1993.

Murray, Albert. *The Omni-Americans: New Perspectives on Black Experience and American Culture*. New York: Outerbridge and Dienstfrey, 1970.

"N. S." [Nathaniel Saltonstall?]. "A New and Further Narrative of the State of New–England, by N.S., 1676." *Narratives of the Indian Wars 1675–1699*. Ed. Charles H. Lincoln. New York: Barnes and Noble, 1913; rpt. 1959. 77–99.

Namias, June. *White Captives: Gender and Ethnicity on the American Frontier*. Chapel Hill: U of North Carolina P, 1993.

Odell, Edson Kenny. *The Romance of Pocahontas.* New York: Cosmopolitan Press, 1912.

One More River: The Mood of the American South in 1964. Dir. Douglas Leiterman and Beryl Fox. Canadian Broadcasting Corporation, 1964.

Person, Leland S., Jr. "The American Eve: Miscegenation and a Feminist Frontier Fiction." *American Quarterly* 37 (1985): 668–85.

Peyton, Thomas. *The Glasse of Time, in the First Age.* London: 1620.

"Plummer, Clarissa." *Narrative of the Captivity and Extreme Sufferings of Mrs. Clarissa Plummer.* New York: Perry and Cooke, 1838. Rpt. in *Garland Library of North American Indian Captivities*, vol. 54. New York: Garland, 1977.

Plummer, Rachael. *Rachael Plummer's Narrative of Twenty-One Months Servitude among the Commanchee Indians.* Intro. William S. Reese. 1838. Austin, TX: Jenkins, 1977.

"Pocahontas" [William Hillhouse]. *Pocahontas; A Proclamation: With Plates.* New Haven: Clyme, 1820.

"Pocahontas" [Emily Clemens Pearson]. *Cousin Franck's Household, or Scenes in the Old Dominion.* Boston: Upham, Ford and Olmstead, 1852.

Pocahontas. Walt Disney Studios, 1995.

Pratt, Mary Louise. "Arts of the Contact Zone." *Profession 91.* New York: Modern Language Association, 1991: 33–40.

Ralegh, Sir Walter. *The Discovery . . . of Guiana.* 1596. Rpt. in *Sir Walter Ralegh: Selected Writings.* Ed. Gerald Hammond. London: Carcanet, 1984. 76–123.

Rasmussen, William M. S., and Robert Tilton. *Pocahontas: Her Life and Legend.* Exhibition catalog. Richmond: Virginia Historical Society, 1994.

Reese, William S. Introduction. *Rachael Plummer's Narrative of Twenty-One Months Servitude among the Commanchee Indians.* Austin, TX: Jenkins, 1977. N. pag.

Rich, Adrienne. "An Atlas of the Difficult World." *An Atlas of the Difficult World: Poems 1988–1991.* New York: Norton, 1991. 1–26.

———. "Song." *Diving into the Wreck: Poems 1971–72.* New York: Norton, 1973. 20.

Richardson, Samuel. *Pamela, or Virtue Rewarded.* 1740–42.

Robertson, Wyndham. *Pocahontas's Descendants.* 1887. Revised, enlarged, and extended by Stuart E. Brown, Jr., Lorraine F. Myers, and Eileen M. Chapel, 1985.

Rogin, Michael Paul. *Ronald Reagan, the Movie: And Other Episodes in Political Demonology.* Berkeley: U of California P, 1987.

Rolfe, John. *A True Relation of the State of Virginia in 1616.* Charlottesville: UP of Virginia, 1951.

Rountree, Helen C. *Pocahontas's People: The Powhatan Indians of Virginia through Four Centuries.* Norman: U of Oklahoma P, 1990.

Rowlandson, Mary. *A Narrative of the Captivity and Restauration of Mrs. Mary Rowlandson*. 1682. *Narratives of the Indian Wars 1675–1699*. Ed. Charles H. Lincoln. New York: Scribner's, 1913. 109–67.

Russell, Howard S. *Indian New England before the Mayflower*. Hanover, NH: UP of New England, 1980.

Sale, Kirkpatrick. *The Conquest of Paradise: Christopher Columbus and the Columbian Legacy*. New York: Knopf, 1990.

Salisbury, Neal. "Squanto: Last of the Patuxets." *Struggle and Survival in Colonial America*. Ed. David G. Sweet and Gary B. Nash. U of California P, 1981: 228–45.

Schaffer, Kay. "Colonizing Gender in Colonial Australia: The Eliza Fraser Story." *Writing Women and Space: Colonial and Postcolonial Geographies*. Ed. Alison Blunt and Gillian Rose. Series *Mappings: Society/Theory/Space*. New York: Guilford, 1994. 101–20.

The Searchers. Dir. John Ford. Warner Brothers Pictures, 1956.

Seaver, James Everett. *A Narrative of the Life of Mrs. Mary Jemison . . . .* Canandaigua, NY: Bemis, 1824.

Sedgwick, Catharine Maria. *Hope Leslie*. 1827. Ed. Mary Kelley. American Women Writers Series. New Brunswick, NJ: Rutgers UP, 1987.

Seymour, Flora Warren. *Pocahontas: Brave Girl*. Childhood of Famous Americans Series. New York: Bobbs-Merrill, 1946.

Shirreffs, Gordon. *Bugles on the Prairie*. New York: Fawcett Gold Medal, 1957.

Sieminski, Greg. "The Puritan Captivity Narrative and the Politics of the American Revolution." *American Quarterly* 42.1 (March 1990): 35–56.

Sigourney, Lydia. "The Lost Lily." *The Western Home, and Other Poems*. Philadelphia: Parry & McMillan, 1854. 342–49.

———. "Pocahontas." *Pocahontas and Other Poems*. London: 1841. 1–29.

Slotkin, Richard. *Gunfighter Nation: The Myth of the Frontier in Twentieth-Century America*. New York: HarperCollins, 1992.

———. *Regeneration through Violence: The Mythology of the American Frontier, 1600–1860*. Middletown, CT: Wesleyan UP, 1973.

Slotkin, Richard, and James K. Folsom, eds. *So Dreadfull a Judgment: Puritan Responses to King Philip's War 1676–1677*. Middletown, CT: Wesleyan UP, 1978.

Smith, John. *Captain John Smith: A Select Edition of His Writings*. Ed. Karen Ordahl Kupperman. Chapel Hill: U of North Carolina P, 1988.

Smith-Rosenberg, Carroll. "Subject Female: Authorizing American Identity." *American Literary History* 5.3 (Fall 1993): 481–511.

Smits, David D. "'Abominable Mixture': Toward the Repudiation of Anglo-Indian Intermarriage in Seventeenth-Century Virginia." *The Virginia Magazine of History and Biography* 95.2 (April 1987): 157–92.

————. "The 'Squaw Drudge': A Prime Index of Savagism." *Ethnohistory* 29.4 (1982): 281–306.

————. "'Squaw Men,' 'Half–Breeds,' and Amalgamators: Late Nineteenth-Century Anglo-American Attitudes toward Indian-White Race Mixing." *American Indian Culture and Research Journal* 15.3 (1991): 29–61.

Snead, James A. *Figures of Division: William Faulkner's Major Novels.* New York: Methuen, 1986.

Stannard, David E. *American Holocaust: Columbus and the Conquest of the New World.* New York: Oxford UP, 1992.

Stone, John Augustus. *Metamora, or The Last of the Wampanoags.* 1829. Rpt. in *Dramas from the American Theatre 1762–1909.* Ed. Richard Moody. Cleveland: World, 1966. 199–227.

Strachey, William. *Historie of Travaile into Virginia Britannia.* London: 1612.

————. *Lawes Divine, Morall and Martiall, etc.* London: 1612. Ed. David H. Flaherty. Charlottesville: UP of Virginia, 1969.

Taves, Ann, ed. *Religion and Domestic Violence in Early New England: The Memoirs of Abigail Abbot Bailey.* Bloomington: Indiana UP, 1989.

Thomas, David Hurst, et al. *The Native Americans: An Illustrated History.* Atlanta: Turner, 1993.

Thoreau, Henry David. *A Week on the Concord and Merrimack Rivers.* 1849. Ed. Odell Shepard. New York: Scribner's, 1921.

Tilton, Robert. *Pocahontas: The Evolution of an American Narrative.* New York: Cambridge UP, 1994.

Todd, John. *The Lost Sister of Wyoming: An Authentic Narrative.* Northampton: Butler, 1842.

Todorov, Tzvetan. *The Conquest of America.* New York: Harper & Row, 1984.

Tompkins, Jane. "'Indians': Textualism, Morality, and the Problem of History." *"Race," Writing, and Difference.* Ed. Henry Louis Gates, Jr. Chicago: U of Chicago P, 1986. 59–77.

————. *Sensational Designs: The Cultural Work of American Fiction, 1790–1860.* New York: Oxford UP, 1985.

Tompson, Benjamin. "New-Englands Crisis." Boston: 1676. Rpt. in *Colonial American Poetry.* Ed. Kenneth Silverman. New York: Hafner, 1968. 96–111.

Two Rode Together. Dir. John Ford. Columbia Pictures, 1961.

Ulrich, Laurel Thatcher. *Good Wives: Image and Reality in the Lives of Women in Northern New England 1650–1750.* 1980. New York: Vintage Books, 1991.

Unconquered. Dir. Cecil B. DeMille. Paramount, 1947.

The Unforgiven. Dir. John Huston. United Artists, 1960.

Vaughan, Alden T. *Roots of American Racism: Essays on the Colonial Experience.* New York: Oxford UP, 1995.

Walker, Alice. "Am I Blue?" *Living by the Word: Selected Writings 1973–1987.* New York: Harcourt Brace Jovanovich, 1988. 3–8.

———. "Beauty: When the Other Dancer Is the Self." *In Search of Our Mothers' Gardens: Womanist Prose.* New York: Harcourt Brace Jovanovich, 1983. 384–93.

Watson, Larry. *Montana 1948.* Minneapolis: Milkweed, 1993.

Webster, Mrs. M. M. *Pocahontas: A Legend.* Phildelphia: Hooker, 1840.

Webster, Yehudi O. *The Racialization of America.* New York: St. Martin's, 1992.

Weedon, Chris. *Feminist Practice and Poststructuralist Theory.* New York: Basil Blackwell, 1987.

Welch, James, with Paul Stekler. *Killing Custer: The Battle of the Little Bighorn and the Fate of the Plains Indians.* New York: Norton, 1994.

Whitford, Kathryn. "Hannah Duston: The Judgement of History." *The Essex Institute Historical Collections* 108.4 (October 1972): 304–25.

Whittier, John Greenleaf. "A Mother's Revenge." *Legends of New England.* 1831. Gainesville, FL: Scholars' Facsimiles and Reprints, 1965. 125–31.

Wilde, Richard Henry. "The Lament of the Captive." 1813–14? Rpt. Edward L. Tucker. *Richard Henry Wilde: His Life and Selected Poems.* Athens: U of Georgia P, 1966. 98–107.

[Willard, Joseph.] "Mrs. Rowlandson." *Collections Historical and Miscellaneous* 3.4 (April 1824): 105–14, and 3.5 (May 1824): 137–49.

Williams, John. *The Redeemed Captive, Returning to Zion.* 1707.

Williams, Roger. *A Key into the Language of America.* 1643.

Williams, Walter L. *The Spirit and the Flesh: Sexual Diversity in American Indian Culture.* Boston: Beacon, 1986.

Winthrop, John. *The History of New England from 1630 to 1649.* 2 vols. Ed. James Savage. Boston: Phelps and Farnham, 1825.

Woodward, Grace Steele. *Pocahontas.* Norman: U of Oklahoma P, 1969.

Woolf, Virginia. *To the Lighthouse.* 1927. New York: Harvest Books/Harcourt Brace, 1989.

Yellin, Jean Fagan. Introduction. *Incidents in the Life of a Slave Girl, Written by Herself.* By Harriet A. Jacobs. Cambridge: Harvard UP, 1987. xiii–xxxiv.

Young, Philip. "The Mother of Us All: Pocahontas Reconsidered." *The Kenyon Review* 24.3 (Summer 1962): 391–415.

Zeskind, Leonard. "White–Shoed Supremacy." *The Nation* 262.23 (June 10, 1996): 21–24.

Index